Phaidon Encyclopedia
of Impressionism

Phaidon Encyclopedia of
Impressionism

Maurice Sérullaz

with contributions by

Georges Pillement
Bertrand Marret
François Duret-Robert

Phaidon

Translated by E. M. A. Graham

Phaidon Press Limited
Littlegate House, St Ebbe's Street, Oxford

Published in the United States of America by
E. P. Dutton, New York

This edition first published 1978
English Translation © 1978 by Phaidon Press Limited

ISBN 0 7148 1897 6   Hardback
ISBN 0 7148 1911 5   Paperback
Library of Congress Catalog Card Number: 78–62588

Original French edition *Encyclopédie de l'Impressionnisme*
© 1974 by Editions Aimery Somogy, Paris
Illustration © S.P.A.D.E.M. and A.D.A.G.P.

Printed in Italy

Table of Contents

Introduction

Impressionism is the name given to a school of painting which started in France and subsequently spread to other countries in the second half of the nineteenth and the first quarter of the twentieth century. It was a real revolution in painting. It was 'a method of painting that consists in reproducing an impression exactly as it is experienced', and the Impressionist artist 'aims at representing objects according to his own personal impressions without bothering about generally recognised rules'. The Impressionists painted out of doors, using a technique of separate, fragmented brush strokes and pure prismatic colours; they aimed at rendering changing effects of light and reflection with vivid immediacy and intensity.

The Impressionists were innovators but they had their forerunners too, both long ago and in more modern times. For instance one can think of the Venetian Renaissance painters trying to express reality as it actually was and using brilliant hues and complementary colours. Then certain Spanish painters, particularly El Greco, Velazquez and Goya, express these new tendencies to an even greater extent; indeed Manet and Renoir were very strongly influenced by their work.

Camon Aznar, in his analysis of what he calls the 'Spanish Impressionism' of those early days, declares that 'we can call it by the name *instantism*. The chief characteristic of Spanish Impressionism is the way it seizes on the living luminous moment, leaving gaps between the brushstrokes; painting in the open air or using only primary colours were not considered essential and black was freely used'.

The Spanish author Quevedo, who was a contemporary of Velazquez, analysed the painter's technique in penetrating words, speaking of 'a few scattered brush-strokes that here represent truth'. And the historian Ortega y Gasset went as far as to say that 'just as Descartes reduces thought to what is rational so Velazquez reduces painting to what is visual'.

Quite recently Lafuente Ferrari declared: 'If one can speak of Velazquez's Impressionism, the term means he succeeded in representing objects as they actually appear to the eye, as shapeless conglomerations of coloured planes. The volumes of his earlier paintings, with their hard clearly-defined contours, have now become apparitions that are none the less ghostly for being at the same time real and present to the spectator'.

At about the same period, in Flanders, Rubens was painting shadows that were transparent and full of colour. Delacroix remarks how, in his paintings, light is made up of fresh delicate tints, while the tints of his shadows on the other hand are very warm, and their usual essential reflections add to the chiaroscuro effect. Rubens never used black for shadows, and here he was at one with the Impressionists.

In Holland, Frans Hals, with his technique of broken separate brush strokes and brilliant colours standing out against the deep black, had a definite influence on the Impressionist Edouard Manet.

The English School of painters played an important part in the evolution of French painting as it developed towards Impressionism. During the war of 1870, Claude Monet, Sisley and Pissarro went to London to study the work of the great English landscape artists, Constable, Bonington and Turner. As Pissarro remarked: 'Turner's and Constable's watercolours and paintings and Old Crome's canvases certainly influenced our painting'. And Constable already anticipated Monet when he said that what he aimed at in painting was 'light, dews, breeze, bloom and freshness', and 'neither were there ever two leaves of a tree alike since the creation of the world; and no two days are alike, nor even two hours. The genuine productions of art, like those of nature, are all distinct from one another'.

Delacroix, who was a great admirer of Constable, confirmed this view when he stated: 'Constable says that the green of his meadows is much better because it is made up of a number of different greens', a method that Claude Monet and his friends were to use subsequently. As

TURNER *Yacht approaching the coast. c.* 1840-1845

DELACROIX *The sea from the heights of Dieppe.* 1852

for Turner, the titles he gave his paintings correspond very closely to those the Impressionists gave theirs: *Sunrise in fog* (1807), *Morning frost* (1813), *Yachts on the Solent* (1827), *Snowstorm* (1842) or *Rain, steam and speed* (1844).

Claude Monet and the artists of his circle were also influenced by certain French painters— for instance, Cézanne said he wanted to imitate Poussin; while Renoir was particularly attracted to Watteau's evanescent charm and the style of Boucher and Fragonard.

But the most immediate influence on the Impressionists was that of Delacroix, with his belief that everything is a reflection in painting. One realizes from an entry in his *Journal* how his attitude and vision corresponded with those of the Impressionists, when he distinguished particular local colour from colour as light: 'You have to reconcile colour as colour with colour as light'.

In his watercolours painted in North Africa in 1832 or at Étretat in 1835, and particularly in his painting of *The Sea at Dieppe* (1852), there are clear anticipations of Impressionism; this latter picture above all others anticipates by twenty years Claude Monet's *Impression: Sunrise* painted at Le Havre in 1872. The poet and writer Jules Laforgue felt this when he wrote in the *Revue Blanche* (15 May 1896): 'The quivering effects the Impressionists attain (their marvellous innovations) and innumerable dancing specks of light are foreshadowed by Delacroix, the great lover of movement. Amidst the passionless distortions of Romanticism, he was not satisfied with

9

mere wild contortions and violent colouring, but defines his forms with vibrant hatching' (*Posthumous Notes*). Signac's book *From Eugène Delacroix to Neo-Impressionism* was published in the year 1899.

The landscape painters who worked at Barbizon in the second half of the nineteenth century, and particularly Daubigny and Diaz, had a definite influence on the Impressionists. Daubigny, one of the earliest of the Barbizon school, used to go along the river Oise in his boat called 'Le Botin' and paint; he was practically the first artist to paint in the open air.

However it was the painters Corot and Courbet who played the most important part in leading up to Impressionism.

Corot believed that 'beauty in art consists of truth, bathed in the impressions we receive from contemplating nature'. And this original direct vision and poetic, sensitive contact with nature became progressively more and more important in his painting. Corot was originally drawn to study effects of light, but later became more and more absorbed in expressing a feeling of atmosphere; his tints became more delicately shaded and melting into one another, to express the imponderable all enveloping quality of air, and he uses infinite gradations of shaded greys. Delacroix used to say that 'grey was the enemy of painting' but Corot took the opposite view. To make his greys he did not mix black and white but used the various colours of the prism to produce all sorts of grey tints, as he mingled his colour 'values' with extraordinarily delicate skill. The painters of the Honfleur and Saint-Siméon Schools, Eugène Boudin in particular, esteemed Corot's work, and Boudin wrote: 'People thought that after three years' absence I should reappear as a kind of artistic phoenix; but actually, as the great men of those days made a fuss of me, I came back more bewildered than ever, vacillating between Rousseau, who was always attractive, and Corot, who was beginning to show us a completely different way of painting'.

The followers of the new way were the artists we would call 'painters of atmosphere', particularly those who worked in Normandy and on the Seine estuary, between Honfleur, Trouville, Deauville and Le Havre. Impressionism originated here, and a group of painters, gathered round Boudin and Jongkind, decided that from now on, they would paint *entirely and completely* out of doors. They settled at the Ferme Saint Siméon, very close to Honfleur, where mère Toutain kept an inn and there inaugurated what has become known as the Saint-Siméon or Honfleur School. Actually Diaz, Troyon, Cals, Daubigny and Corot had worked there before them, and in 1859 Courbet and Schanne came there through Boudin, who settled there himself in 1862. He persuaded the Dutch painter Jongkind to join him in 1863 and to stay several years. Claude Monet came later and spent the autumn of 1864 there, and it was in or near Honfleur that Boudin executed his enchanting and brilliant pastel and watercolour sketches of skies and the sea that were so much admired by Baudelaire for their delicate poetic quality. It is there too that Jongkind painted his delightfully vibrating watercolours, and both Boudin and Jongkind encouraged the young artist Claude Monet to experiment with painting in the open air, and to use bright light colours.

Courbet's influence was as important as Corot's. Courbet was the leader of the French realist school that originated during the 1848 Revolution; he was an exceptionally gifted landscape painter who is known above all as the painter of light.

Courbet was bold and perceptive, and in the brief instructions he gave his pupils, he told them: 'Paint what you *see*, what you *want*, what you *feel*'. Surely these are the key words of Impressionism. Courbet actually always painted in his studio, even when he tried to give the feeling of being out of doors, and with his deep sense of light and intensity of vision he adopted a kind of quivering, brightly coloured *tachisme* in rendering reflections and light effects, that is particularly noticeable in his famous picture *La Rencontre, ou Bonjour M. Courbet* (1854) or in some

MONET *Impression, sunrise.* 1872

of his landscapes such as *Cliffs at Étretat* which was exhibited in the Salon of 1870. We have already seen how Courbet went to paint in the Seine estuary, especially in 1854 when he went to Honfleur and there met Boudin.

Courbet's influence was however particularly strong among a group of more or less realist painters who worked in Provence, such as Paul Guigou and Frédéric Bazille. They were very much influenced by Courbet's style, his brilliant light effects against deep shadows, and his bright light colours contrasting with the heavy black tones he used. It is interesting to notice how in Bazille's paintings, like in some early works of Claude Monet, there are often out-of-doors scenes with figures.

Édouard Manet however is the painter on whom the direct influence of Courbet is most marked. The close connection between the two painters, which had already been noticed by contemporary critics, is most obvious in their 'modern' realistic subjects, their portraits and in the strong definite influence of Spanish painters, as well as in their choice of 'beautiful' subjects, their touches of *tachisme* and the light bright colours, that appear specially brilliant by contrast with the warm tones of black they use.

The part Manet played in launching Impressionism is well known, particularly after the 1863 *Salon des Refusés* where he exhibited his *Déjeuner sur l'herbe*. He used to go too to the café Guerbois,

11 Grande-Rue des Batignolles (later re-numbered as 9 Avenue de Clichy, and known as 'brasserie Muller'). Here various artists and poets used to meet regularly, originally under the leadership of Manet and Zola. These meetings probably began about 1866 and were extremely popular between 1868 and 1870. Manet and Zola were both supporters of the new trends in art, and a number of writers and critics used to join them at the café—men such as Duranty, Théodore Duret, Paul Alexis, a friend of Zola's, the sculptor and poet Zacharie Astruc, Edmond Maître the musicologist, Nadar the photographer, and various painters and engravers of different schools such as Constantin Guys, Alfred Stevens, Guillaumet, the engraver Bracquemond, Fantin-Latour, Bazille with his friend Lejosne, as well as Degas, Renoir, Claude Monet, Sisley, Pissarro and Cézanne.

Manet was from the first the enthusiastic spokesman for the new revolutionary tendencies in art, but actually it was only a year or two later, after the 1870 war, that Claude Monet persuaded him to start painting out of doors himself. However he absolutely refused to show at any of the eight Impressionist exhibitions; he always considered himself an 'independent' painter not belonging to any particular school.

In this way, although for different reasons, his ambiguous position is not unlike that of Degas. Degas called himself 'the classical painter of modern life' and took part in seven out of eight of the Impressionist exhibitions, but all his life he firmly refused to paint out of doors and so cannot strictly speaking be considered an Impressionist. Like Manet, he is really more of an independent painter. Within the general setting of Impressionism, he was a traditionalist but also an innovator, classical as well as modern in his approach to his art. At that period, 'modern' painting was in favour with artists like Manet and Degas and later Toulouse-Lautrec. Baudelaire wrote, in his book *Romantic Art*, with reference to Constantin Guys: 'You have no right to despise what is modern or to avoid it—fleeting and transitory and changing as it is'.

Photography, a recently discovered technique, also had a good deal to do with fixing the modern image. Some people considered photography to be an art; others, like Baudelaire, attacked it violently, but it certainly opened up new aspects of life, with its original approach and direct spontaneous vision. Photographic effects like close-ups and takes from unusual angles, distortions of detail, especially with nudes, or racing scenes, snapshots that caught the fleeting moment and inspired artists to do the same in their painting, immediate effects of light and reflections, all helped to modify the way Impressionists looked at things.

But on the whole photography was more a rival to painting than a help. Artists were stimulated by the new technique and were determined to attain the same kind of results not just mechanically, like the camera, but by effort and art and genius. Photography could produce black and white prints, but artists could do better and seize the immediacy and actuality of life and vision through the use of brilliant and varied colours and shimmering light effects.

Finally there was one last and very marked influence on the young painters of the time, and that was Japan and everything Japanese. From 1854 onwards, diplomatic relations between France and Japan had been re-established, and several exhibitions of Japanese art were held as a result. At these exhibitions, French artists got to know Japanese prints, and the great Japanese engravers such as Utamaro (1755-1806), Hokusai (1760-1849) and Hiroshige (1797-1858). To Western eyes, the general appearance of these prints with oblique off-centre effects, simplified forms and presentation, as well as their delicate colouring, were unusual and fascinating, and many artists, among them Manet, Monet, Renoir, van Gogh, Toulouse-Lautrec, Gauguin and especially Degas, as well as the Symbolists and the 'Nabis', were influenced by Japanese art. In the Rue de Rivoli there was a famous new shop called *La Porte Chinoise (The Chinese Door)* devoted to Japanese and Chinese art, which fascinated the young Impressionists and influenced many of their works.

CARRIÈRE *Portrait of Paul Verlaine. c.* 1895.

BAUD-BOVY *Portrait of Charles Morice*

Historically speaking, an obscure journalist, Lucien Leroy, was responsible for the word *Impressionism*, as applied to the artists in question. He wrote an article about the first exhibition of the 'Société coopérative d'artistes, peintres, sculpteurs, graveurs' in the *Charivari* for 25 April 1874 under the title *L'Exposition des impressionnistes* (Impressionists' Exhibition). The show took place in the photographer Nadar's premises at 35 Boulevard des Capucines, from 15 April to 15 May of that year. The term Impressionism was taken from the title of one of Claude Monet's pictures shown in the exhibition, *Impression, sunrise* (1872) representing the harbour at Le Havre in early morning mist. The word was intended to show Leroy's scorn and disapproval of those artists who were giving up the traditional approach to painting and were merely aiming at expressing their own personal visual impressions. However, it should be mentioned that Antonin Proust, in his *Recollections* devoted to Édouard Manet and published in the *Revue Blanche*, remarks that 'the term Impressionism does not come from Monet's painting entitled *Impression*, as Monsieur Bénédite states, but it actually originated during our 1858 discussions about art.'

COURBET *La Rencontre, ou Bonjour Monsieur Courbet*. 1854

However that may be, Impressionism has to be considered as a new kind of painting, following on a new kind of vision—and as a sort of apologia for sensation pure and simple. Painters, who, as usual, were ahead of composers and authors, could have taken André Gide's famous remark in *Les Nourritures terrestres* as theirs: 'I *feel*, therefore I am' rejecting the rationalism of Descartes when he said: 'I think, therefore I am'. Impressionism is a purely visual, instinctive form of art. This continually renewed vision is generated by light and its manifold shifting changes, and becomes to a great extent the true subject of the picture. As a result of this, landscapes tended to predominate over all other types of painting, and religious, mythological and historical painting more or less vanished. Painters tended to work from then onwards almost exclusively out of doors, and aimed at getting their pictures on to canvas as fast as possible, as nature continually changes and they wanted to seize every fleeting impression. So Impressionist painters would just stop and paint somewhere at random without having planned anything beforehand, setting up their easel casually wherever their fancy took them. Suddenly on a walk they might be attracted by some fleeting and ephemeral effect of light in nature and decide to paint it then and there. The motion of the waves, the far horizon of the sea, rivers with their flowing murmuring waters, the sky with its ever-changing clouds, the glistening effects of sunlight, wreathing smoke and the pearly iridescent brilliance of snow; all these were subjects they loved to paint.

They were particularly attracted to painting reflections and light effects, and above all, water. Their vision was extraordinarily fresh and keen, and they noticed every shifting tone and fleeting movement. They would try to seize the effect of a breeze playing on water and rippling its surface, lightly stirring the leaves of the trees or moving across a grassy meadow. It was not just the seasons they painted, as did their predecessors, but also the detail of the actual hour and place, one particular month, one exact moment in time. Several of the Impressionist artists and particularly Claude Monet, did whole 'series' of paintings of the same subject under different conditions; poplar trees, or a cathedral, or water lilies, in different lights from dawn to dusk, almost from hour to hour, showing a constant renewal of colours, shapes and light transparent shadows.

In this connection it is interesting to notice that in April 1874, just at the time of the Impressionist exhibition which was open from 15 April to 15 May, Verlaine wrote his *Art Poétique* at Mons. It was dedicated to Charles Morice and was first published in *Paris Moderne*, a review started by Vanier on 10 November 1882, later re-printed on 3 January 1885, in *Jadis et naguère* (Long ago and the other day), also published by Vanier:

> Music first and foremost
> So choose the odd numbers
> That drift and dissolve better in the air,
> With nothing heavy or static about them.
>
> Shaded tints we desire,
> No colour, only tints and hues.
>
> Nothing lovelier than a grey song
> Where uncertainty and precision meet.
>
> Beautiful eyes veiled and dim,
> The quivering bright light of noon,
> And the blue tangle of the clear stars
> In a mild autumn sky.
>
> Only the shaded tint can link
> Dream to dream and flute to horn.

Technically speaking, the Impressionist painters no longer represented form and colour as they believed them to be, but as they actually saw them under the distorting effect of light. This led them to abandon several of the traditional principles of art. Clear contours, to outline shapes and suggest volume, were henceforward rejected, and single broken touches with separate fragmented brush strokes were adopted instead. Perspective founded on the rules of geometry was no longer used, but instead, graded tones and tints were employed to define space and volume, working back from the foreground to the horizon. We must explain here that the word *tint* is used for the actual quality of a colour—with greens for instance there are emerald green, viridian, olive and so on; while *tone* defines the intensity of the colour, as it ranges from dark to light. Painters gave up using *chiaroscuro* with its strong and violent contrasts. Blacks and greys, pure white, the various brown and 'earth' colours such as ochre, umber and burnt Sienna were excluded from their palettes and they only used the pure prismatic colours, blues, greens and yellows, orange, red and violet. They painted what they saw and not what they knew was there; earth for instance could be represented as purple or violet, blue or pink or orange as it appeared, and not just brown as before. They often tended to use the technique of optical blending, with colours—that is, they would place two pure colours in juxtaposition on the canvas, rather than mixing the pigments themselves on the palette, and the eye of the spectator then had to recompose the colour the painter required. For example, small red and blue brush strokes in juxtaposition will suggest violet to the eye of the beholder, through the vibrations set up by the two colours. This is in accordance with the theories of famous physicists such as Chevreul (1839), Helmholtz (1878) and N. O. Rood (1881).

The solar spectrum is made up of the following seven colours: violet, indigo, blue, green, yellow, orange and red, but as indigo is a kind of blue, there are really only six colours. Three of the colours, blue, red and yellow are known as primary or fundamental colours. Three are known as binary or mixed colours: green, violet and orange. They are made up by mixing two primary colours together; blue mixed with yellow produces green; blue and red together make violet, and red and yellow make orange. Each of the three binary colours is complementary to the colour which is not included in its composition; so green is complementary to red, violet to yellow, and orange is complementary to blue. Every colour tends to tinge the space surrounding it with its complementary colour. As a result, the shadow of any object is always slightly tinged with the complementary colour of the object itself; a red object will have a shadow very slightly tinged with green, and according to the particular tint of red, so the greens will vary.

We may add that according to the law of simultaneous contrasts stated by Chevreul, two complementary colours (such as for example red and green) or two binary complementaries (violet and green) become much more intense when in juxtaposition with each other, while they would obliterate each other if the pigments were mixed. The complementary colour of each one of the two colours used affects the other colour. In the case of two complementaries, green and red for instance, the complementary colour of red (that is, green) exerts its action on the green and increases its intensity; and the same applies to red, the complementary of green. In the case of two binary complementary colours (say violet and green, for example) the complementary colour of green, that is red, acts on the violet which becomes more red, and the complementary colour of violet (that is yellow) acts on the green which becomes more yellow. On the other hand, violet and green, which both contain blue, become less blue. In fact one finds that when two tints which both contain the same pure primary colour are placed in juxtaposition the primary colour will in both cases be attenuated and lightened.

The best brief summary of Impressionist vision and technique can be found in Jules Laforgue's article Art criticism: impressionism (*Critique d'art, l'impressionnisme*) in his *Posthumous Miscellany* (*Mélanges posthumes*) of 1903: '*The physiological origin of Impressionism—Prejudice and drawing*. It is generally conceded that a work of art depends ultimately on the soul and the intellect, but it can only do so through the agency of the human eye. The eye is, therefore, just as the ear is in music, the first essential in art. An Impressionist painter is a modernist painter endowed with unusual visual sensitivity. He forgets all the vast accumulation of pictures he has seen in museums, and all the visual education he has received in art schools about correct perspective and drawing and colour. Living and working out of doors instead of in a studio, viewing his subjects directly and plainly, whether in the country or inside a house or out in the street, he has managed to see things naturally and freshly with an innocent eye, and to paint them simply and unaffectedly just as he sees them (pp. 133-134). *The academic eye and the Impressionist eye—Colour polyphony*. In a landscape drenched in light, where objects stand out in relief like tinted grisaille, where an academic can only see plain diffused white light, the Impressionist will see light in a quite different manner. He sees light suffusing everything not with a kind of blank dead whiteness, but with a rich interplay of prismatic colours and innumerable quivering fragments. Where the academic painter only sees a bare outline enclosing some form or relief, the Impressionist sees living vibrating strokes struggling and moving, that lack any definite geometrical form but are made up of innumerable irregular touches that together, when seen from far off, are built up into a living entity. An academic painter sees objects in perspective, placed regularly according to plan in their respective planes, a mere framework with no life in it, a purely theoretical thing; but an Impressionist sees perspective as something established by innumerable almost imperceptible touches and tones, not fixed but ever in motion.

So in the scale of human evolution, the Impressionist eye, in its capacity to seize and render the most complicated combinations of tone and colour, is the most fully developed and the most advanced. The Impressionist sees and paints nature as it is, that is pure colour vibrations. No drawing or light or modelling or perspective, nor chiaroscuro—none of these childish categories; instead it is all really resolved into colour vibrations and must be obtained on the canvas by colour vibrations only' (pp. 136-137).

MAILLOL *Woman with a sunshade. c.* 1895-1900

Several of the Impressionist painters were sculptors as well. Degas modelled figures of dancers and horses in wax, and Renoir did a number of nudes. Then there were Renoir's friend, the sculptor Maillol, who had a very great influence on him at the end of his career, and Auguste Rodin, who was a friend of Claude Monet and his circle, and whose art has sometimes been, wrongly it would seem, taxed with being Impressionist—they were more or less on the fringe of the group. The painters came first; then the writers and poets, and it is to them we must turn to find the same type of subjects: sunshine and light, reflections, vibrations, water and wind and rain. In André Gide's *Nourritures terrestres*, published in 1897, there are a number of passages which show how intensely absorbed he was in the same sort of things as Claude Monet and his friends were—subtle feelings and fleeting impressions. 'Shall I tell you what was my joy and delight that day', André Gide wrote, 'and will you understand me if I tell you that it was purely and simply the exaltation of light? I was sitting there in the garden. I could not actually see the sun, but the air was sparkling with diffused light as if the blue of the sky were becoming transparent and falling like rain . . . It really seemed as if light were streaming down, in that broad alley walk, and all the tips of the branches were touched with frothing gold that lingered there among all the streaming rays of light'. Or again 'The sea ever moving and formless . . . the great waves advance noiselessly one after the other, following each other, and each wave brings up the same drop of water almost without moving it. Only their shape moves forward; the water yields and then falls back and never moves on with them'.

Marcel Proust however is the best example we have of Impressionism in literature. When Proust describes a landscape—or rather his feelings as he looks at a landscape—an Impressionist painting seems suddenly to appear before our eyes. 'The sun had set, and the sea, seen through the branches of the apple trees, was mauve. As light as pale faded wreaths and persistent as regretful thoughts, little pink and blue clouds were floating on the horizon. A long melancholic line of poplars plunged into the shadows, their tops were caught up as it were in the rose window of a church, and the last rays of the sun tinted the branches of the trees with colour, leaving the trunks untouched, and hung bright garlands of light on the pillars of shadow'. (*Les Plaisirs et les jours*, 1896). In his sequence of novels, *À la recherche du temps perdu* (*Remembrance of things past*) which began to come out in 1913, Proust based his character, Elstir the painter, on features taken from several Impressionist painters, particularly Claude Monet and Renoir: 'I could see that the particular charm of Elstir's paintings consisted in a kind of transformation of whatever he was representing,—something not unlike what in poetry is known as "metaphor". God is said to have created things by giving them names; but Elstir created them anew by abolishing the names they were originally known by and giving them fresh ones. There are rare moments in life when we see nature as it is, in a poetical way, and Elstir's work was made up of that sort of moment, for instance, in the seascapes that he was working on just then. One of his most usual metaphors involved the comparison of land and sea, leaving out any differences between them; and it was this comparison, tacitly repeated over and over again in the same painting, which gave it its manifold and powerful unity.'

Proust gave an excellent description of this new school of painting when he wrote: 'Really and truly, surfaces and volumes are independent of the names of objects that spring up and come to our mind as soon as we have recognized them . . . Elstir tried to dissociate whatever he actually knew about things from what he felt about them, and tried often to dissolve and break up into its essential elements the total of thought and reasoning that we normally call vision'.

Another art to be influenced by Impressionism was music. Émile Vuillermoz says of Debussy that 'he was wonderfully attuned, as it were, to the pitch of the Impressionist painters as they struggled to capture the essence of light as the dominant element in their language, and this struggle had led them to a kind of painting we can call *microstructure*. Debussy, like them,

Blanche *Portrait of André Gide*. 1912

practised every kind of fragmentation, breaking up and subdividing, analysing the quality of sounds and tones, and his liking for the 'divided quartet' and for mutes corresponds to colour fragmentation in painting. The Impressionist painters discovered all the magic of atmospheric vibrations and quivering living light; yet people often accused them of sacrificing precision and clarity of outline to enchantment and atmosphere. In fact their enemies accused them of not knowing how to draw. In the same way Debussy was misunderstood, and for the same reasons; people have often stupidly declared that his music was a perpetual monotonous *grisaille* with no sort of melodic line'. Even the titles of many of Debussy's works suggest the kind of subjects the Impressionist painters used to choose; for instance *Nuage* (*Cloud*; from *Nocturnes*, 1898), *Esquisses* (*Sketches*), *Jardins sous la pluie* (*Gardens in the rain*; from *Estampes*, 1903), *La mer* (with *De l'aube à midi sur la mer*, *Jeux de vagues*, *Dialogues du vent et de la mer*, 1905), *Reflets dans l'eau* (*Reflections in the water*, *Images*, 1905–1907), *Des pas sur la neige* (*Footsteps in the snow*), *Voiles* (*Veils*; from *Préludes*, Book I, 1910), *Brouillards* (*Mists*; from *Préludes*, Book II, 1913).

Gabriel Fauré was another composer whose style, with its shifting tones, was subtle and delicate with an almost imperceptible rhythm. His music suggests the sea, waves, clouds and wind.

The Impressionist painters were trained either at the Académie Suisse or at the Gleyre studio. The Académie Suisse—so called from the name of its founder—was situated on the Quai des Orfèvres. It was an independent academy where students could study for very little, using live models; no advice was given and there were no corrections and no examinations. Both Édouard

Manet and Claude Monet spent some time there, but the most important artists to work regularly there were Pissarro, Cézanne and Guillaumin. Thus the original group of three painters was formed.

At about the same time, a second group of four painters came together at the Gleyre studio at the end of 1862. The studio was founded by the painter Gleyre who taught at the École des Beaux-Arts, and, although independent, was rather vaguely connected with the École. It was not an expensive course. Bazille was the first student to join along with Claude Monet, Renoir and Sisley following soon after. However two years later, Gleyre gave up the studio, and Monet and his friends were unattached again.

The first Impressionist manifestation was held, as we have already noticed, in 1874 when the 'Société anonyme coopérative d'artistes, peintres, sculpteurs, graveurs' held an exhibition in the studios belonging to the photographer Nadar, at 35 Boulevard des Capucines. Thirty artists took part. Both critics and the public reacted violently, and Louis Leroy used the term 'Impressionism' there for the first time. Two years later, in April 1876, a second exhibition was held at the Durand–Ruel Gallery at 11 Rue Le Peletier, this time with only twenty exhibitors. There was general misunderstanding on the part of the public as we can see from Albert Wolff's famous and extraordinarily unperceptive article in *Le Figaro* (3 April 1876): 'The Rue Le Peletier is really very unlucky. First there was the great fire at the Opéra and now a second disaster has come to upset the district. An exhibition—supposed to be an exhibition of paintings—has just been opened at the Durand-Ruel Gallery. The innocent passer-by, attracted by the display of flags in front of the shop, goes in, and immediately a ghastly sight meets his eyes. Five or six madmen—with one woman among them—have met here to exhibit their works. Some people just burst out laughing when they see the stuff shown. But I am not like that. I am deeply pained and grieved. These so-called artists call themselves Impressionists and radicals. They just take canvas, paints and brushes, hurl a few colours onto the canvas and then sign their name. So you get a set of misguided lunatics at Ville-Évrard picking up pebbles on the road and thinking they are diamonds. It really is frightful seeing such an aberration of human vanity and lunacy. Do tell Monsieur Pissarro that trees aren't really purple and the sky isn't really the colour of butter; tell him the things he paints don't really exist anywhere and no intelligent person can be expected to accept such rubbish. You might just as well waste your time trying to make one of Dr. Blanche's inmates at the asylum, who has an idea he's the Pope, believe that he lives in Paris and not at the Vatican. Try and make Monsieur Degas see reason and tell him there really are such things in art as drawing and colour and technique and meaning. He will only laugh at you though, and tell you you are an old stick-in-the-mud. Try and explain to Monsieur Renoir that a woman's body is not just a bundle of decomposing flesh with green and purple patches that show what an advanced stage of putrefaction the corpse is in. There is also one woman among this group of painters, someone called Berthe Morizot (sic), very odd; because she still keeps her feminine grace, in spite of her lunatic ravings'. The Impressionists did have one or two supporters, however, among them Armand Silvestre, Castagnary and particularly Duranty. In 1877 there was a third Impressionist exhibition, again in April, held at 6 Rue Le Peletier this time, and there were eighteen exhibitors.

The next year, 1878, the first analytical study of the new school of painting was published, under the title *Les Peintres Impressionnistes* (*The Impressionist Painters*) by Théodore Duret.

In 1879 came a fourth exhibition, held between 10 April and 11 May at 28 Avenue de l'Opéra, and this time sixteen artists exhibited; this was followed by a fifth show in 1880, from 1 to 30 April at 10 Rue des Pyramides, with eighteen exhibitors. The sixth exhibition took place from 2 April to 1 May, at 35 Boulevard des Capucines; this time thirteen artists exhibited, but at the seventh exhibition in March 1882 at 251 Rue Saint-Honoré, in premises rented by Durand–

BLANCHE *Portrait of Marcel Proust*

BLANCHE *Portrait of Claude Debussy*

SARGENT *Portrait of Gabriel Fauré*

Ruel, there were only nine painters showing. The eighth and final exhibition took place at 1 Rue Laffitte, from 15 May till 15 June, this time with seventeen exhibitors: these included Neo-Impressionists and also Symbolist painters.

In that same year, 1886, the art dealer Durand-Ruel went over to New York with a consignment of three hundred Impressionist paintings, by artists he was especially interested in, and managed to sell quite a number of them.

Impressionist painting which was so much disparaged and disliked when it first appeared, has been fashionable now for something like fifty years, so much so that one is inclined to think of it as an end in itself when it was merely a tendency in art, a revolutionary tendency, certainly, but with nothing final about it. It is important to realise how several painters who belonged to the Impressionist group soon came to see short-comings in the new style of painting, although they were far from denying its great qualities and value. Renoir, for instance, tried to react by going back to drawing, and by stylising forms, but it was Cézanne who reacted most strongly against Impressionism, and with him were the Neo-Impressionists.

Cézanne, while implicitly admitting the importance of the Impressionist movement, also felt the dangers of over-free, over-spontaneous painting. He declared that his aim was to 'make something solid out of Impressionism, and permanent, like museum art'. He pursued his ideal with endless perseverance in a spirit of broad synthesis, combining spontaneity and strictness, immediacy with permanence, an instantaneous vision of nature with feelings well under control, evanescence with structure, colour and form. He sought to go beyond appearances and to reconstitute the essential world, in a poetical as well as a philosophical sense, and ever reaching out towards the absolute. Although in some ways Cézanne was conservative and conventional, in others he was extraordinarily modern. He was forward-looking and open to new ideas, so we can rightly consider him to be the first great modern painter, the immediate predecessor of the Fauves and Cubists, as well as of independent avant-garde painters. For instance Georges Braque's *Les Paysages de l'Estaque* from which Cubism derived its name, are directly derived from Cézanne.

In 1886 came a new theory of art, inspired by Impressionism. The group of artists who belonged to this 'Neo-Impressionist' movement did not reject the theories of Monet and his friends; on the contrary, they wanted to continue what the Impressionists had begun, without however entirely accepting their casual attitude or their purely instinctive conception of art. The method they advocated was rational, founded on strict rules and principles. Although they were quite definitely innovators, they also believed in tradition and were strongly influenced by Delacroix. As far as theory was concerned, their spokesman was Signac, and in an article published in 1899 in *La Revue Blanche* under the title *D'Eugène Delacroix au néo-impressionnisme* (*From Eugène Delacroix to Neo-Impressionism*) he gave a clear account of the sources, aims and principles of the new movement. In the articles he uses two words that he compares: 'divisionnisme' which is an actual theory of art, and 'pointillisme' which is only a technique inspired more or less by Byzantine mosaics. 'Neo-Impressionism' he wrote 'does not make use of pointillisme or stippling, but divides and separates instead. By the use of division, one has all the benefits of colour, light effects and harmony by (1) the optical blending of pure pigments, i.e. all the colours of the prism; (2) the separation of the different elements one from another, i.e. the different kinds of colour and their reactions; (3) the proportion and balance between these various elements, according to the laws of contrast, gradation and irradiation; and (4) the choice of a style and the type of brushstroke used, according to the size of the picture'. We may also notice that their strokes were applied methodically in dots set close together (pointillisme) and also that the Neo-Impressionist painters used to practise the optical blending of tones. They followed the development of modern physics with great interest, and Chevreul's famous

BRAQUE *L'Estaque, the landing-stage.* 1906

treatise *De la loi du contraste simultané (On the law of simultaneous contrast)* was reissued in 1889.

As a result, when Claude Monet painted a picture of red tiles, he would quite spontaneously paint in the shadows in greenish tints, green being the complementary colour to red. His exceptionally keen eye noticed the colours and transferred them straight on to the canvas. But the Neo-Impressionists would not just put any red and any green together. If, for instance, the red in question is tinged with orange then they would put a more bluish green with it, but if the red is purplish, then the green would contain more yellow. They based their choice of colouring on Chevreul's chromatic circle, a diagram with seventy-two segments, and when they used one particular red, then they also had to use the only green that corresponded exactly to it on the diagram.

We have just seen that the eighth and last Impressionist exhibition, in which the Neo-Impressionists also joined, was held from 14 May to 15 June 1886. Among the Neo-Impressionists exhibiting was Seurat, who showed his large canvas *Un Dimanche après-midi à la Grande Jatte (Sunday Afternoon on the Island of La Grande Jatte)* as a manifesto for the new movement in painting. Soon after, Seurat showed the same picture again at the second Exhibition of Independent Painters, from 21 August to 21 September. There was a group of other artists who followed his ideas and theories about art; these included Signac, Dubois-Pillet,

Henri-Edmond Cross, Lucien Pissarro and Angrand. We find the word Neo-Impressionist being used for the first time on 19 September by Félix Fénéon in the Belgian review *La Vie moderne*, and it appeared again in *L'Événement* on 10 December in an article by Arsène Alexandre.

In February 1887, Signac and Pissarro exhibited in Brussels, at the Salon des Vingt, with M. Petitjean, Maximilien Luce, Lucie Cousturier as well as the Belgian painters Henri van de Velde and Théo van Rysselberghe.

Then there were several other artists connected with, and influenced by, both the Impressionist and Neo-Impressionist movements, but who nevertheless remained uncommitted and independent, like Édouard Manet, Degas and Fantin-Latour, two of the most important being van Gogh and Toulouse-Lautrec.

In 1890, the same year that the great painter van Gogh died, Georges-Albert Aurier wrote about him in the *Mercure de France*: 'Beneath skies now carved out in the dazzling brilliance of sapphire or turquoise, now made up of scorching, blinding, noxious, infernal sulphur; skies that seem to be like the casting of metals or crystals in fusion, irradiated by torrid suns; beneath the fearful incessant streaming of innumerable lights in a heavy, blazing, scorching atmosphere, that seems to have been exhaled by grotesque, fantastic furnaces for distilling gold and diamonds and precious stones . . . the disquieting disturbing outpourings of a strange personality, a character combining elements of straightforward sincerity with what one might call an almost supernatural quality. Van Gogh's nature was given to exaggeration. Everything he comes in contact with, whether it be objects or living creatures, light or shade, form or colour, all seems to be possessed, asserting its will in a wild and furious determination, yelling and shrieking in that intense, shrill voice—the unique and individual manifestation of a disturbed character. Here matter and nature are frantically twisted in a wild paroxysm of distortion; form has become a nightmare, colour is flames of hot spilling lava and precious stones; light is fire, and life itself is feverish and hectic. We may think all this is an exaggeration, but it really does give the impression we first get from these strange, intense, feverish paintings of Vincent van Gogh, who is a not unworthy successor and compatriot of the old Dutch masters'.

Not long after, on 31 March 1891, Octave Mirbeau declared, writing in the *Écho de Paris*: 'He could never forget his personality or suppress it, whatever external sights or visions he contemplated. Everything he saw or touched or felt was stamped with the burning intensity of his imagination. Van Gogh was not absorbed in nature, but he absorbed nature into himself. He took the natural forms and forced them into strange shapes, bending and moulding them into extraordinary manifestations of his ideas, and the characteristic deformities we associate with his art. Van Gogh possessed to an extraordinary degree the quality that differentiates one person from another, style. He throws all the weight of his approach into painting trees and sky and flowers. His forms are twisted and contorted into innumerable strange shapes, wild skies where intoxicated suns and moons whirl and stagger and stars stream with light like dishevelled comets; fantastic flowers rise and rear themselves up like great demented birds. Yet, beyond all this, van Gogh preserves his extraordinary qualities as a painter, with his moving nobility of vision and terrifying tragic genius'.

Toulouse-Lautrec was not connected with any group or movement, in fact he sometimes seems not even to belong to his own generation of painters. 'I have tried to depict truth and not an ideal' he wrote. 'Of course this may be a mistake as I paint people warts and all, and even give them the odd hairs and a shiny nose thrown in'. This may be why his friend Tristan Bernard used to assert that his excessive naturalness made Lautrec supernatural. He had an extraordinary gift for detail, sometimes important, sometimes not, but it is always indelibly imprinted on his models and somehow marks them as individuals and real people. This can be

ToULOUSE-LAUTREC *Tristan Bernard au Vélodrome Buffalo.*
1895

proved by the way Paul Leclercq, whose portrait Toulouse-Lautrec painted, gives these details about his method of working: 'When he painted my portrait, I realised his extraordinary facility. For about a month I went regularly to his studio in the avenue Frochot two or three times a week, but I can only really remember posing for something like two or three hours in all. As soon as I arrived, he used to make me sit in a huge wicker basket chair. He would then take up his position by his easel, wearing a funny little soft felt hat that he always had on in the studio. He would then fix me with his eyeglass, wink and then pick up his paintbrush. When he had had a good look at what he wanted, he would make a few very slow, light brushstrokes on the canvas; then he would put his brush down and say peremptorily: "That's enough. Too fine to stay indoors". Whereupon we would go out and have a walk instead'.

So far, most of the artists or groups we have been dealing with have been connected either technically or ideologically with the Impressionists. But when we come to the Symbolists, there is a definite break, at least as far as aesthetic and pictorial principles are concerned, although Gauguin and his circle did fraternise with the Impressionists and even exhibited along with them.

From then onwards, 'sensation' which had been such an essential element in Impressionist painting, was no longer considered important, and the concept of the 'idea' took its place. Exact visual reality and naturalism gave way to an intellectual approach and the use of symbols. The fragmented, brilliant colours and stippling used by the Impressionists were now replaced by a quite different style of painting with clear contours and definite outlines, and flat uniform surfaces all one colour. From 1879, parallel to the equivalent movement in literature, painters used the new method. Gustave Moreau (1826-1898) and Puvis de Chavannes (1824-1898) may be considered as the originators of this new movement, at least in some of their works. In 1881, which was the year Paul Verlaine's *Sagesse* was published, Puvis de Chavannes painted the *Poor Fisherman* (*Le Pauvre Pêcheur*) now in the Louvre, the most 'Symbolist' of all his pictures, while Odilon Redon first exhibited his work at *La Vie Moderne*.

In 1884 Seurat and Signac founded the *Société des Indépendants* and Odilon Redon agreed to be President. The next year Henri de Régnier and Jules Laforgue both brought out their first books of poems, and in 1886 Jean Moréas published the first *Symbolist manifesto* in the *Figaro* (18 September). In it he declared: 'Symbolist poetry seeks to clothe ideas in an outward form. This however is not its fundamental aim; Form must be subordinate to Idea while helping to express it. On the other hand the idea must never give up its sumptuous garments of outward analogy and comparisons, because the essential characteristic of symbolic art consists in never reaching the concept of the idea itself. Symbolism needs a very complex archetype if it is to express its synthesis properly. Objectivity can never be anything more than a mere starting-point for art'. Jean Moréas saw Symbolism as an artistic revival, whose characteristics included 'far-fetched metaphor, exaggerated pomp and ceremony, and a new vocabulary where harmony, line and colour were merged into one'.

Various Symbolist reviews were started, such as *la Pléiade, le Décadent, le Voyage* and *le Symboliste* which was founded by Jean Moréas and Gustave Kahn. In 1888 Gauguin went to Pont-Aven in Brittany, where he joined Émile Bernard, and together they launched what they called *synthetism* and *cloisonnism*—which might be translated as 'partitionism'. Gauguin painted *The Vision after the Sermon, or Jacob's struggle with the Angel* (*La Vision après le Sermon ou La Lutte de Jacob et de l'Ange*), as a manifesto of Symbolist painting. This same year saw the foundation of a new group called the 'Nabis'. At the beginning of 1889 at the Café Volpini on the Champ-de-Mars, where the Exposition Universelle took place, an 'Exhibition of paintings by the Impressionist and Synthetist group' was held as a public manifestation of the new artistic theories. Gauguin exhibited seventeen paintings and Émile Bernard twenty-three. Then in May a new Symbolist review, entitled *la Plume* appeared, founded by Léon Deschamps. In January 1890 the first number of the *Mercure de France* came out, with a most enthusiastic article on Gauguin by Georges-Albert Aurier. Maurice Denis published his famous manifesto on the *Definition of neo-traditionalism* in the review *Art et Critique* (23 and 30 April). He praised the 'triumph of feeling for the Beautiful over the deceit of naturalism', and concluded his article by saying: 'We must remember that a painting is essentially a surface covered with colours arranged in a certain order, before being the nude figure of a woman, or a picture of a horse or some sort of story'. In the *Mercure de France* for March 1891, which was entitled *Symbolism or painting: Paul Gauguin*, Georges-Albert Aurier declared: 'To sum up and conclude: a work of art, as I like to think of it logically, should be: (1) *ideist* ('*idéiste*'), as its one aim will be the expression of an idea; (2) *symbolist*, since it will express this idea by means of forms; (3) *synthetic* as these forms and signs will be expressed in a way that can be universally understood; (4) *subjective*, as the object will never be considered just as an object, but as a token of an idea perceived by the subject; (5) (and this follows as a consequence from the other four points) *decorative*, because painting which strictly speaking is decorative, as the Egyptians, the Greeks and the Primitives understood it, is merely a manifestation of art which is, at one and the same time, subjective, synthetic, symbolist and ideist'. Finally he adds that an artist who has all these talents must 'unite to his power of understanding another even more excellent gift . . . the gift of *emotivity* (*emotivité*—the capacity to experience emotion)—this transcendent capacity which is so precious and so great, and which stirs the soul as it contemplates the ever-changing drama of abstractions. Thanks to this gift, perfect, complete and absolute art exists at last'.

In the same year 1891, the two Natanson brothers, close friends of Toulouse-Lautrec and the Nabis, founded the *Revue Blanche*, and many Symbolist gatherings were held at the Café Voltaire. In December, the first of a series of fifteen exhibitions, all held at the Le Barc de Bouteville Gallery in the Rue Le Peletier, and lasting right up to 1897, was held; it was called 'Exhibition of Impressionist and Symbolist painters'. It included work by artists of various different tendencies: Impressionism, Neo-Impressionism, Symbolism, Nabism and even work by academic artists.

In 1893 Lugné-Poë founded the Theatre de l'Œuvre and Vuillard, Bonnard, Maurice Denis, Ranson, Sérusier, Toulouse-Lautrec, and Munch contributed designs for programmes, scenery and costumes. In the same year Maurice Denis illustrated André Gide's *Le Voyage d'Urien*.

In 1896, the year Verlaine died, Bonnard exhibited for the first time, and André Mellerio published *Le Mouvement idéaliste en peinture* (*The Idealist Movement in Painting*). He classes what he calls the idealist painters in four different categories, Gauguin, who now lived on his own in Tahiti, being excluded:

1. The chromo-luminarists: Angrand, Maximilien Luce, Lucien Pissarro, Théo van Rysselberghe, Seurat and Signac.
2. The Neo-Impressionists: Anquetin, Guillaume, Ibels, Maufra, Schuffenecker, Toulouse-Lautrec.
3. The Synthetists or neo-traditionalists: Bonnard, Ranson, K. X. Roussel, Sérusier, Vallotton, Vuillard.
4. The mystics: Meyer, Ballin, Émile Bernard, Maurice Denis, Filiger and Jean Verkade.

In 1897, Sérusier met Verkade at the monastery of Beuron in the Black Forest, and there they studied the theory of *sacred measurements* and the *Golden Number* together.

In 1898 two of the forerunners of Symbolism in painting, Gustave Moreau and Puvis de Chavannes died, as well as the great Symbolist poet Mallarmé.

In 1899 an exhibition in honour of Odilon Redon was held, and André, Émile Bernard, Cross, Maurice Denis, d'Espagnat, Ibels, Luce, van Rysselberghe, Sérusier, Signac, Vallotton and Vuillard all contributed paintings.

Sculptors such as Rodin, Maillol and others were very much involved in the aesthetic problems of their painter friends, and their sculpture is often very close in conception to contemporary painting. Forms as well as colours can be subtle and fleeting impressions of a passing moment.

Many foreign artists have been influenced by Impressionism, Neo-Impressionism and Symbolism; some were in close contact with the movements in France, while others worked independently. Whether they came from Europe or America, they all felt in their own particular way how important painting out of doors was; they were also influenced by the Symbolist movement.

German Impressionism, which began to appear during the last years of the nineteenth century, was very different from French Impressionism. Although German painters were very much interested in the Impressionist exhibition of 1879, they were more influenced by Corot, Courbet and Daubigny in their approach to painting out of doors, than by Claude Monet and his circle.

Adolf Menzel, Max Liebermann, Max Slevogt, Hans Thoma and Fritz von Uhde did not, strictly speaking, practise fragmentation or stippling, but their feeling for nature and the bright, light tones of their palette show how much they were influenced by the French Impressionists and their ideas about painting, which helped them to break away from an excessively academic approach.

Fundamental changes took place in the realm of art during a period of more than fifty years, and it is interesting to notice that it was painters who led the way, before sculptors, musicians, authors or poets. The painters who originated the artistic revolution by painting out of doors emphasized the value of feeling and sensation, which was such an important element in the period that produced Impressionism. Then, by an almost inevitable process of reaction, came the triumph of the idea and the theory of correspondences introduced by Baudelaire, which in its turn led directly to Symbolism. This was an extraordinarily prolific period, when direct contemplation of the subject was counterbalanced by interior contemplation and by the predominance of the idea and of an inner dream world.

It is interesting to notice that, whatever the reason—whether direct influence, or the inevitable swing of the pendulum—all the important movements in contemporary painting derive from this extraordinarily fertile and productive period; Nabism, Fauvism, and Cubism, as well as the art of independent painters; it all goes to show the amazing richness of French painting.

The Precursors
of Impressionism

ACHENBACH Oswald (1827-1905) was born in Düsseldorf on 2 February 1827 and died on 1 February 1905. After studying for twelve years at Düsseldorf Academy, where he was a pupil of his elder brother Andreas, he specialised in the study of nature. In 1845 he lived for a while in Bavaria and then moved to the north of Italy; later he went to Naples, then to Venice and Verona, and subsequently worked in Switzerland and the Rhine Valley.

His best and most original work however was done in the South of Italy where his subjects included various scenes of local life, religious festivals and processions. Like the French forerunners of the Impressionists, he made a special study of light and shade effects, his subjects ranging from dawn, twilight and moonlight to landscapes painted in brilliant sunshine, all most carefully and truthfully observed.

At that time the Düsseldorf School was still definitely classical in spirit; landscapes tended to be painted laboriously in the minutest detail, but Achenbach's work, with its delicate touches of tone and colour, was entirely different.

His fresh and lively approach to nature is accompanied by something poetical and romantic in his attitude, as we can see in his *Boat by the Lorelei* painted in 1862, where he portrays his brother Andreas with several other members of his family.

APPIAN Adolphe (1818-1898) Jacques Barthélemy, better known as Adolphe Appian, studied at the École des Beaux-Arts at Lyons, and was a pupil of Corot and Daubigny. He exhibited at the Salon in 1835, and then not again until 1855, after which he became a regular exhibitor until his death in

ACHENBACH *Monastery garden in Italy. c.* 1857

APPIAN *Landscape in Provence*

BLECHEN *Former Studio of Rudolf Schadow.* 1829

1898. His delicate and sensitively painted landscapes, with their feeling for the play of colour and light often vividly portrayed, come very close to Impressionism. Much of his work was done in the countryside near Lyons, at Optevoz and Virieu and in the Ain district, but he also painted along the south coast, at places like Collioure, Toulon and Les Martigues, and as far as Venice.

His beautiful engravings show a deep feeling for the poetry and melancholy of his native land. He chose simple and familiar things, such as a farm wagon in a forest clearing, a lakeside scene or a group of isolated trees, and he obtained unusual and attractive effects by his skilful technique in inking and wiping.

Although his engravings are still known and appreciated, Appian as a painter has been unjustly neglected. Yet in a number of his paintings he reveals himself as a true Impressionist.

BLECHEN Karl (1798-1840) Blechen studied at the Berlin Academy and with the landscape painter Lütke; he then worked for the Königstadt Theatre as a scene-painter. In

1828 he visited Switzerland and Italy, and later succeeded Lütke as Professor at the Berlin Academy, becoming a full member of the Academy in 1835. Well before Menzel, Blechen chose subjects that tended to be prosaic and far from picturesque, perhaps a view of roof tops or a factory with its tall smoking chimney. But his real feeling for changing lights and shadows and his sensitive and delicate touch made him an Impressionist before his time. In his painting *Palmarium on Peacock Island*, for instance, he uses a whole range of different green tints that merge into delicate shades of blue.

BONINGTON Richard Parkes (1802-1828) In 1817 Bonington's family went to live in Calais, where they set up a lace factory. There he studied with François-Louis Francia, a French watercolour painter who had lived in London during the time of the French Revolution, and had there met Girtin. In 1818 Bonington's family moved to Paris, and young Richard joined the painter Gros in his studio. He then travelled in France and Italy, and exhibited at the Paris Salon as well grace and elegance are French.

Bonington also did *genre* and historical paintings, mostly rather romantic in style and painted in the homely intimate manner of Dutch painting. His style is here inventive while as a landscape painter he paves the way for the Impressionists, just like Turner and Delacroix did.

BONINGTON *Fishing on the Normandy coast.* 1827

BONVIN François (1817-1887) was the son of a soldier who later became an innkeeper and a *garde-champêtre*, and whose second wife was inclined to be harsh with her small stepson. François had a difficult and unhappy childhood and eventually ran away from

BONVIN *Girls' School.* 1873

as elsewhere in France and in England. In spite of his English origin, he can in some respects be considered as a French painter, being also a friend of both Huet and Delacroix. His landscapes however are in the true English tradition, with their sense of space, their feeling for sky and clouds and their luminous, misty atmosphere. They are often reminiscent of Constable and Turner, but his

BONINGTON *Riva degli Schiavoni, Venice*

home. He had trained as a printer, found a job as a junior clerk at the Law Courts, and exhausted himself working in his clerk's office by day and at the printers' by night. Finally he found a rather better-paid job at 1000 francs a month and was able to spend his evenings studying drawing. In 1845 he began to study painting with François Granet who specialised in painting monks, but Bonvin preferred nuns as subjects, particularly the Sisters of Charity who had once nursed him devotedly when he was ill in hospital. In 1847 he exhibited for the first time at the Salon.

Bonvin can well be compared to Chardin or Peter de Hooch in his deep sincerity of approach and in the type of subjects he chose. His paintings, like theirs, have an atmosphere of stillness and recollection, and his love of plain and simple things, such as a candlestick, a coffee mill or a plain copper bowl, comes out in his still-life painting. Although he is a master of realism, he is also a forerunner of Manet, whom he befriended and encouraged in his early days; his studies of light remind one of the Impressionists, while his charcoal drawings are extraordinarily like those of Seurat.

In 1886 his friends organised a retrospective of his work; six months later he became blind. A sale was arranged to give him financial help but he died the following year.

Bonvin's approach to art was sincere and unassuming, and the simplicity of his subjects and the humility and modesty of his style are touching evidence of his patient search after truth.

CALS Adolphe (1810-1880) was born in Paris into a poor working-class family, and even as a small child showed a gift for painting. He began by doing drawings for various engravers, and in 1828 went as a student to Léon Cogniet, who was known as a painter of historical subjects. Corot however was his real teacher. Life was not easy. The young woman he married went mad and their only daughter was also mentally ill; his only comfort and joy was in painting. Whatever the weather, winter or summer, Cals would set out, in his heavy wooden clogs, to explore the countryside, taking the poor country folk as models, while his unpretentious interiors remind one very much of Chardin. One day when he was visiting his usual dealer, Père Martin, he met Count Armand Doria, who was a great lover and connoisseur of painting and invited him to stay at his country house at Orrouy. At last Cals was free to devote himself to his great love of nature, and moreover, he was able to sell his pictures. His daughter's health gradually improved but in 1871 his wife died; he then moved to Honfleur where he had a group of painter friends—Hervier, Vignon, Boudin and Jongkind. The last few years of his life were peaceful and happy; he spent all his time

CALS *Portrait of a Young Woman.* 1874

painting and actually showed his pictures along with the Impressionists, who accepted him as one of themselves.

In his landscapes he is the forerunner of Boudin and Jongkind, with the same spontaneity and freedom of approach, the same quivering sensitivity and often dazzling intensity of vision. He also painted some fine still lifes; here his technique is amazingly rich and modern while his studies of peasants and fishermen have the authentic ring of truth.

CARPEAUX Jean-Baptiste (1827-1875) was a great sculptor who had however many jealous enemies and detractors, and as a result developed a kind of persecution mania. But he was also a powerful and original painter; indeed many critics look on him as one of the forerunners of Impressionism.

His father was a poor stonemason. His childhood was wretched and deprived; he was often ill and misunderstood by his teachers,

CARRAND *Lyons, the Cours du Midi*

but in spite of all these difficulties, in the end his genius triumphed over all obstacles. In 1854 he won the Prix de Rome, and in 1863 attained general recognition with his *Ugolino*. He was a hard and dedicated worker; his total output includes more than eighty groups, statues and busts, as well as a large number of unfinished projects and sketches, more than three thousand drawings, and a number of paintings in oils.

His paintings are all too little known. They reveal Carpeaux's nervous and vigorous approach, and his violent, brutal brushwork reminds one of painters such as Frans Hals, Magnasco and Manet. He paints like a sculptor, emphasising the harsh and rugged aspect of his models by the play of light and shade, or giving faces and limbs a shiny, indeed almost oily surface so that they seem to be made of terracotta. We see this technique, for instance, in the portrait he painted of his son. His intense and powerful light effects remind us of Expressionism and underline the truth of what the Goncourt Brothers wrote of him: 'the hectic violence of genius in a sculptor's skin'.

CARRAND Louis-Hilaire (1821-1899)
Carrand was born at Lyons, the son of a rich silk merchant. He inherited a considerable fortune from his father, and was therefore able to take up painting. In 1840 he visited Italy with his brother. In 1865 his brother got into financial difficulties and was threatened with bankruptcy; Louis gave up his entire fortune to meet the creditors' demands, and was left practically ruined. As a result he had to take any job he could find, and even though his prices were as low as 30 francs, he had the greatest difficulty in selling his pictures.

He painted both at Crémieux and Optevoz, where he met Ravier and Daubigny, and also near his country house at Collonges-le-Haut. He used to get up very early, dressed in his blue artist's smock, and go down towards the river Saône; and the canvases he painted by the water reflect all the changing moods of nature and the seasons. His very personal experiments with colour remind one of Ravier; indeed one can see in him the true forerunner of modern painting, going far beyond the Impressionists or the Fauves and even, in some of his works, experimenting with abstract painting. He did not expect his pictures to be understood by the local people who were completely baffled by his approach; indeed the critics declared his paintings to be nothing but ghastly daubs and scribbles.

A few days before his death he declared: 'I have spent my life facing the sun; now I shall see what there is on the other side'. And so he died, unknown and unappreciated.

CHINTREUIL Antoine (1814-1873) Like Cals and Hervier, was a disciple of Corot's. He was particularly interested in the different aspects of light, sunset and sunrise, and was one of the most outstanding among the forerunners of the Impressionists in his sensitive approach to subtle changes of light and atmosphere. He first went to Paris as a penniless lad in 1838, and lived a Bohemian life with a group of other artists, but he was a serious and reserved man, and his one aim was to observe nature. He would spend long hours at Igny on the banks of the river Bièvre, sitting on the wet grass in all weathers exposed to rain and wind, and there he contracted pleurisy which left his lungs permanently affected.

Various friends, such as Champfleury and Béranger, took an active interest in him and helped him. He first went to live at La Tournelle-Septeuil near Mantes in the Seine valley—he came back there to die at the end of his life—and then at Millemont. There he painted most of his landscapes, catching the fleeting moods and gradations of light, and the great wide spaces, as we see in the painting entitled *Space* and in his last painting, *Rain and Sun*. Here the rain and cloud effects and the iridescent play of light illuminate the receding planes of the landscape with loving delicacy and tenderness.

Chintreuil tends to ignore detail; feeling and impressions predominate in his work, and he builds up great masses and volume in broad sweeps of brushwork. He loves to conjure up all the poetry of silvery mists and sparkling dew and frost; indeed one of his biographers speaks of his attaining strange and uncanny effects almost impossible to express.

COLIN Gustave (1828-1910) came from a legal family. He showed his talent for painting when still very young, and became a pupil of Corot's friend Constant Dutilleux. He first exhibited at the Salon in 1857, and then went to the Pyrenees to work. There he met an

COLIN *Le Torrent*

CHINTREUIL *The Seine and the Mont Valérien*

attractive local girl; they married in 1860 and settled at Ciboure. In 1863 he was showing at the Salon des Refusés (paintings that had been turned down by the Salon) and it was not until 1867 that the Salon Hanging Committee overcame their dislike of his work and began to appreciate him. He became a regular exhibitor at the Salon, but even then he was not really appreciated, and he found life difficult. Meanwhile he had become a friend of Corot's and went with him first to Arras and then to the Pyrenees. In 1874 he showed some canvases at the Impressionist Exhibition. Count Doria took an interest in him but he still had to sell his works through the salerooms at the Hôtel Drouot, like Corot's two pupils, Lavieille and Lépine.

In his early work we see Colin using thick layers of paint and stippling in muted tones; later he developed a frankly Impressionist style, with a lighter clearer palette. His studies of women are not unlike Corot's, while his genre paintings are full of life, and his landscapes are full of sparkling changing light.

CONSTABLE John (1776-1837) was born at East Bergholt in Suffolk, the son of a rich miller. He began to study painting with some friends who were artists, but most of what he learnt came from his observation of nature. In 1799 he was accepted as a student at the Royal Academy, where he spent most of his time copying landscapes by artists such as Claude Lorrain and Ruisdael. He first exhibited at

CONSTABLE *Salisbury Cathedral*. 1819

the Royal Academy in 1802, and in 1819 became an A.R.A., but it was not until after he had won a Gold Medal at the Paris Salon

with *The Haywain* and another at the Lille Exhibition for the *White Horse* that he was elected a member of the Royal Academy. In 1806 he visited the Lake District, and in 1811 went to Salisbury for the first time, while in 1816 he spent his honeymoon in Dorset. He also stayed in Brighton several times, and bought himself a house in Hampstead, each new place giving him fresh inspiration for his painting. Although he made sketches from nature both in oils and in pencil, he actually worked his pictures up in his Charlotte Street studio in London.

His deep sense of nature, his understanding of *chiaroscuro* and his free handling of paint are all remarkable. His exhibits at the 1824 Paris Salon made a great sensation and, as a result, in France alone he sold more than twenty paintings. Incidentally Constable was much admired by Delacroix who paid him a visit in 1825. Constable is undoubtedly one of the greatest forerunners of the Impressionists.

COROT Camille (1796-1875) Corot, the real forerunner of modern landscape painting, brought back from Rome, as did his two friends Édouard Bertin and Caruelle d'Aligny, a number of closely observed but somewhat austere studies of the Roman Campagna that showed a fresh vision and attitude to the classical landscape. These paintings are small in size, but are real masterpieces. However the large compositions he painted for the Salon to please the Hanging Committee are definitely still in the neo-classical tradition, and lack his usual typical spontaneity and freshness.

He also shows his originality as a portrait painter, though indeed he sometimes reminds us of Manet. His *Woman seated with her breast bare* painted in 1835, *Marietta* (1848) and the portrait of the *Reverend Mother of the Annonciade Convent* reveal a deep sense of hidden life such as one finds in Vermeer, in spite of his apparently effortless simplicity.

At the same time as he was working on a series of *Souvenirs* of Mortefontaine and Ville d'Avray, with peasant women carrying wood, or mythological figures added just to please the authorities at the Academy, he also painted landscapes in various other parts of France: Chartres, Brittany, Douai or the Isère

Corot *View of Marissel*

Valley. These landscapes are very moving in their simplicity, and have an extraordinarily fresh and youthful appeal.

COTMAN John Sell (1782-1842) was the son of a Norwich barber. In 1798 he went to

Corot *Marietta in Rome.* 1843

London where a friend of his, Dr Monro, introduced him to various watercolour and landscape artists. Cotman's early water-colours, painted between 1800 and 1803 during visits to Wales and the West Country, are rich and sombre in tone. In the years between 1803 and 1805, he was working in Yorkshire. Cotman's technique was always individual, and his very original colour harmonies show a spirit of synthesis which is completely different from the naturalism of most of his contemporaries. In 1806 Cotman went back to Norwich, and between 1807 and 1833, exhibited regularly with the Norwich Art Society. In 1812 he went to live in Yarmouth where he worked at a series of etchings of East Anglian buildings. He visited Normandy in 1820 again, and as a result published his *Architectural Antiquities of Normandy*. In 1834 he was appointed to the staff of King's College, London, as professor of drawing; among his pupils there was the Pre-Raphaelite painter Dante Gabriel Rossetti.

Cotman's watercolours are bold and free in style, while their dramatic light effects and stormy atmosphere remind one of Turner.

COTMAN *After the Storm*

COURBET Gustave (1819-1877)
Although Courbet was the achnowledged
leader of the Realist school of painting, his
work also has a certain affinity with the
Impressionists. He influenced Monet, who
painted with him at Fécamp and Étretat in
1867, and together with Boudin and Jongkind, played a definite part in guiding and
training the younger painter. After all,
Realists and Impressionists alike share a love
and appreciation of nature, and Courbet is
closest to the Impressionists in his Honfleur
paintings with their expanses of sky and ever-
changing colouring. The critic Roger Marx,
speaking of *The Amazon*, a portrait of Louise
Colin painted out of doors says: 'It fulfils in
anticipation all the aims of impressionism'.

Courbet, like Corot, was one of the first
artists to paint out of doors, and the green of

COURBET *The cliff at Étretat.* 1870

COURBET *Fishing boats on the shore at Trouville*

his fields is even more convincing, fresher and more vivid than Constable's. It is particularly noticeable after 1854, when he stayed at Montpellier with his friend Bruyas, that his palette became lighter and brighter in tone. Zacharie Astruc remarks that Courbet's seascapes 'express all the shifting light effects of the sea throughout the day, with mist and sunlight, the wind on the waves, the pearly light of early morning, the bright translucent calm of noonday, and the stillness and mystery of evening'.

COX David (1783-1859) came to London in 1804, and as a pupil of John Varley, experimented with sketching in oils out of doors. In 1826 he visited various parts of England, and also went to Holland and Belgium; in 1829 and again in 1832 he went to Calais and Paris, and finally, in 1841, settled at Harborne near Birmingham.

Cox was a contemporary of Cotman and Peter de Wint, and like them, sought to catch all the fleeting moods of nature, rather in the manner of his immediate predecessors, Turner and Constable. The paintings he exhibited in France were very much appreciated there, particularly at the 1855 Salon. His beach scenes already anticipate those of Boudin, while his street scenes, with their delicacy and softness, remind us of Monet and Pissarro.

CROME John (1768-1821) better known as Old Crome, was the son of a Norwich weaver. He was apprenticed to a sign-painter, and there learnt the elements of painting. He and his friend Robert Ladbrooke used to sketch together in Norfolk, and his meeting with Thomas Harvey of Catton, who had a fine collection of seventeenth-century Dutch paintings as well as works by contemporary British artists, was a turning-point in his career. He set up as a teacher of drawing, and was one of the founder members of the Norwich Society of Artists, becoming its President in 1808. He exhibited there regularly from 1805 till 1820, and also showed at the Royal Academy between 1806 and 1818.

Apart from three oil paintings executed after a visit to the Continent in 1814, all his works represent scenes in East Anglia.

Crome belongs to the tradition of English landscape painting, beginning with Cuyp and ending with Turner, with its increasing emphasis on changing light effects. *The Fishmarket at Boulogne, Yarmouth Water Frolic* and *Moonrise over the Yare* are three examples of his style.

DAUBIGNY Charles (1817-1878) was five or six years younger than Dupré and Rousseau, and more than any other painter of his generation, can be called the real fore-runner of Impressionism. Like Corot, he work-ed mostly out of doors. He exhibited at the Salon in 1838, but his first real success was in 1844, with his *Crossroads in the Forest of Fontaine-bleau*. After making a journey to Rome on foot, he came back to Barbizon where he stayed with Rousseau; he then painted in Normandy and in the Isère, and finally settled down and lived on a barge at Auvers on the river Oise. He is like Sisley in his fondness for riverbanks as a subject. In his painting *Harvest*, now in the Louvre, he still shows the strong influence of the Dutch School; later he used much clearer and brighter tones. Yet his sketches tend to be dim and subdued in colouring, broad and flexible in treatment but without much sense of light. His actual technique, however, was very close to that of the Impressionists, and this is in fact the main reason why he was so disliked by the critics and the general public.

During the time of the Commune he went to London, and subsequently visited Holland; the result was some very fine paintings. Daubigny died at Auvers in 1878, twelve years before Van Gogh.

DELACROIX Eugène (1798-1863) When Delacroix began his career as a painter, neo-classicism, with David as its chief exponent, was fashionable; but both Delacroix and Géricault abandoned this style and led French painting towards romanticism. In this way he showed himself to be a true forerunner of Impressionism. Like his friend Bonington, and the other English painters of his day, he experimented with colour and light effects. George Sand tells us how, when he was paint-ing at Nohant, he noticed how the flowers he was painting would change in tone and even in outline, throughout the various stages of their flowering; they were different from one day to another. We see the same close observation of nature in Monet's studies of

DAUBIGNY *The Sluice at Optevoz*. 1859

waterlilies.

We can see from Delacroix's letters and Journal how he was attracted to what he called 'pure painting'; in fact, Maxime du Camp goes as far as to use the expression 'abstract colour' when writing about his work. Delacroix believed that painting had a kind of individual 'soul' and a personal language by which it was able to express itself, even without the use of form. He used to say of Bonington that his works were 'a kind of diamond that delighted and charmed the eye, quite independently from any actual subject or

DELACROIX *Death of Ophelia*

DELACROIX *Vase on a console table. c.* 1848

imitation of reality'. Delacroix discovered the way and the Impressionists followed it.

DIAZ DE LA PEÑA Narcisse Virgilio (1807-1876) was born at Bordeaux where his parents, middleclass Spaniards, had fled at

the time of King Joseph's persecutions. They both died when he was still a child, and he was adopted by a Protestant pastor. Like Jules Dupré, he began his career in a china factory, and then started painting small panels that he sold for sixteen to twenty-five francs each; later he exhibited at the 1831 Salon. He was a great admirer of Correggio and Delacroix. He particularly deserves to be numbered among the pre-Impressionists for his woodland scenes, with their bold colour contrasts and vigorous handling. Indeed André Billy wrote of him: 'Diaz was born before his time, an Impressionist before Impressionism existed; if he had lived thirty years later, he would have been the most outstanding painter of his generation. Of all the Barbizon school he is the one most admired by lovers of modern art, and in many ways, can be said to anticipate Renoir. No other artist of his generation could convey the freshness and grace of flowers or woman's flesh with such charm and felicity'.

He worked in the same studio as Millet, sharing his life and his poverty, but, as he said: 'Millet paints nettles but I prefer painting roses'.

Diaz pandered to contemporary taste by putting melancholy love-lorn maidens and

DIAZ DE LA PEÑA *Landscape on the edge of the Forest of Fontainebleau.* 1869

DIAZ DE LA PEÑA *Landscape with pond*

mythological goddesses in his woodland scenes, but he is a marvellous colourist and has been called a forerunner of *tachisme*; he would paint patches of colour that did not represent anything in particular, and then go out of doors and work them up into paintings.

FRIEDRICH Caspar-David (1774-1840) was born on 5 September 1774 at Greifswald and died on 7 May 1840 in Dresden. In 1794 he joined the Copenhagen Academy with Quisdorf before moving on in 1798 to Dresden. There he saw a good deal of P. O. Runge and was in close touch with the romantics under Tieck and Novalis, while later his style was not unlike that of the painters Dahl and Carus. He left Dresden to travel and went to the North Sea, the Riesengebirge and the Harz mountains. He was a simple sensitive character, something of an introvert and tending to be withdrawn and to avoid social life. He would meditate on the great ultimate realities, life and death and the existence of God, and find the inspiration for his landscapes in the contemplation of nature.

He loved to paint ruined Gothic churches, romantic landscapes, desolate shores and steep mountain peaks, and shows a wonderful feeling for nature.

He also did engravings of landscapes. In 1817 he was appointed Professor at the Dresden Academy and in 1840 was elected a member of the Academy in Berlin.

FRIEDRICH *Rocks at Ruegen.* 1820

GENSLER Johann-Jacob (1808-1845) Born in Hamburg on 21 January 1808, he died there on 26 January 1845, and is chiefly known as a *genre* and a landscape painter. Like the English watercolourists, he was able to discover and anticipate the special qualities of Impressionism through an intense love of nature and close attention to the changing effects of light.

Gensler was first a pupil of Wilhelm Tischbein at Eutin; in 1826 he went to study at the Munich Academy, and in 1830 in Vienna. From 1830 onwards he exhibited in Ham-

burg, Munich and Dresden. In 1841 he visited Holland and Belgium. There he was particularly successful, with his delicately dreamy and melancholy style, in capturing light effects and portraying dawn and twilight scenes, and the iridescence of sky and clouds reflected in water, by lakes and by the sea. His best works are to be found in the Kunsthalle in Hamburg.

GENSLER *The Old Willow tree.* 1842

GIRTIN Thomas (1775-1802) was apprenticed at the age of fourteen to a topographer. He was then encouraged to take up painting by some of his patrons and eventually became the leading English watercolourist of his time. His free technique and subtlety of approach influenced Turner, Constable, Cox, Peter de Wint and Cotman, and Bonington. Bonington in his turn influenced Delacroix and the French Romantics. Girtin can thus be considered the leader of that movement in painting which finally turned away from neoclassicism and led towards a greater freedom of technique and a more luminous vision, so opening the way eventually to the coming of Impressionism.

GUIGOU Paul (1834-1871) Paul Guigou, like Monticelli, can be looked on as a true

GIRTIN *Kirkstall Abbey, evening.* 1800

forerunner of Impressionism in the nineteenth-century Provençal school. Guigou was originally intended to be a solicitor, but with the encouragement of the head of the École des Beaux-Arts at Marseilles, Emile Loubon, decided to give up law and take up painting instead. The two canvases he first exhibited at Marseilles in 1854 show him to be an outstanding colourist. He came across Courbet's work in 1856, during a brief visit to Paris, and when he returned to Provence, he began to paint in the most desolate and barren parts of the countryside. He went back to Paris in 1862. His work was accepted for exhibition at the Salon the following year, and from then until 1870 he showed there regularly, visiting Provence whenever he could and often painting there with Monticelli. Each of the two artists interpreted the Provençal landscape in his own individual way; Guigou's style gradually became lighter and brighter. The subjects he chose were less sombre, while he often painted on wooden panels to obtain richer and warmer effects. He always pays great attention to detail in his paintings, with brilliant colour and light effects. When in Paris, he painted large canvases of the kind he thought suitable for the Salon, and also gave painting and drawing lessons. Life was not

GUIGOU *La Route de la Gineste.* 1859

easy financially and when he could not afford to go back to Provence, he painted by the Seine and the Marne instead. He was just beginning to be better known and the future at last seemed promising, when he suddenly had a stroke and died at the age of only thirty-seven.

HARPIGNIES Henri (1819-1916) was a pupil of Jean Alexis Achard, who belonged to the Lyons school of painters, and often travelled about with him. Harpignies' first works, particularly his delicate and sensitive watercolours, show an affinity with the Fontaine-bleau School and the Pre-Impressionists of the period.

After a visit to Italy to study art, he exhibited a *View of Capri* at the 1853 Salon, but in 1868 the Hanging Committee turned down his *Wild Ducks*, whereupon he destroyed it. Later he achieved great success as a painter, and, unlike most other forerunners of Impressionism, won a number of medals.

HARPIGNIES *Autumn scene.* 1884

HERVIER Adolphe (1818-1879) was the son of a painter who had been a pupil of David. Adolphe himself was taught first by Léon Cogniet and then by Isabey. He was always poor, living a solitary bohemian existence, like his contemporary Rodolphe Bresdin, also an engraver, whose genius is now fully recognised and appreciated. The two artists influenced each other in their engravings, while both had a particular admiration for Rembrandt.

Hervier, like his teacher Isabey, chose subjects such as farmyard scenes, rustic wooden houses or boats on the seashore. He would wander from one place to another, looking for picturesque subjects to paint, but although he started sending canvases to the Salon in 1838, he was turned down twenty-three times, and when a painting of his was finally accepted, it

HERVIER *The Potato pickers*

was very badly hung. Théophile Gautier much admired him, and in fact he was an excellent landscape artist as well as a remarkable *genre* painter. His village scenes, with their old buildings, stone walls and winding country lanes, have an atmosphere of real poetry and charm; he has a convincing sense of colour with a vigorous lively technique. His watercolours particularly have a unique inimitable grace, and among them are some that are worthy of the great masters of Impressionism.

HUET Paul (1803-1869) was a pupil of Gros and Pierre Guérin. He painted out of doors in the Île Seguin, which was then quite wild and unspoilt, and also in the country round Paris.

He later met Delacroix who had admired one of his sketches. Huet's style, with its contrast between heavy shadows and clear light, reminds us of English painting, then very fashionable in France. Huet actually met Bonington in Gros' studio, and in the 1824 Salon he came across Sir Thomas Lawrence's portraits and Constable's *Haywain*, which made a great impression. Huet can be considered one of the real forerunners of Impressionism, along with Delacroix and the painters of the English School, and from now on, Delacroix and Huet frequently met. Huet travelled extensively in France, Normandy, the Auvergne and Provence, and in the 1838 Salon his painting *High Tide* was much admired, while in the 1853 Salon he showed *Flood at Saint-Cloud* which Delacroix praised as a masterpiece.

Huet's work reveals a deep sense of communion with nature and an extraordinarily lyrical and poetical atmosphere. Impressionism can indeed be said to have begun with Huet. His free inspiration and the freshness of his approach are even more clearly expressed in his landscapes than in his oil paintings, and his original engravings and lithographs are also remarkable.

LAMBINET Émile-Charles (1815-1878) was a pupil of Drolling, Boisselier and Horace Vernet, but more particularly, a disciple of

HUET *The Footbridge*

Corot and Daubigny. Starting in 1833 right up to the year of his death he showed landscapes of the country round Paris, especially of the Chevreuse valley, as well as paintings of Brittany and Normandy, and his light effects particularly show great delicacy and charm.

Salon Libre in 1848; in the 1849 Salon Exhibition he won a medal for third prize. In 1855 an art-lover friend invited him to live in the outbuildings of his house at La Ferté-Milon that had once been an old Leper Hospital, and there he worked hard at his land-

LAMBINET *Autumn morning.* 1850

Several of his landscapes painted after 1854 remind us of Camille Pissarro and already anticipate Impressionism.

LAVIEILLE Eugène (1820-1889) Lavieille was the son of a Paris upholsterer, and like Georges Michel, Hervier and Chintreuil began by sketching such things as tumble-down cottages on the Butte Montmartre. He then became Corot's favourite pupil. He settled with his wife and children in a cottage at Barbizon, where life was anything but easy; he used to get up very early to capture the changing light effects of dawn. He first exhibited at the Salon in 1844 and again at the

scape painting, going out into the forest and countryside in all weathers, winter and summer. When he was at Barbizon his tones tended to be subdued and melancholy; in the Valley of the Ourcq they became brighter and fresher. But like Chinetreuil, his health suffered from painting out of doors in all weathers, even sketching village scenes in the snow, and his chest was permanently affected after having bronchitis and pleurisy. The *Night Scene* he exhibited at the 1878 Salon was very well received, and this encouraged him to do as Jongkind had done and paint a number of moonlight scenes, as well as snow scenes, sunrises and sunsets, and attractive sunny landscapes.

LAVIEILLE *The Pond*

Like other landscape painters of his generation, such as Cals, Hervier and Chintreuil, Lavieille had a very deep love of nature. His landscapes show her infinitely varying moods, and are painted in a lyrical, yet lovingly faithful spirit. He is indeed one of the most authentic forerunners of Impressionism.

LÉPINE Stanislas (1835-1892) Like Boudin, this pupil of Corot's was originally self-taught. Though he spent part of each

LÉPINE *Sailing boats in Caen harbour*

summer in Normandy, he lived in Paris, and the banks of the Seine provided the chief inspiration for his painting. He knew Cals, Vignon and Dutilleux, and in 1874 showed his work along with the Impressionists. In many ways, his painting anticipates theirs, although with its soft and delicate colouring, it is far removed from the bolder approach of Monet and his friends.

What is chiefly attractive about Lépine's work is the delicacy of his colouring and his light touch, something between Corot and Jongkind. Like Jongkind he painted a number of moonlight scenes. He was always hard up and as he had no dealer to sell his works for him, he was obliged to hold auctions of his paintings, as did several of his contemporaries. It was only towards the end of his life that his real originality began to be recognized.

MENZEL Adolf (1815-1905) was the son of a Breslau lithographer, and hence a direct descendant of the Berlin school of Krüger and Blechen. When visiting an exhibition in Berlin in 1845, he came across Constable's paintings, and they were a revelation to him. The two great Universal Exhibitions in Paris, in 1855 and 1867, gave him the opportunity to get to know French painting. His finest and most striking picture was *Le*

MENZEL
*Afternoon in the Tuileries
Gardens.* 1867

Théâtre du Gymnase which he painted in 1856 after his first Paris visit; it was inspired by Daumier's *Le Drame*. This little German dwarf—he was about Toulouse-Lautrec's height—is indeed an Impressionist before his time; one can see this in his delightful *Room with a balcony*, a bright sunny interior, where a long net curtain is blown into the room by a breath of wind, and in *The Tuileries Gardens* which reminds one very much of Manet.

MENZEL
The Room with a balcony. 1845

Menzel is also famous for his historical paintings; it was on account of these that he was made a member of the academies of Berlin, Vienna, Munich, Dresden and Brussels.

MICHALLON Achille Etna (1796-1822) who won a prize for an historical landscape in 1817, is considered by many critics to be a

MICHALLON *Woman struck by Lightning.* 1857

forerunner of Romanticism, while others think of him rather as anticipating Impressionism. He was only fifteen when he began to be well known, and the Russian Prince Youssoupoff became his patron and gave him a regular pension. In 1812, when he was only sixteen, he exhibited several landscapes at the Salon and won a silver medal. Five years later, he won the Prix de Rome for his historical landscapes, and went to Rome as a result. Soon after his return he died prematurely.

Michallon had the great honour of being Corot's teacher, and it was he who urged Corot to start painting in the open air. He brought back a number of sketches of the Roman Campagna with him from Italy. They were all painted out of doors, and remind us very much of Corot's work as well as the English landscape painters who were his contemporaries, in their skilful handling of light effects.

MILLET Jean-François (1814-1875) was the son of a peasant from Normandy, the eldest of eight children. He began to draw very early when he was still working on the farm. In 1833 he started lessons with the painter Bon Dumoncel, otherwise known as Mouchel, in his Cherbourg studio, and in 1885 went to Langlois de Chèvreville to study. He was awarded a scholarship by the municipality of Cherbourg, and so was able to go to Paris. He settled there in 1837 and became a student at Paul Delaroche's studio as well as working at

MILLET *Spring.* 1868-1873

the Louvre and the Académie Suisse. When he returned to Cherbourg, he painted mostly portraits and shop signs, and also attempted some nudes. After his marriage he went to live at Barbizon, where he became known as one

MILLET *Woman bathing*

of the artists of the realist school, his subjects being mostly simple workers and peasants. The critics were unfavourable and he was called 'a painter of low life' and a revolutionary. But his friends, including the painter Théodore Rousseau, supported him, and towards the end of his life he finally became famous.

Like Courbet and Rousseau, he may be considered as anticipating Impressionism in some of his paintings, in his love of nature and his feeling for light. This was particularly evident in his final period, when his tones became lighter and he made more use of bright reflections and highlights; at the same time his opaque shadows were lightened through his 'multiplicity of close, lively brushstrokes that made his surfaces shine and reflect the light'.

Later he came across an illustrated book with Hokusai wood-cuts; in 1864 he began a collection of Japanese prints which he kept in a folder along with some Delacroix drawings, and they influenced and inspired his subsequent work.

MONTICELLI Adolphe (1824-1886)
After beginning his studies at an art school in Marseilles, in 1846 Monticelli went to Paris to

MONTICELLI *The Trumpeter*

study at the Louvre and in Paul Delaroche's studio. In 1849 he went back to Marseilles and from 1851 to 1862 lived alternately there and in Paris. He was influenced at first by the painter Henri Baron and later by Diaz whom he got to know personally. He was much impressed too by the work of Delacroix and this had a great influence on his technique. From 1862 to 1870 he was working in Paris where a dealer undertook to buy any pictures he might produce, at a very low price, and then sold them again to English and American clients. He went back to live permanently in Marseilles in 1870, and eventually died there in 1886 after a stroke. He was a real bohemian, living from hand to mouth and selling his paintings for very little; he was a very prolific painter whose only joy was in his work.

His light effects are produced by a combination of pure unmixed colours, dotted on to the canvas with stiff brushes. His landscapes are painted with thick oily strokes, like a kind of coloured mosaic done with heavy impasting. His favourite subjects were richly-coloured sunsets, autumn tints, with early morning scenes and the brilliant scarlet of dawn. His still-lifes are aglow with light and colour, with rich brocades, flowers in full bloom and vivid shades of porcelain. He also executed a number of *genre* paintings, flirtatious encounters and fair-grounds, as well as several portraits. Germain Bazin declared that he was 'the missing link between Delacroix and van Gogh' and there is a good deal of truth in this.

PALMER Samuel (1805-1881) Palmer was the son of a bookseller who brought him up to love English literature and especially Milton. He learnt the rudiments of painting from William Wate, and first exhibited in 1819, when still under the influence of Turner and William Cox. In 1822 he met John Linnell who interested him in naturalist painting, and in 1824 introduced him to William Blake. He became Blake's disciple and under his influence illustrated Thornton's *Virgil*. From 1826 to 1832 he was living at Shoreham in Sussex, and became the centre of a group of artists who called themselves the Ancients. It was at Shoreham that he painted his most unusual works, where his inner vision is expressed through a very individual interpretation of nature. In 1837 he married Hannah, Linnell's daughter, and they left England for Italy where they spent two years. After his return, Samuel Palmer concentrated on watercolour painting, and towards the end of his life recovered something like Blake's vision and atmosphere in his illustrations to Milton and Virgil.

His youthful work however gives the best impression of the visionary spirit of English Romanticism.

PALMER *View of Tivoli. c.* 1839

RAVIER Auguste (1814-1895) was born at Lyons and came from a rich merchant family. He gave up studying law when still very young to dedicate himself to painting. In 1839 he first met Corot at Royat, and like Corot, it was during a visit to Rome in 1840 that he became aware of his real gift for painting. He stayed more than a year in Rome on that first visit, and went back several more times. He particularly admired the works of Caruelle d'Aligny, and his views of the Roman Campagna are reminiscent of those of Corot.

After some time spent working in the Forez and Velay districts he settled down at Crémieu about 1850. There he married, and he often went back to his old haunts. Corot, Daubigny and Français joined him there, but in 1867 he decided to move to the neighbouring little town of Morestel where he went on living his independent and solitary life. Ravier was a painter of dawn and twilight, and brilliant colours flashing across the sky and reflected in pools and water. Here we can see the beginnings of 'pure painting'. Ravier taught Carrand who will take even further his studies of the effects of light reflected in mists and of the thickets and undergrowth along the banks of the Saône. He loved autumn with its changing tints, and his watercolours have a delicate transparent quality that reminds one of Turner. He is an imaginative painter and a visionary, to an even greater extent than Monet, while his capacity for conveying a sense of space and the immensity of a landscape is unequalled.

He was very little known during his lifetime, partly because he lived at Lyons, and was always unassuming and independent.

RIBOT Théodule (1823-1891) Like Bonvin and Vollon, Ribot is considered to be a predecessor of Manet. He found it very difficult to get started in his career, even more so than most of the Impressionists. He attempted various things—working with a looking-glass maker, decorating blinds, doing copies of Watteau and Pierrot pictures to send to America. Finally he began to paint his own family, doing small pictures of his wife and children, and also those kitchen scenes that eventually made him famous. His colouring,

RIBOT *La Charbonnière*

and especially his use of blacks and pinks, remind one of Velazquez, and he rivals Chardin and Le Nain in his delightful domestic scenes.

Towards 1865 his use of contrast and of strongly marked chiaroscuro became more marked, and his work is reminiscent of the Spanish painters Ribera and Zurbaran, who favoured the same kind of effects. In fact Ribot's painting reminds one very much of theirs, particularly in his religious pictures, such as his *St. Sebastian*, exhibited at the 1865 Salon, or *Christ among the doctors*.

About the year 1876 Ribot went back to painting interiors, but with a distinct change in his use of colour; he still made considerable use of black but otherwise his palette had lightened. He used clear whites with brilliant greens, blues and yellows as well as bright reds, and the whole effect was now different. He paid a visit to the country near Calais and brought back paintings such as *Inn in Nor-*

mandy, where his models tended to be either fishermen or peasants with weathered faces. He also painted a number of fine portraits. The style of these last works is extraordinarily vigorous but at the same time delicate, with warm rich tones and a generous use of paint; his brushwork is determined and strong, though never deliberately impasted.

By contrast with his difficult beginnings, Ribot's work was much appreciated in his latter years, and now, after an intervening period of neglect, he was once more acknowledged as a great painter. Unlike Manet, who chose attractive subjects such as lovely women in the nude enjoying a meal al fresco, or a fashionable lady at her balcony or dressing table, Ribot took unpretentious models, simple folk, gypsies and peasants, or people in a kitchen; but his penetrating, indeed spiritual approach makes him Manet's equal.

ROTTMANN Carl (1797-1850) was born on 11 January 1797 at Handschuchsheim near Heidelberg, and died on 6 July 1850 at Munich. He learnt painting first with his father, then with Johann Xeller at Heidelberg. In 1822 he went to live in Munich. At first he was much influenced by Poussin and Claude Lorrain, and he paid several visits to Italy. In 1827 he visited Rome and Palermo, and in 1829 went back to Rome where he

ROTTMANN *View of Cefalù*

painted a series of frescoes. In 1834 he went for a long journey through Greece and came back with a number of paintings he had done there. Later he was appointed official painter to the Court of Bavaria. King Ludwig I commissioned him to paint a series of twenty-three Greek landscapes; several of these are executed in a technique using pyrogravure. He also decorated the arcades at the Hofgarten with twenty-eight frescoes of Italian landscapes.

A study for the painting known as the *Battlefield at Marathon*, now in the Berlin museum, is not unlike some of Turner's landscapes, and gives a good idea of Rottmann's approach, romantic but yet anticipating Impressionism. His views of Greece and Italy have a nostalgic brooding quality.

ROUSSEAU Théodore (1812-1867) was leader of the Fontainebleau school and together with Millet and Courbet, one of the

ROUSSEAU *Cows at the watering-place*

chief French realist painters of the period. He was at the same time a forerunner of Impressionism; it is difficult to make rigorous distinction between different types of painting that are all inspired by love of nature and tend to overlap. Rousseau appears closest to Impressionism: it is difficult to make rigorous of doors, and his landscapes and woodland scenes, done in different lights and seasons, already have something of the Impressionists' luminous quality and sensitivity. He was influenced by Constable and Bonington as well as by Ruisdael and Hobbema, as is evident in the brilliance and clarity of his painting.

STIFTER Adalbert (1806-1868) After spending his childhood at Oberplan, he went in 1819 to a school kept by a religious community, and in 1826 to the University of Vienna. He was at the same time poet and artist, although he was entirely self-taught and never learnt painting. He showed his work at two exhibitions, in 1840 and 1862. In 1849 he became provincial Inspector of Primary Schools at Linz, continuing to live there till his death. He did not travel much, but in 1841 went to Hungary, in 1846 to Munich and Regensburg, in 1857 to Trieste, in 1860 again to Munich; then in 1865 he visited Carlsbad (now Karlovy Vary in Czechoslovakia), Prague and Nuremberg, returning to Carlsbad in 1866 and 1867. In 1851 he began writing reviews of art exhibitions.

In spite of a certain amateurishness, both his painting and writing show delicacy and sensitivity, and his pictures, with their very individual range of colouring, are fresh and graceful. The best of his landscapes were painted between 1835 and 1845. Although he had no knowledge of contemporary French painting, we can see in him a certain affinity with Corot; later on he tended to aim at a more realistic treatment of detail. Very little remains of his later work, and practically all we have left is some sketches for paintings he subsequently destroyed.

TROUILLEBERT Paul Désiré (1829-1900) was a disciple of Corot's; he first exhibited at the Salon in 1865 and started his career as a

TURNER *Crossing the brook.* 1815

portrait painter, but from 1881 onwards he concentrated on painting landscapes with delicate silvery grey tones and a misty atmosphere. He was particularly drawn to painting lake and riverside scenes, often with figures of men fishing.

TURNER Joseph Mallord William (1775-1851) Turner's landscapes are bold and impressionistic. He was the son of a barber, and taught himself to paint. He began by colouring architectural drawings and engravings, and in 1789 was admitted as a student at the Royal Academy. There he met Girtin, Reynolds, Fuseli and Loutherbourg, and through them attained his imaginative and fantastic conception of landscape. He then did some research into optical light effects, and his investigations went even further than the famous experiments of the Impressionists. He travelled widely in Europe, visiting the

Netherlands, Switzerland and Italy in his search for picturesque sites and spectacular scenery. In 1870 Monet and Pissarro, who were then in London, discovered Turner's work. He had already worked with Bonington in 1820 and in 1835 had met Delacroix. Towards the end of his life he came to paint those characteristic magical light effects, where his memory transfigured visual impressions into enchanting, fantastic hallucinations.

Turner's development was deliberately slow. He liked to go back to places he had already known and painted, and treat them again in an increasingly abstract manner, allowing the play of light to give a symbolic value to the scene. This is why Symbolists such as Huysmans and Gustave Moreau, as well as the Impressionists, thought so much of Turner's painting, and used him to justify their own theories about art. It was through Ruskin and his writings that aesthetes such as Proust came to admire Turner so much.

The painting *Great Western*, which had much impressed Monet and Pissarro, and represents a train rushing along at full speed, was admired by Romantics, Impressionists and Symbolists alike. Théophile Gautier described it as 'The Beast in the Apocalypse, the steam-engine, opening its great red glassy eyes in the dark and hauling its long backbone of coaches like an enormous tail. It is a wild demented picture where earth and sky are thrown into confusion together with furious brushstrokes—a strange extravagant picture, but the madman who painted it is a genius'.

VALENCIENNES Pierre Henri de (1750-1819) Valenciennes was one of the most outstanding representatives of Neo-Classicism,

VALENCIENNES *View of Rome*

and in his book *Elements of practical perspective for the use of artists* he appears completely academic in outlook, yet in spite of this, his studies of nature contradict his own theories. In fact he wrote: 'Alas, whenever a man of genius contemplates nature he hardly finds anything there; he sees nature exactly as it is, and although he admires what he sees, he is not really satisfied. The rocks seem to him mean and unimpressive . . . Happy is the artist who lets himself be swayed by the delights of illusion and so imagines he sees nature as it

ought to be. Such a man really is satisfied; he feels a noble pride at being able as it were to create something which is almost impossible to find in a state of perfection. His heated imagination is excited and fed by what the poets describe, and he produces all kinds of new things in infinite profusion'.

This describes the kind of imaginary landscape that was so dear to eighteenth century artists.

Valenciennes came from Toulouse and had been a pupil of Doyen. He taught perspective at the École des Beaux-Arts and was known as the direct inheritor of Poussin's 'grand manner'. He travelled in Italy where he made a special study of Claude Lorrain and Poussin, and later founded a successful school of classical landscape. In 1789 he was elected a member of the Royal Academy of painting, and also in that same year exhibited at the Salon for the first time.

VERNAY François (1821-1896) was born at Lyons. His mother was a cloth-maker and he started as a designer himself, but soon abandoned industrial design for art. Berjon taught him ornamental design, and he was also influenced by Ravier whom he met in

VERNAY *Still Life*

1850 on his return from Italy. Vernay learnt his independent outlook from Ravier, and really preferred to work alone. He was a natural colourist, varying his palette from bright and dazzling colours to softer muted tones, like his two favourite painters, Delacroix and Ravier.

The work he has left us consists of landscapes, charcoal or pencil drawings touched up with watercolour, but chiefly still lifes; he loved to paint fruit arranged on rich sumptuous materials.

Towards the end of his life he practically gave up painting in oils and worked at stylized landscape drawings rather after the manner of Rouault and Derain. He was misunderstood and unappreciated, like Ravier and Carrand, and died as he had lived, poor and wretched, in a public hospital ward.

VEYRASSAT Jules Jacques (1828-1893) Veyrassat did a number of *genre* paintings such as *Reapers*, *Cider drinkers*, and *Peasants* working

VOLLON Antoine (1833-1900) Vollon. the son of a decorator of Lyons, descended from good old artisan stock. He was twenty-six when he first went to Paris, where the Empress' chamberlain saw and liked his still lifes and bought several of them for one hundred francs each. He exhibited at the Salon in 1864, where the critic William Burger approved of his work. Vollon was influenced first by Ribot and later by Corot, and soon became expert in painting still life. Here he was a forerunner of Manet, while the style of his landscapes anticipates Impressionism.

A number of his still lifes with elaborate jugs, oriental earthenware and sumptuous brocades were the type of thing that attracted the rich bourgeois of the time, but we tend to prefer his simpler subjects that recall Chardin and Bonvin, with ordinary pots and pans.

Like Cézanne, he used to study his subjects—perhaps just a single apple—for weeks

VEYRASSAT *Les 'Cascaroles' du Lavoir*. 1863

in the fields etc., but he is chiefly known as a painter of horses, especially carthorses. His rustic scenes, and farm yards with sturdy horses in harness, remind one of Hervier both in subject and technique, and in their minute attention to detail. Like Chintreuil and Lavieille, he was very much interested in light effects, sunsets and sunrise.

at a time. 'In this way' he declared, 'I taught myself how to model things and how to put everything in its proper place'.

His style is bold and free in his still lifes, while his landscapes are much more delicately painted. Puvis de Chavannes went as far as to say his skies were as lovely as those of Backhuysen.

VOLLON *Daubigny's house.* 1883

Vollon was a fine colourist and an impulsive, tormented personality who sought to penetrate into the secret of things. Waldemar George wrote of him: 'The freshness of Vollon's visual perception reminds one of Corot; on the other hand his charcoal drawings, odd as it may seem, anticipate Maurice de Vlaminck's sketches'.

WASMANN Rudolph Friedrich (1805-1886) was born in Hamburg and was a pupil of Naecke in Dresden. He subsequently studied at Munich and then in Rome. He made friends with Cornelius, then leader of the 'Nazarenes', a German school of painting famous for its large historical works, such as *The Story of Joseph* which was painted for the Bartholdys. Wasmann however was particularly drawn to landscape painting, and went to live in a remote part of the Tyrol where he spent the rest of his life. He was completely forgotten when a Norwegian painter, Bernt Grönvold rediscovered him, pub-

lished his *Journal* and collected his works; they include some beautiful landscapes and mountain scenes in the Upper Adige and the Tyrol. Wasmann had a strong sense of colour, and felt the deep harmony between the greens of mountain pastures and the dim misty blues of the peaks and distances; he was also a distinguished portrait painter.

WHISTLER James Abbott McNeill (1834-1903) His father, Major George Whistler, was an army engineer. When he was commissioned to plan the St. Petersburg to Moscow railway he took his wife and child with him. After his father's death James entered West Point Academy, but he was an undisciplined character unsuitable for army life, and instead he was appointed a naval map-designer to the state of Washington. He also experimented with his first engravings. In 1855 he left America and worked first in London and then in Paris, where he studied with Gleyre. His fellow students in Gleyre's studio included Degas, Legros, Bracquemond and Fantin-Latour. In 1858 he brought out his first set of engravings. In 1859 his canvas *At the piano* was turned down by the Salon Hanging Committee, and Bonvin instead organised an exhibition in his studio, with works by Whistler, Legros and Ribot. In 1860 he sent his *White Girl* to the Salon; it was also refused. As his relations with the London Royal Academy were better than with the Salon, he decided to settle in England, and in 1859 brought out a series of engravings of the Thames. He also became an excellent portrait painter. He was influenced by Velazquez as well as by Dante Gabriel Rossetti and the Pre-Raphaelites, and by Japanese art. The quality of sober understatement in his work probably derives from this Japanese influence, but Whistler was also a forerunner of Impressionism. Writing about the Impressionists, he declared: 'Nature contains the elements in colour and form of all pictures, just as the keyboard contains the notes of all music. But the artist is born to pick and choose, and group with science those elements, that the result may be beautiful, as the musician gathers his notes and forms his chords, so he brings forth from chaos glorious harmony.' He went on to speak of 'The fantastic balancing of form and irregular spaces, the arbitrary choice of a viewpoint and the faded splendour that reveals a symbol of the spiritual' in Japanese drawing. Whistler's was a very individual talent, who tended to sacrifice line and form in favour of luminous masses and volume.

He was also a distinguished portrait painter, as can be seen in the fine portrait of his mother first shown in 1872 at the Royal Academy, and those of Carlyle, Miss Alexander, Théodore Duret and the comte de Montesquiou Fezensac. He decorated Mr Leyland's dining room with his famous *Princess of the land of porcelain*. In 1877 he exhi-

WHISTLER *Portrait of the Artist's Mother.* 1871

bited his *Nocturnes*, with their almost musical quality, but the critics were unfavourable. He visited Venice in 1884 and in 1896 settled in Paris again where his work was now much appreciated. He was connected with various art movements of the time, and may rightly be considered as one of the forerunners of Impressionism.

WILSON Richard (1714-1782) Ruskin remarked that with Richard Wilson there took place, fifty years before Constable, 'the birth of the history of an art of landscape painting, founded on a contemplative love of nature'. With Girtin, Cozens and Gainsborough, he is one of the originators of the renewal of landscape painting in England.

After working for some time in London as a portrait painter he set off for Italy where he met Joseph Vernet and Zuccarelli, and came to love the works of Claude Lorrain, Nicolas Poussin and Gaspard Dughet. He then gave up portrait painting to dedicate himself entirely to landscapes, some imaginary but others more realistic and sensitive in their approach. It is through his landscapes that Wilson has earned the right to be numbered among the forerunners of Impressionism, although his inspiration was more inclined to be romantic, with landscapes reflecting states of mind. His tones however tended to be clear and cold, and he paid very great attention to detail.

ZIEM Félix (1821-1911) Towards the end of his life Ziem became a well-known painter and tended to repeat himself for the sake of popularity, but earlier, particularly in his sketches, he was a genuine forerunner of the Impressionists.

ZIEM *The Grand Canal, Venice*

WILSON *Cader Idris. c. 1774*

With his 'fluttering brushstrokes à la Guardi' as Louis Gillet called them, he managed to achieve extraordinary light effects. Martigues and Provence, Constantinople and the East, and the polders and canals of the Netherlands, all provided him with subjects and inspiration.

His first appearance at the Salon in 1849 was with a *View on the Bosphorus* and *The Grand Canal, Venice* which both attracted favourable attention. He showed there regularly until 1868; but over the next twenty years he exhibited nothing.

He bequeathed part of his work to the Municipality of Paris, including a representative collection of studies and drawings.

The Impressionists

BALLA Giacomo (Turin 1871—Rome 1958) Balla was influenced by what he saw of Impressionism and Neo-Impressionism during the course of a visit to Paris. In 1904, when he returned to Rome, he passed on the knowledge he had acquired of modern painting to his two pupils Boccioni and Severini.

On 11 February 1910, there appeared in Milan the 'Manifesto of futurist painters', signed by Balla, Boccioni, Carrà, Russolo and Severini, followed on 11 April by the 'Technical manifesto of futurist painting'. In France, the review *Comoedia* published the complete text of the manifesto in the issue for 18 May of that year, and an article on *Futurist Venice* on 17 June. Balla however went back to his traditional way of painting, and continued to live in Rome.

The most important of Balla's paintings from his futurist period are: *Dynamism of a dog on a lead* (1912), *Injections of futurism* (c. 1912), *Speed of a motor car + light, noise* (1913).

BAZILLE Jean-Frédéric (Montpellier 1841—Beaune-la-Rolande 1870) Bazille went to Paris in 1862 to take up painting, and met Claude Monet at Gleyre's studio where he was a pupil. In 1863 he and Monet went together to Chailly to paint out of doors. In 1864, Monet took him to Honfleur where they met Boudin and Jongkind, and in 1867 both Bazille and Monet began experimenting to-

gether, with the idea of substituting figures painted out of doors for the traditional use of models in the studio. The two artists tried to persuade their friends and relations to pose for them in the open, and often used family photographs as a basis for their work. Bazille's great canvas *The Bazille family*, usually known as *Family Reunion* but exhibited at the 1867 Salon under the title *The X Family*, was a painting of this kind, and in the same year, 1867, Monet painted his group of *Ladies in the garden*. In the 1868 Salon, Bazille showed *Village Scene* based on his previous picture *The pink dress* (1864). Berthe Morisot wrote after visiting the 1869 Salon, and seeing Bazille's work: 'It is full of light and sunshine. Bazille is looking for what we have always wanted to find; how to paint a figure out in the open. This time I think he really has succeeded'.

BAZILLE *View of Castelnau.* 1868

BAZILLE *Negress arranging flowers.* 1870

BAZILLE *Family Reunion*. 1867

After this, Bazille experimented with painting nudes out of doors, and in 1869 produced *Summer Scene* or *Bathing in the river Lez*, which he showed at the Salon the following year, ahead of all the other Impressionists. In 1870 he painted two canvases inspired by Courbet, *Toilette* and *Black woman arranging flowers*. Bazille was killed in the 1870 war, leaving an unfinished *Landscape on the banks of the Lez*.

BERNARD Émile (Lille 1868—Paris 1941) has been described by Roger Marx as the father of 'pictorial symbolism', but Albert Aurier, in a famous article published in the March 1891 number of the *Mercure de France*, actually written at Bernard's request, gave the title to Gauguin. This started off a quarrel between the two artists, Bernard indignantly reclaiming the title, and breaking off relations with Gauguin immediately. The incident demonstrates well Bernard's impetuous and uncompromising character. His talent for painting and drawing developed very early,

and he was only twelve when he made a copy of Frans Hals' *The Witch*. He was admitted as a pupil in Cormon's studio in 1885 and there met Anquetin, Lautrec and van Gogh, who remained a close friend. He also got to know Cézanne's works at Père Tanguy's studio. The following year he was expelled from Cormon's for insubordination: he then went to Concarneau where he met Schuffenecker and was then introduced to Gauguin. It was not however until August 1888 that he really got to know him well, and in September supported him in his famous meeting with Sérusier. In 1889 Bernard exhibited twenty-three landscapes of Brittany and the country round Paris, at an exhibition in the Café Volpini, and in 1891 and 1892 he showed at the *Indépendants'* Exhibition. On this occasion he was very much upset by Gauguin's refusal to recognize his early investigations into, and involvement with, Synthetism. The fact was that Bernard had in 1887 and the years immediately following set up with Anquetin a movement of 'personal and lively simplism', which soon came to be known as 'Synthetism', as a reaction against both Impressionism and Divisionism. (See *Portrait of the artist's grandmother*, painted about 1887, and *Still life*).

After another visit to Brittany, Bernard set off in March 1893 on a long journey which took him to Italy and Greece, then on to Constantinople, Jerusalem and Egypt. Apart from a few months in Spain, he then spent the next eleven years in Cairo and did not finally return to France until 1904, after a stay of eight months in Venice. He visited Cézanne at Aix-en-Provence and in 1905 founded the 'Aesthetic Revival' movement. He then went on to exhibit at the Salon de la Nationale in Paris, where his great painting *Moses and the daughters of Midian* made a great sensation. He continued to travel abroad, especially in Italy, right up to his death, and his *Human Cycle* was painted in Venice. Towards the end of his life he abandoned his Symbolist ideas and reverted to an academic, classical style based on the great Renaissance masters.

Among his most outstanding works, all painted in the first half of his life, are *Madeleine in the Forest of Love* and *Breton women in the fields*, both painted in 1888 when he was only 20.

BERUETE Aureliano de (Madrid 1845-Madrid 1912) was a Spaniard; he was a pupil of the landscape painter Carlos de Haes, a Belgian living in Spain, and of Martin Rico. Beruete was both a prolific painter and a scholar; for instance, he was the author of the first descriptive catalogue of the complete works of Velazquez. As time went on, his palette became lighter, brighter and more luminous, as he tried to capture the transparency and clarity of the atmosphere, and it is this attitude towards light that brings him very close to the Impressionists. He painted views in the country round Madrid, and also Toledo, Avila and Cuenca—for example his *View of Madrid from the Manzanares*, as well as landscapes in France, Holland and the English coast.

BOUDIN Eugène (Honfleur 1824-Deauville 1898) Boudin is one of the most important figures in the history and development of Impressionism. He seems to have been the person who first suggested painting out of doors, when he started an art centre at an inn kept by Mère Toutain near Honfleur known

BERNARD *Pont-Aven*

BOUDIN *The Pier at Deauville.* 1869

as the Ferme Saint-Siméon. Here a group of artists which included Jongkind, Monet and Bazille used to meet, and Boudin would encourage them to experiment with open-air painting.

BOUDIN *St Mark's Square, Venice, seen from the Grand Canal.* 1897

BOUDIN *Woman with a sunshade.* 1880

Boudin took up painting at the suggestion of Millet and Troyon about 1848. He began by producing a series of pastels and watercolour

BOUDIN *Beach Scene*

October 8th, noon; north-west wind. If you have ever had time to look at them, you will remember Boudin's detailed notes and observations. Even if you put your hand over the caption, you would easily be able to guess what season of the year it was, the time of day and the prevailing wind. I am not exaggerating, I have actually seen it'.

Boudin then, was really responsible for the beginning of Impressionism. Now what was needed was to specify the aims and methods of the new movement and to gather a group of artists together, who would subscribe to its tenets—painting out of doors, direct sensation, fragmentation and broken brushwork.

sketches invariably painted out of doors, which he later worked up into canvases. Baudelaire, who was staying at Honfleur in 1859, was very much struck with them and wrote in his *Salon of 1859:* 'These astonishing studies, so quickly and so faithfully executed, these sketches of things that are almost imperceptible, of what is most fleeting and changeable in shape and colour, of waves and clouds, they always have a note in the margin giving the exact date and time of day and the prevailing wind when they were painted. For instance:

BOUDIN *Sailing boats*

BOUDIN *Honfleur, entrance to the Harbour.* 1896

'Tones must be clear and fresh, brilliant if possible', Boudin wrote in a letter dated 3 April 1866; but actually he preferred using delicate shades of grey and subdued tints and harmonies.

Boudin is unrivalled as a painter of seascapes and beach and harbour scenes, while a number of his paintings are sketches of the Seine estuary. Among them are *The jetty at Deauville* (1869), *Cliffs at Étretat* and *The Harbour at Honfleur* painted in 1896. He showed at the first Impressionist exhibition in 1874, and Durand-Ruel held a retrospective of his works in 1883.

CASSATT *The Box at the Theatre.* 1879

CASSATT *Portrait of Mademoiselle C.*

CASSATT Mary (Allegheny City, Pennsylvania 1845- Château de Beaufresne at Le Mesnil Théribus, Oise, 1926) The daughter of a rich Pittsburgh banker, she decided to take up painting and in 1866 went to live and work in France. In 1872 she went to Italy and spent eight months at the Parma Academy studying with the painter and engraver Raimondi. That same year she visited Seville, as well as going to Belgium and Holland, and under the name Mary Stevenson exhibited *On the Balcony* at the Salon in Paris.

CASSATT *Young woman sewing. c.* 1886

In 1877 Degas, who had noticed her *Portrait of Zola* in the 1874 Salon, suggested her joining the Impressionists. She showed two paintings at their fourth exhibition in 1879, *The Box at the Theatre* and *The Cup of Tea*, and also had pictures in their fifth (1880), sixth (1881) and eighth (1886) exhibitions. In 1891 and 1893 one-man shows of her work were held at the

Cassatt *Two women seated in a landscape*

Durand-Ruel Gallery. Mary Cassatt did engravings as well as paintings and pastels. Her main work was portraits, and she also painted a number of pictures of a mother holding her child in her arms. Degas, who was normally an admirer of her work, saw one of these mother-and-child pictures of hers one day, where the baby was rather too pretty and immaculate and well scrubbed, and he exclaimed in exasperation: 'Look! There's baby Jesus with his nanny!' However Mary Cassatt's work has a delicate sensitive texture, particularly in her landscapes; for instance *Two women seated in a landscape*.

CÉZANNE Paul (Aix-en-Provence 1839-Aix-en-Provence 1906) Although he was much involved with Impressionism, Cézanne soon developed a kind of resistance and even reaction against the movement, which he considered lacking in structure. Unlike most of the Impressionists, he cared just as much for drawing and composition as for painting, and for the solidity and permanence of forms, as he did for tone and colour. He felt the two aspects of painting were inseparable and should not be dissociated. To Émile Bernard he wrote: 'As one goes on painting a subject, so one is also gradually drawing it too, and the more colour harmonies are developed, so the clearer does the drawing become. So when colour attains its full brilliance and richness, then form reaches its fulness too. The secret of drawing and modelling lies in contrasting and corresponding tones'. In this last statement of his, Cézanne comes very close to the theories of Seurat, Signac and the Neo-Impressionists. He wanted to 'do Poussin from nature' but he realised how fleeting the 'immediate impressions' were, which were so dear to Monet and his circle. His mind refused to accept mere

CÉZANNE *The Magdalen, or Grief. c.* 1866-1868

CÉZANNE *Portrait of Boyer with a straw hat.* 1869-1870

CÉZANNE *Melting snow at l'Estaque. c.* 1870

CÉZANNE *Portrait of the painter Achille Emperaire. c.* 1866

of paintings of the same subject, was obliged to paint extremely rapidly, to try and express the inexpressible and the transience of things in nature, particularly fleeting light effects. Cézanne, on the other hand, was a slow worker; he kept going back to his pictures, sometimes after an interval of several years, so as to capture not merely the appearance but the very essence of things. His work does not merely seek to convey the passing moment, as Impressionism does, but also the past and the future. This explains why his art is timeless and why it has had such repercussions on modern art, particularly Fauvism and Cubism.

Cézanne, like most of his contemporaries, started with a rather subdued and sombre period before he went on to bright colours, as he did later. This first period, which has been called romantic or baroque, goes from about 1861 to 1871. Cézanne and Émile Zola were at school together at the College Bourbon in Aix-en-Provence, and remained friends until 1886, when they quarrelled. Cézanne had taken umbrage over Zola's novel *l'Œuvre* (*The Work*) where he thought he recognized

CÉZANNE *Self Portrait.* 1858-1861

visual sensitivity and, unlike the Impressionists, he aimed at conveying the essence and permanence of things. He declared that 'nature is always the same, but nothing remains of what actually appears to us in nature. Our art has to convey the sense of duration, along with the outward appearance of all these changes'; and again: 'In painting there are two elements, the eye and the mind, and these two must assist each other. We have to work at their mutual development, but we must work as painters—first on the eye through our vision of nature, then on the mind through the logic of well-regulated sensations producing the means of expression'.

In this connection we may recall that Claude Monet, particularly in his linked series

CÉZANNE *A modern Olympia. c.* 1873

himself in the character of the unsuccessful artist Lantier.

After studying drawing at Aix, Cézanne went to Paris in April 1861, to the Académie Suisse. He spent his time there copying Italian Old Masters, and also painted portraits, still lifes and occasional landscapes. Among the works of this period are the following: *Portrait of the painter's father, Louis-Auguste Cézanne, reading l'Événement* (1866), *Man in a cotton night-cap* (1865-67), *Portrait of the painter Achille Emperaire* (c. 1866), *Paul Alexis reading to Zola* (1869), *Portrait of Boyer with a straw hat* (1869-1870), and *The Magdalen, or Grief* (c. 1866-1868), while among the still lifes were *The black marble clock* and *Still life with a tin kettle*, both painted about 1869 or 1870. His land-scapes of that period include *Melting snow at l'Estaque* (1870) and the *Wine Market* (1872).

All these works are distinguished by the use of heavy thick paint, with strong shadows, often in pure black. The tones are subdued and sombre, with black, grey, brown and Prussian blue predominating, and the odd touch of white; now and then patches of green or red brighten the almost monochrome se-verity of the picture.

Cézanne's contact with the Impressionists, particularly with Pissarro whom he met at the Académie Suisse, convinced him to give up his sombre style for the clear colours of the Impressionists. He abandoned his heavy im-pasto technique and began to use stippling, juxtaposition of brushstrokes and the rough, almost clotted surfaces they used. These years, roughly between 1872 and 1882, are known as his Impressionist period.

The painting *A modern Olympia* marks the transition from one period to another. Pissarro's influence gives some idea of the new direction his art was taking. Claude Monet and Sisley tended to concentrate on light effects and fleeting reflections in water, but Cézanne would not only do this. He wanted to experiment with planes and structured forms in space, to capture what was unvarying and stable in the universe, not merely the outward appearance of things. He used to discuss these questions with Émile Bernard and K. X. Roussel, and once declared: 'Light is some-thing that cannot be reproduced; it can only be represented in terms of something else— colour, for instance. When I worked this out, I was really quite proud of myself!' The first

CÉZANNE *Still Life with a Soup Tureen. c.* 1883

evolution. He soon came to consider the Impressionist formula as being out of date and needing to be revised according to fundamental principles, where intelligence corrected and modified vision. His chief aim was to achieve a balance between colour and design, tone and form, so as to reach a broad spirit of synthesis. This explains why the expression 'period of synthesis' is often applied to what he produced roughly between 1883 and 1895. Cézanne painted several *Views of l'Estaque*

CÉZANNE *Self Portrait.* 1880-1881

important picture to show Cézanne's new ideas about art was *La Maison du pendu à Auvers-sur-Oise* (or *House of the Hanged Man*), painted in 1873. Cézanne showed this painting at the first Impressionist exhibition in 1874, and it was shown again later at the Exposition Universelle in 1889. There are several other landscapes of Auvers dating from the same period, one being now in the Chicago Art Institute, and a number of views of Pontoise where he often painted with Pissarro, for instance the *Côte du Jalais at Pontoise* (1879-1882), *Poplars* (1879-1882) and the *Bridge at Maincy* (*c.* 1882). In these last two canvases, Cézanne conveys perfectly 'that shuddering sense of duration'; art, for him, is 'a harmony running parallel to nature'.

He treated still lifes, portraits and other compositions in the same way; for instance *Dahlias* (1875), *Still life with a Soup Tureen* (*c.* 1883), several *Self Portraits* and *Portraits of Madame Cézanne*, one of the most celebrated of these being known as *The Red Armchair* (1877), the *Portrait of Victor Chocquet* (1876-1877) and finally several studies of *Women bathing*, the famous *Baigneuses*.

Cézanne conceived of art—and particularly his own—as being always in a state of

CÉZANNE *The Poplars.* 1879-1882

near Marseilles, in which his new theories are applied. In a letter to his friend Gasquet he tried to explain what he meant: 'Planes—surfaces in colour. The sweep of colour where you get the inner soul of a plane, thrilling and stirring, the heat of prismatic colour strikes you and planes meet and clash in the sun. Do you see what I mean? I make my planes with the colours on my palette. You have to see the planes—and clearly; but you must group them and rearrange them, getting them to merge into each other ... the whole thing must turn and be blended and interwoven together. Nothing matters but volume'. He sought to 'render perspective by colour alone' in his beautiful drawings, watercolours and oil paintings of the *Montagne Sainte-Victoire* partly done between 1885 and 1887, but on which he worked up to the end of his life. He tended more and more towards a kind of cubism: 'To paint nature in cylinders, spheres, cones, all in perspective ... for us humans, nature consists more in depth than in surface'. He does not actually use the word cube, but some of the houses in *La Montaigne Sainte-Victoire* are really cubes, the trees are rendered as cylinders and

CÉZANNE *Self Portrait.* 1880-1881

the mountain itself as planes superimposed and defining its mass, structure and volume.

CÉZANNE
The Gulf of Marseilles seen from l'Estaque.
1883-1885

CÉZANNE
Mount Sainte-Victoire with large pine tree.
1885-1887

CÉZANNE *The Card Players. c.* 1890-1892

In some of his *Views of l'Estaque,* too, he conveys the sea both horizontally, on the surface, and vertically in depth, with its dense liquid mass and volume.

In his still lifes, Cezanne adopts the same procedure, suggesting the nature and essence of an object by the quality and intensity of his tones and colours, greater or less fluidity, and successive layers of paint. Examples are *The Chest of Drawers* (1883-1887), *The Kitchen Table* (1880-1890), *Pot of Geraniums and Fruit* (1890-1894), and *the Vase of Tulips* (1890-1894). He deals in the same way with his figures, whether portraits or nudes, and tries to integrate them into their proper background. The artist must go beyond mere outward appearances

and reveal his sitter to himself, through Cézanne's own conception and feelings about him. The *Portraits of his Wife, Woman with a Coffee-pot* (1890-1894), *Boy in a Red Waistcoat* (1890-1895), *Portrait of Gustave Geffroy* (1895) and *A Harlequin* (1880-1890) are all conceived in that spirit. We find the same approach in his different paintings of *Card Players,* with five, four or two figures (*c.* 1890-1908) as well as in his various groups of men or women bathing.

The work of his last ten years (1896-1906), known as his lyrical period, confirms Cézanne's tendency to achieve an even more balanced synthesis between severity of composition and structure, and an almost poetic attitude. His art becomes less and less sponta-

CÉZANNE
Woman with a coffee-pot. c. 1890-1894

CÉZANNE
Still Life with a basket. c. 1888-1890

CÉZANNE *Les Grandes Baigneuses*. 1898-1905

neous, showing signs of incipient Cubism in its strictly intellectual approach, and also of Fauvism in its lyrical use of colour and form. Among his landscapes, further paintings of the *Montagne Sainte-Victoire*, the *Lake of Annecy* (1896), *Rocks and branches at Bibémus* (c. 1904) and *The Black Castle* are in this style. His beautiful *Still Life with Onions* reveals the fundamental elements of Cubism—the glass in the picture is seen from two sides at once, while the famous *Portrait of Ambroise Vollard* (1899) also anticipates Picasso's well known Cubist portraits, particularly his own portrait of the same Vollard, and the portraits of *Kahnweiler* and *Wilhelm Uhde*. However his painting

Les Grandes Baigneuses (1898-1905) is closest of all to Cubism. It is a splendid picture; its rhythmic composition, clearly defined superimposed planes and general sense of harmony directly anticipate Picasso's *Les Demoiselles d'Avignon* painted very nearly at the same time (1906-1907). Cézanne's declared ambition: 'I wanted to make something solid and permanent out of Impressionism, like art in museums' was here finally achieved.

CORDEY Frédéric (Paris 1854-Paris 1911) Before joining the Impressionists he worked with Franc-Lamy, particularly at the École des Beaux-Arts where he was taught by Lehmann who was a pupil of Ingres. About 1876 he attended Renoir's studio in the Rue Saint-Georges, and also went to his newly acquired house in the Rue Cortot. Renoir put Cordey among several others also dancing, in his painting *Le Bal au Moulin de la Galette*. Soon after, at the time of the third Impressionist exhibition in 1877, Renoir invited Cordey and Franc-Lamy to join them, but this was the only Impressionist exhibition in which Cordey showed. In 1881 he went to Algeria, where he met Renoir, and on his return, exhibited in Paris at the 1877 Salon des Indépendants. Among Cordey's works are several landscapes in private collections as well as his *View near Auvers-sur-Oise*, *A Lane at Auvers-sur-Oise* and *Millstones at Neuville-sur-Oise*. His style recalls Renoir, Pissarro and Sisley.

CORDEY *A Lane at Auvers-sur-Oise*

CORINTH Lovis (Tapiau, East Prussia 1858-Zandvoort, Holland 1925) Corinth studied painting at the Königsberg Academy with Otto Günther and then at Munich with Ludwig von Löfftz, but received his main training in Paris, where he stayed from 1884 to 1887. He worked at the Académie Jullian and was a pupil of Bouguereau and Robert Fleury, who introduced him to the Flemish painters, Frans Hals and Rembrandt. He was enthusiastic about Millet and realism, but so far he had made no contact with the Impressionists. When he returned to Königsberg (1887-1891) he worked hard to acquire his powerful realistic, very individual style, expressing himself in landscapes, portraits and still lifes, which he painted better than anything else: he also painted mythological and religious scenes. In 1890 he obtained an honourable mention for his painting *The Body of Christ* at the Paris Salon. The following year he went to Munich and there painted mainly nudes and portraits, and also attempted some large-scale religious paintings. In 1895 he sold a picture for the first time, a *Descent from the Cross*. After 1900 he lived in Berlin and joined the Sezession movement which had been founded ten years previously by Franz von Stuck, Wilhelm Trübner and Fritz von Uhde, as a reaction against the academic style of painting then prevalent in Germany. In 1901 he married Charlotte Barend, who was his pupil and twenty-three years younger, and who became his favourite model.

Together with Max Slevogt, Corinth became one of the chief Berlin Impressionists, and experimented especially with light effects. He began to use fragmentation, and his palette gradually became richer and more brilliant without losing its depth of tone. *After the bath* (1906), *View from the studio in Munich*, *Emperor's Day at Hamburg* (1911) are examples of his style at the time. In 1911 he had a stroke which left him physically incapacitated at first, but his energy helped him to make a good recovery and in that same year he painted more than sixty canvases in a rather different and more sensual style than before, where his material is more important than the subject, and he seeks to merge his spaces into powerful sweeps of colour. He was an indefatigable traveller and visited Italy, France, Switzerland, Denmark and the Netherlands. After 1918 he spent his summers in Bavaria, at Urfeld on the Walchensee, and the lakeside there appears in several of his paintings (*Walchensee—landscape with a cow*, 1921; and

CORINTH *Reclining Nude.* 1899

CORINTH *Emperor's Day at Hamburg.* 1911

The Walchensee seen from Wetterstein, 1921).

Towards the end of his life he gave up his Impressionist technique and adopted a more violent style and more intense tones anticipating Expressionism (*Portrait of his son Thomas in armour*, 1925). Corinth died in 1925 during a last visit to Holland to see the works of Frans Hals and Rembrandt. His fame increased after his death up to the coming of Nazism,

when most of his work was rejected as being subversive and decadent, and a good number of his paintings in German museums were then sold. Corinth was a complicated, unconventional personality and never really attached himself to any movement. His work centres on his love of nature which he calls 'our master, guide and comfort during the many dark hours of our life'.

CORINTH *View from the Studio, Munich.* 1891

CORINTH *After the bath.* 1906

CROSS *Nude in a garden*

CROSS Henri-Edmond (Douai 1856-Saint-Clair, Var, 1910) Cross was the pseudonym adopted, at Bonvin's suggestion, by Henri-Edmond Delacroix whose mother was of British origin. He began studying at the Lille Académie des Beaux-Arts and in 1876 went to Paris. His early work, exhibited at the 1881 Salon, was sombre in colouring, but his *Corner of a garden at Monaco* which he exhibited at the first Salon des Indépendants in 1884, showed an entirely different approach. He had obviously come under the influence of the Neo-Impressionists and the theories of Seurat, Signac and their followers, and now painted in clear brilliant colours. He did not however exhibit at the eighth and last Impressionist exhibition where the first important paintings of the Neo-Impressionists, particularly

Seurat, Signac and Camille Pissarro, were hung.

Signac admired in Cross 'his progress towards logic in colour and synthesis of form . . . He is a cold, methodical thinker and yet has a strange disturbed dream-like quality'. Cross explained his position to his friend Théo van Rysselberghe: 'Harmony always implies sacrifice. We start with some impression of nature, but we cannot put everything there is in nature into our paintings. It is not so much that we cannot put in everything, but that there is so little we can put in, and this very little becomes everything—that is, man's work. We have to sacrifice form or value or colour, according to the ideas behind the work

in progress'. Later on he wrote—here disagreeing with Seurat: 'I wonder whether these fragments of nature arranged more or less tastefully in a rectangle do really constitute the aim of art? Then I come back to the idea of chromatic harmonies arranged as a whole, and external to nature, as a starting point'. Among Cross' most important works are *Les Îles d'Or* (*c.* 1891-1892), *Cypresses at Cagnes* (*c.* 1908), *la Ronde* (1894-1895) and *Antibes* (1908).

DEGAS Edgar (Paris 1834-Paris 1917) Degas described himself as being 'the classical painter of modern life'. In this way he sets

CROSS *Cypresses at Cagnes*

himself apart from the Impressionists, although he was closely connected with them and frequently showed at their exhibitions. However, unlike his Impressionist friends, he firmly refused to paint out of doors, and he stressed composition and drawing, which they tended to underestimate and neglect in favour of colour and tone. '. . . A painting must first of all be a product of the artist's imagination. It must never be a copy (here Degas agrees with Delacroix and Baudelaire). If he adds one or two accents from nature, that obviously does no harm . . . it is much better to draw things that one only sees in one's mind's eye. Imagination and memory collaborate in the transformation effected and you only paint what has struck you, that is, what is really necessary'.

It seems rather surprising that after this uncompromising statement of his artistic aims and ideas, Degas should have taken part in seven out of eight Impressionist manifestations (he did not exhibit anything at the seventh) and have been in such close touch with the group. Unlike Edouard Manet, who let himself be persuaded by Claude Monet to start painting out of doors after 1870, Degas absolutely refused all his life long, even when painting his few landscapes.

His training was classical and traditional. At school he studied classics and in 1854 became a pupil of the painter Lamothe, a disciple of Ingres; the next year he started at the École des Beaux-Arts. He worked at the Louvre copying Old Masters and paid two visits to Italy, in 1856 and 1858. In this early period he confined himself to portraits and historical paintings, following the usual tradition, but even then he showed great originality in the boldness of his composition and in his feeling for rhythm and balance. He did a lot of drawing too, and when Paul Valéry asked him what he meant by drawing, he explained that 'drawing is not form; it is the way in which we see form'.

By this he meant that true classicism does not imply constriction or constraint, nor does it limit the freedom of forms, but on the con-

DEGAS *The Bellelli Family.* 1860-1862

trary it gives them true liberty so that they can live and be themselves. During this period, Degas' colours tend to be restrained and his paintings, with their fluid sense of rhythm, almost give the impression of frescoes. Among his best work of this period are his *Portrait of the Bellelli Family* (1860-1862), several *Self portraits*, and paintings of his family, particularly *Mme Edouard Morbilli*, while among his historical paintings are *Young Spartan girls inciting the boys to fight* (1860), *Semiramis building the hanging gardens of Babylon* (1861 Salon) and *The plight of the city of Orléans* (1865 Salon). The Louvre Department of Drawings houses a wonderful collection of studies Degas made for the last two of these paintings. Most of them are in lead pencil and are among the most beautiful drawings of groups and figures, female nudes and draperies to be found anywhere in the world. The purity and intelligence of the drawing, the realism and subtlety of curves and strokes, the skilful variations of line and stress all make of this collection of drawings a series of undisputed masterpieces.

DEGAS *Portrait of a Young Woman*. 1867

DEGAS *Self Portrait. c.* 1854

About 1865 or 1866, Degas made the acquaintance of Édouard Manet and the Impressionists who invited him to their gatherings at the Café Guerbois. From that time onwards Degas decided to be 'The classical painter of modern life', and gave up his historical painting, without however giving up his classical approach. He did however begin to use lighter tones although his colouring was still subdued, while there appeared a change in his rather glossy surfaces as he used heavier brushstrokes. His 'modern' approach can be seen particularly in the influence of photography and Japanese prints. Right up to the end of his life he continued to paint off-centre compositions with extraordinarily bold effects, both on canvas and on paper. In several of his works Degas goes so far

DEGAS *Femme à la potiche*. 1872

DEGAS *The Absinthe Drinkers*. 1876

seaside, but even so he never worked out of doors and he was much more interested in composition than in the actual subject he was painting. Examples are: *Sea bathing* (1876-1877) and *By the seaside* (pastel, 1869).

From about 1874, Degas started to paint series of pictures, limited to five in each series. Because their scope was so restricted, he felt this allowed for almost unlimited interpretation. Degas hoped in this way to be able to concentrate on actual form, and to show how infinite variations could be constructed out of one single theme. Here he moved right away from the Impressionists and particularly from Claude Monet who had tried to show, in his own series of paintings on a single subject, how everything—even a cathedral—is changed and transformed by reflections and light.

Degas believed that art involved thought and that applied intelligence corrected vision; visible, mobile forms had to be dwelt on and considered so as to make them intelligible here and now. Although Degas' paintings belong quite definitely to his own period, his art is timeless; it belongs to yesterday, today and tomorrow. He used to think of his series as a continually renewed succession of forms in which all possibilities could be explored without limits or bounds, and where he could discover new rhythms and curves and impressions, felt as well as seen. He aimed at

DEGAS *Women in a café, evening*

as to cut off part of the body, or even of the head of his models so as to prolong his picture beyond the frame, as it were, in the imaginations of artist and spectator.

During this transition period (*c.* 1865-1877) with its continued research and experiments, Degas produced the following: *Woman with chrysanthemums* (1865), *Mademoiselle Fiocre in the ballet La Source* (1868), *Portrait of Madame Camus* (1870), *The Cotton Merchants' Office, New Orleans* (1873), *Sulks* (*c.* 1874), *Madame Fèvre or the singing rehearsal* (*c.* 1873), *The Absinthe Drinkers* (1876), *The Café des Ambassadeurs* (1876-1877), *Women in a café, evening* (pastel, 1877) and *Singer with a glove* (1878). Degas like all the Impressionists, loved the sea and the

DEGAS *At the Races, before the stands.* 1869-72

expressing in oils, pastels and in pencil drawings some shred of the living truth that he had
caught in a fleeting moment and later restored
in its most perfect essence. Every being is at
the same time both one and many: so Degas
sought to capture the one essential moment in
the rich multiplicity of existence.

Apart from a few portraits, and several
scenes of café and theatre life and prostitutes,
Degas painted five complete series: *The Races*;
Laundresses or *Washerwomen*; *Milliners*, and the
two best known of all, *Dancers* and *Women at
their toilet*. The series on horse-racing recalls
Degas' classical leanings. The jockeys on their
mounts remind us of the horsemen of anti-
quity, especially the Parthenon frieze. The
formal sculptural appearance of the man who
seems to be one with his horse, the supple

rhythmic movements, the jockey's disjointed
body, looking like a puppet—all this allows
the artist to 'distort' his models and reconstruct them again more perfectly. *Gentlemen's
race, before the start; Racehorses by the Stands*
(1869-1872); *Racehorses at Longchamp* (1873-
1875) and *Training* (pastel, 1894) are
examples of his style from 1862 onwards.
Particularly in some of his pastels, Degas'
bold approach and colours help us to appreciate his connection with the Impressionists, slight though it might be.

The *Laundresses* and *Women ironing* have a
classical quality although they depict modern
life. The best of this series are *Woman ironing,
against the light* (1874), *Laundresses carrying linen*
(1876-1878) and *Women ironing* (1884).

There are not so many sketches in the

Degas *Jockeys*

Degas' reputation depends largely on his *Dancers* series, a varied and important set of works which again show his classical taste. It was about the time that Toulouse-Lautrec was doing his *French Cancan* pictures and Renoir was painting his *Bal au Moulin de la Galette* that Degas executed his studies of dancers at the Paris Opera. His deliberate choice of classical ballet as his subject once more bears witness to his taste for arabesque (a term applicable in ballet as well as in art), rhythm, and harmony. He wanted to express simultaneously what is immediate and what is enduring; in fact he prolonged the immediate so that it does actually endure. In his rendering of the dance he succeeded in breaking down and analysing every movement and every attitude of a single dancer or group. He then recomposed and reconstituted the forms so that they became perfect in expression, absolutely and strictly true. They no longer depend on contingency or chance, but are full of fantasy and imagination and ecstasy—a state where balance and instability almost touch, to achieve an ideal, sculptural quality—in short, perfect living beauty.

Milliners series, but they offer the artist the pretext to create a brilliant set of original compositions, full of humour and charm. Degas has an extraordinary gift for somehow creating, out of innumerable odd hat shapes and amorphous caps and bonnets, the essential quality and appearance of a hat—what Paul Valéry calls the 'shapeless shapes' in Degas' work. Most of the *Milliners* series of paintings and pastels date from between 1882 and 1885, and are to be found either in the Metropolitan Museum in New York or in the Art Institute, Chicago; there are also some in American private collections.

From then onwards, and particularly towards the end of Degas' life, colour became as important to him as line. Degas' eyesight deteriorated progressively until in the end he was almost blind, and this partly explains his

Degas *Training. c.* 1880

DEGAS *Women ironing.* 1884

preference for pastel, which allowed him to use heavier and thicker strokes and hatching for rendering forms and light and shade. But neither his colouring nor his chiaroscuro make any concession to Impressionism. His choice of intense and unusual colour always depends on the forms chosen and is part and parcel of them, while his luminous reflections and highlights come from artificial light and footlights, never from daylight. The strong light from projectors alters tones and paintings and gives them that unique immaterial appearance that so fascinated Bonnard. The most outstanding

works of this series are the following: *Ballet rehearsal room at the Opera, rue Le Peletier* (1872), *Ballet rehearsal on the stage* (1874), *End of an arabesque* (pastel, 1877), *Dancer with a bouquet taking a curtain call* (pastel, 1878), all in the Musée du Jeu de Paume, and *Dancers at the bar*. There are also some series of *Dancers*, mostly pastels in bright colours, to be found in various large museums or in private collections; these dancers are in gay tutus, blue, green, mauve, yellow, red, orange or pink.

The last series of all is of *Women at their toilet*. Some people call Degas a misogynist because of the realistic and sometimes unflattering attitudes of his models in these sketches. I cannot agree; in fact I believe Degas loved and understood women and in spite of appearances to the contrary, succeeded in conveying their essential femininity, their sensitive supple grace, and their noble grandeur and dignity. Degas notes his models' natural ease in the most extravagant, as well as in the simplest poses and attitudes. He somehow recreates woman in her hidden life, in her modesty and immodesty, in her reserve as well as in her sensuality, creating an enchanted wonderland of gestures and attitudes, of expressions and emotions, intelligence and receptivity, indeed a whole world of feminine life. The world he conveys is full of truth and mystery, the eternal woman, Eve. *Women combing their hair* (c. 1876), *La Toilette* (1885), *The tub* (1886), *After the bath; woman wiping her feet* (1886),

Woman doing her hair (1887-1890), *After the bath; woman wiping her neck* (1898) or *La Coiffure* (1892-1895) are among the best of this series.

As well as paintings, pastels and drawings, Degas also did engravings, especially in monotype, and sculpture; he liked to model little wax figures of female nudes, dancers or horses. Paul Valéry sums up Degas' art perfectly in his book *Degas, Danse, Dessin*: 'He has a passionate longing to achieve the one exact line to express a face; and he finds this face in the street or at the Opera, at the milliner's, anywhere. He always captures it in some characteristic attitude at some special moment, never without movement, always expressive; this is the general impression I get of Degas. He dared to attempt combining instantaneous impressions with endless toil in the studio, capturing the fleeting moment by studying it in depth.'

DEGAS *At the milliner's.* 1885

DEGAS
Ballet Rehearsal Room at the Opera,
Rue Le Peletier. 1872

DEGAS *Four Dancers.* 1899

DEGAS *The Tub.* 1886

DEGAS *Dancer seen in profile*

DEGAS *Two Dancers*

DEGAS *Three Dancers. c.* 1898

DEGAS *Four Dancers. c.* 1905

DEGAS *Woman in her bath, sponging her leg. c.* 1883

DEGAS *Woman having a bath. c.* 1886

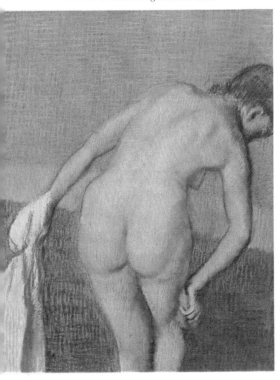

FANTIN-LATOUR Henri (Grenoble 1836-Bure, Orne 1904) Fantin-Latour used to say of himself: 'The blood in my veins is much too mixed for me to be upset by questions of nationality and schools of thought'. He was never committed to any of the great movements of the period, and always remained independent. He was first taught to paint by his father and then by Lecoq de Boisbaudran, copying Old Masters in the Louvre. He was a friend and supporter of Manet and went to the Café Guerbois, and so became involved in the intellectual and artistic movements of the period. He is chiefly known as a painter of portraits, 'intimate' scenes and still lifes; his flower paintings are famous, especially his roses. The first paintings he sent to the Salon were portraits; his canvases were turned down in 1859 but accepted in 1861. He made friends with the American painter Whistler and visited England with him in 1859; he went there again in 1861 and 1864. In both England and France he was much admired as a flower painter, and from about 1872-1874, he concentrated on flower subjects: examples of his work are *Narcissi and Tulips* (1862), *Flowers*

FANTIN-LATOUR *The Studio at the Batignolles.* 1870

(1865), *A June rose, Richesse* (1886), *Roses* (1890) and *Studies of roses*.

His large canvases with several portraits are famous, somewhat reminiscent of seventeenth-century Dutch painters, especially Frans Hals. An outstanding example is *Homage to Delacroix*, painted in 1864 a year after the great artist's death and exhibited in the 1864 Salon. It represents various artists and critics gathered round a self-portrait of Delacroix: Duranty, Fantin-Latour himself in a white smock, Whistler, Champfleury, Manet, Baudelaire, Cordier, Legros, Bracquemond and de Balleroy. There is also *The Studio at the Batignolles*, painted in honour of his friend Manet. Here Manet sits at his easel, with Zacharie Astruc, Otto Schölderer, Renoir, Emile Zola, Edmond Maître, Bazille and Monet. *A corner of the table* (1872 Salon)

shows a group of friends celebrating Baudelaire's birthday; they include Verlaine, Rimbaud, Léon Valade, Ernest d'Hervilly, Camille Pelletan, Elzéar Bonnier, Émile Blémond and Jean Aicard.

Apart from *The Dubourg family* (1878), his last great multiple portrait; this time of musicians, was *Round the piano* (1885 Salon), with Chabrier at the piano, Edouard Maître, Adolphe Jullien, Boisseau, Camille Benoît, Lascaux, Vincent d'Indy and Amédée Pigear. Fantin-Latour loved music and was a great admirer of Wagner, as can be seen in *The Three Rhine maidens* (pastel, 1876, inspired by the opera *Rheingold*, Scene I) and *Tannhaüser* (1886 Salon). Fantin-Latour also did lithographs, and the lyrical individual quality of his work is outstanding.

GAUGUIN Paul (Paris 1848-Atuana, Dominica, Marquesas Islands 1903) Gauguin was conscious of his originality early in his career. In a letter dated 6 October 1888, he wrote to a friend, the painter Schuffenecker: 'What does it matter if I am different from other people? Most people will be completely baffled; a few will think I'm a poet, but sooner or later I shall be appreciated.'

Gauguin did not start painting until comparatively late in life. In 1865 he went into the navy, where he remained till 1871, when he left to join a firm of stockbrokers with the Bertin Bank. He began collecting pictures by

GAUGUIN *Harvest in Brittany.* 1889

GAUGUIN *Self Portrait with the Yellow Christ. c.* 1890

young Impressionist painters, but did not show anything himself until 1876, when he had a picture in the Salon. He showed paintings in the last four Impressionist exhibitions, between 1880 and 1886, and during this period the influence of Claude Monet, Sisley and Pissarro is very noticeable, as in *The Seine at the Pont d'Iéna* (1875) and *Entrance to a village* (1884). But he was hankering after something more primitive, and Brittany, with its ancient granite crosses and sense of remoteness, attracted him. In 1886 he stayed at Pont-Aven from June to November, and there met Émile Bernard. After a short visit to Martinique, Gauguin went back to Brittany where he met Émile Bernard again. Bernard had just completed his *Breton women in a meadow* at Saint-Briac, and it was not long after, in August, that Gauguin painted his famous picture *Vision after the sermon*, or *Jacob's struggle with the Angel*, which became the manifesto for the new developments in painting. The two artists claimed to have found a new form of art, 'synthetism' and a new technique which they called 'cloisonnisme' ('partitionism'), so leading on to Symbolism in painting. Later on, Maurice Denis declared that 'synthetising does not necessarily mean simplifying in the

sense of leaving out various parts of a thing, but rather simplifying in the sense of making it easy to understand. It means classifying things so that every picture has the same rhythm; it means sacrificing details, rearranging them in order and generalizing'. Émile Bernard explained cloisonnisme: 'Dujardin called this first stage "cloisonnisme" because each tone was surrounded by a dark line, which gave a sense of its being separated by a partition, more like a great stained-glass window than a picture, with the same decorative effect of line and colour.'

A complete and definite break with Impressionism encouraged Gauguin to paint a whole series of very decorative canvases, with paint applied in broad flat sweeps, and detail suggested rather than defined; the general impression is something like stage scenery. Two examples are *Still life at the fête Gloanec* and *Decorative landscape*. In October 1888 he went to see van Gogh at Arles and there painted several pictures in an increasingly bold style, like *Landscape at Arles* and *Les Alyscamps*. Van Gogh found Gauguin's new manner disconcerting and this let to disagreement between the two artists. In the course of one heated argument, after his first bout of insanity, van Gogh cut off his own ear with a razor.

In the early part of 1889, Gauguin showed seventeen pictures at the Café Volpini at an exhibition of Impressionist and Synthetist art. He then paid another visit to Brittany, going first to Pont-Aven and then to Le Pouldu near Quimperlé, where he stayed in a small inn kept by Marie Henry, known as Marie Poupée, from April 1889 to November 1890. His painting here tended to be more decorative and primitive in style than ever, emphasising his ideas rather than pure visual quality—for instance in *The Yellow Christ* (1889), *La Belle Angèle* (1889), *Bonjour Monsieur Gauguin* (1889), *Self Portrait with the Yellow Christ* (c. 1890). After returning to Paris, he painted *The Awakening of Spring* (1890-1891) and *Nirvana, or Portrait of Meyer de Haan*, a Dutch painter (1890).

In March 1891, Georges-Albert Aurier published an important article in the *Mercure de France* for 9 February 1891, entitled *Symbolism in painting: Paul Gauguin*. Ignoring Émile Bernard, Aurier declared: 'To sum up

GAUGUIN *Les Alyscamps*. 1888

GAUGUIN
Bonjour Monsieur Gauguin. 1889

and conclude, a work of art as I like to imagine it ought to be: (1) *ideist*, as its one aim will be the expression of an idea; (2) *symbolist*, as it will express this idea by forms; (3) *synthetic*, as it will put down these signs and forms in a generally understandable manner; (4) *subjective*, because the object will never be considered merely as an object, but as the expression of an idea perceived by the subject;

(5) *decorative*, because decorative painting, such as the Egyptians and also probably the Greeks and Primitives conceived it, is no other than a manifestation of art which is at one and the same time subjective, synthetic, symbolist and ideist.'

Gauguin did not however find the inspiration he needed among the Symbolists; he really wanted to get back to an unspoilt primitive way of life. Like Mallarmé and many other artists, he dreamed of 'going far away to distant lands', and with the aim of leaving civilization behind, he set off for Tahiti on 4 April 1891 and stayed until July 1893. There he found a primitive world that seemed to resolve at least some of his problems. He did not find a fresh vision of nature, but he found the symbols it produced; not just people with picturesque customs, but simple folk whose way of life was primitive and noble. Their attitude to life was profoundly religious, and Gauguin found their beliefs agreed with his own philosophy. 'Primitive art' he wrote 'proceeds from the spirit, and nature is its servant. So-called civilized art proceeds from sensuality and serves nature. Nature is the servant of the first kind of art and the mistress of the second. Nature degrades the spirit when it allows itself to be worshipped, and that is how we have fallen into the abominable errors of naturalism.'

Many of Gauguin's paintings during this period show a new approach to art, which has strongly influenced certain tendencies in modern painting. Gauguin's decorative, stylised work, his spirit of synthesis and his pure, vibrant colours applied in broad flat surfaces foreshadowed much that we find in the art of Henri Matisse and his circle. Characteristic examples include: *Orana Maria: Hail Mary*; *The meal: three small Tahitian children at table*; *Tahitian Women on the beach*; *I Rarote oviri*; *Naked Tahitian women on the beach*; *Vahine note vi: Woman with a mango*; *Nafea foa ipoipo: When are you getting married?*; *Ta matete: the Market*. This last picture is especially suggestive. Everything about it: the figures, some of them looking like people in Egyptian bas-reliefs; the flat sweeps of vivid colour, and bright shadows full of blue and purple undertones; the ground like some great carpet spread out and the background like a stage set; all this shows a very definite and striking break with Impressionism.

Gauguin's approach was far from being objective and he was not at all interested in narrative and picturesque subjects. Instead he attained a fresh simplicity of vision, mys-

GAUGUIN *Nave Nave Mahana: wonderful days.* 1896

GAUGUIN *The White Horse.* 1898

terious and wonderfully sculptural in its nobility and harmony. A few more examples:
Hina te Fatou: the moon and the earth; *the Maori's
house*; *Manao Tupapau: the Spirit of the Dead is
watching.*

Gauguin returned to France a sick man, in
August 1893, and henceforth spent his time
between Paris and Brittany. He also organised
an exhibition of his Tahiti paintings at the
Durand-Ruel Gallery. However he could not
settle down in France, and in July 1895 went
back to Tahiti. He became ill again, felt
homesick and wretched, and in 1898 made a
suicide attempt in a state of deep depression.
In spite of all this he did not give up working,
in fact his creative energy seemed greater than
ever. He produced drawings, engravings,

GAUGUIN *Nevermore.* 1897

sculpture, ceramics and paintings, as well as
writing. His most famous paintings of this
period are *Nave, Nave, Mahana: wonderful days*;
The Day of God; *Nevermore*; *The White Horse*;
Breasts with Red Flowers and the huge painting
with its mysterious title: *Where do we come from?
What are we? Where are we going?* dated 1897.
The great picture shows the artist asking
agonizing questions about the origins of life
and the meaning of love and death, but not
necessarily answering them. André Breton
called this painting 'the unravelling of human
life' and indeed it does seem to unfurl itself like
a great frieze. Gauguin himself had a particular affection for the picture, and declared: 'I
do believe this painting is considerably better

GAUGUIN *The Siesta. c.* 1894

GAUGUIN *Fatata te Miti: by the sea.* 1892

GAUGUIN *Aha oe Feii: What, are you jealous?* 1892

than any previous work of mine; in fact I am convinced I shall never do anything better— nor indeed paint anything as good as this again.'

To understand Gauguin and his art one must refer above all to the famous document he produced in collaboration with Charles Morice, during the winter of 1893-1894, entitled *Noa-Noa*. The manuscript of this work is now in the Department of Drawings in the Louvre. It is fully illustrated, and its drawings, watercolour paintings, engravings and photographs make up an extremely important collection. It was published in 1897 in the *Revue Blanche*, and contains a miscellany of artistic, philosophical, religious, symbolic and poetical reflexions collected and related by Gauguin, and including his own beliefs and considerations as well. Another similar book, written rather earlier and with the title *Ancient Maori Religion*, is also an invaluable source for the understanding of Gauguin's personality and art.

In August 1901 Gauguin left Tahiti for Dominica, one of the Marquesas Islands. His health was failing but he still retained his old enthusiasm for work. In November he noted that 'here poetry seems to come unbidden, and if, when you are painting, you let your imagination drift away into dreams, new ideas will follow.' Dreams and suggestion are the key to Gauguin's work. All through his life he kept his simple childlike spirit, his vivid imagination and love of mystery and the supernatural, yet at the same time he was a thinker, a philosopher and a metaphysician. During this period his paintings include *And the Gold of their Bodies* (1901), *Contes Barbares* (1902), *Horsemen on the rose-coloured beach* (1902). He died on 8 May 1903, tormented and harassed by debts, illness and bureaucratic worries.

Gauguin, like the Impressionists, was very little appreciated by most of his contemporaries. People found it hard to understand his new method of painting and his technique which reacted so violently against the theories prevalent at the time. Cézanne, although himself something of a revolutionary in art, was severely critical of Gauguin's work: 'Planes—that is something Gauguin has never understood. I have never approved and I never will approve of his neglect of modelling and gradation. His stuff is absolute rubbish. Gauguin isn't a painter at all, he does nothing but produce incomprehensible nonsense.'

Nowadays we have come to realise how much a number of great contemporary painters, particularly Matisse, owe to Gauguin. He was also the originator of 'Modern Style' and Art Nouveau, while certain aspects of Nabism and decorative art are directly derived from him. He had the courage to break away from a type of art that had lost its sense of direction, and sought out the deep ancestral springs of thought; he discovered a fresh, original and decorative approach to art and influenced many who followed in his footsteps.

GOGH Vincent van (Groot-Zundert, Holland 1853-Auvers-sur-Oise 1890) Van Gogh, like Gauguin, developed late. He was the son of a Protestant minister, and found it hard at first to decide on a career. From the age of about twenty, he worked as an assistant to the picture-dealer Goupil, first at The Hague, then in Brussels, London and finally Paris. He then felt the call to a religious life and for the next two years worked as an evangelist and free-lance missionary among poor miners and peasants. Towards the end of 1878 he began to draw and paint; he had a great admiration for Millet and copied a number of

VAN GOGH *The Road*. 1880-1881

Van Gogh *The Fourteenth of July in Paris*. July 1887

his works. Van Rappard and his cousin Mauve helped him with advice, and he was also influenced by the work of Maris and Israëls.

During this period, up to 1881, van Gogh lived in Belgium; then from 1881 to 1885 he was back in Holland again, staying at Etten, The Hague, Drenthe and for a rather longer period (December 1883-November 1885) at Nuenen. Finally he went to Antwerp (November 1885-February 1886). His pencil studies are mostly realistic in manner and subject, dealing with mine-workers and peasants, simple homely objects, heavy shoes or clogs, looms and workmen's tools; or maybe a heap of potatoes, birds' nests, etc., or sombre landscapes with dark gloomy skies and subdued colouring. We can already see something of van Gogh's strange violent personality in the way he transforms reality into poetry and gives to every object and creature, to every element in nature a terrifying sense of being human. *In the Weaver's House* (1884), *Peasant with a pipe* (1884), *Small jugs* (1884), *Potatoes* (1885), *Nests* (1885), *The Parsonage at Nuenen* (1885), *Cottage at close of day* (1885) are representative of this sombre, gloomy period which also includes his masterpiece in this style, *The potatoeaters* (1885).

His great admiration for Rubens then led him to experiment with colour, from 1885 onwards. 'Colour by itself expresses something,' he said; and in his *Still life with an open bible* we can see the link with Impressionism and what is known as his Paris period.

Van Gogh spent the next two years, from February 1886 to February 1888, in Paris where he associated constantly with the Impressionists; in fact at that time he declared: 'It is as necessary now to spend time regularly with the Impressionists as it used to be to study in a Paris studio.' He was also attracted to Neo-Impressionism and its pointilliste technique, as well as to Symbolism and

VAN GOGH *Fishing in Spring.* 1886-1888

Van Gogh *Restaurant de la Sirène. c.* 1887-1888

the brilliant colouring used by Gauguin and his friends. Another thing he found fascinating was the prevailing fashion for Japanese art, and he copied a number of prints by the great Japanese masters, *Rain* by Hiroshige being one of the most outstanding. *La Guinguette* (*c.* 1886) and *Le Moulin de la Galette* (1886) are more or less transitional works, coming between his sombre Nuenen period and the various Paris influences; while paintings like *Small gardens on the Butte Montmartre* (1887), *At an Asnières Restaurant* (1887) and *Restaurant de la Sirène* (1887) show how van Gogh was gradually developing and moving towards the brilliant colouring and fragmentation of the Impressionists. The *Portrait of Père Tanguy* (1887) and *Woman with tambourines* (1887) on the other hand show the influence of Japanese prints; his famous 'bâtonnets' technique appeared here for the first time, to be developed increasingly as time went on. His new conception of art and his continual longing for something different made him restless and he dreamed of going to a distant land of sunshine,

to far-away Japan. This proved impossible, but he did however leave Paris and go to Arles in Provence. 'I had endless reasons for going to the South of France and working there. I wanted to see another kind of light; then I thought seeing nature under a clearer sky could give a better idea of how the Japanese felt and did their drawings, and finally I wanted to see the stronger southern sunlight.'

Van Gogh's Arles period goes from February 1888 to May 1889, and his powerful creative genius found ample inspiration in that wonderful place. His painting was now violent and forceful, marked by bold chromatic colouring, and he was extraordinarily prolific, producing 190 canvases in a little over a year. He loved and understood the South of France, but unlike Cézanne, who found in the landscape of Provence qualities of classical balance and rhythm, van Gogh felt it was a land of extremes and of tragic violence. He saw in Provence a sunscorched land, burnt by the relentless intensity of the sun and the violence of the wind, the mistral that dries up the countryside and twists the trees in its fury. Everything is shrill and sharp, shapes are tormented and contorted into strange spirals and curves and convolutions; everything seems to be in perpetual motion. Van Gogh is haunted by the sense of space, he is carried away by the idea of a cosmic universe continually renewed because it is continually destroyed. All he can find in this classic land, where he had hoped to discover balance and harmony, is a kind of wild furious exasperation. He felt completely exhausted and tormented by nervous tension and a kind of frenzied creativity; finally, on Christmas Eve 1888, he broke down completely, and cut off his own ear, after an argument with Gauguin. Not long after this he asked to be admitted as a voluntary patient at the local asylum of Saint-Rémy.

It is not easy to select among so many works executed during this period; but these are some of the most outstanding: *La Crau* (1888); *Starry night* (1888); *Café at evening* (1888); *Gauguin's armchair*, *Sunflowers*, *The Drawbridge* and *Vincent van Gogh's house at Arles* (all 1888);

The Arlésienne (1888), *Roulin the Postman* (1888); *Portrait of the Belgian poet Boch* (1888); *Vincent's chair* (1888-1889); *Flowering trees* (1889) and *Self Portrait with bandaged ear* (1889).

Vincent continued painting throughout the year (3 May 1889-16 May 1890) he spent in the asylum. His works of that period are remarkable for their intensity of form and colour and a tender lyrical beauty: Émile Bernard believed he had 'never painted so well nor with such assurance'. His technique is astonishing, with its impasted brushwork, broken up into specks and dots and commas and lines. There is a pathetic sense of hallucination about his work at this time: *Vincent's room at Arles* (1889), *Starry night* and *Cypresses* (both 1889), *The Olive trees* (1889), *Cornfield with cypresses* (1889), *Hospital ward at Arles* (1889), *Olive orchard* (1889), *Road with cypresses near the Alpilles* (1890), *The Paviors* (1889), *Head Superintendant at the Hôpital Saint-Paul* (1890), *Girl from Arles, after Gauguin, On the threshold of eternity* (both 1890) and *Prisoners' round* after Gustave Doré (1890). These last two paintings seem to symbolise his own tragic destiny.

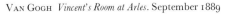

VAN GOGH *Vincent's Room at Arles*. September 1889

VAN GOGH
Le Pont de Langlois. May 1888

VAN GOGH
The Starry Night. June 1889

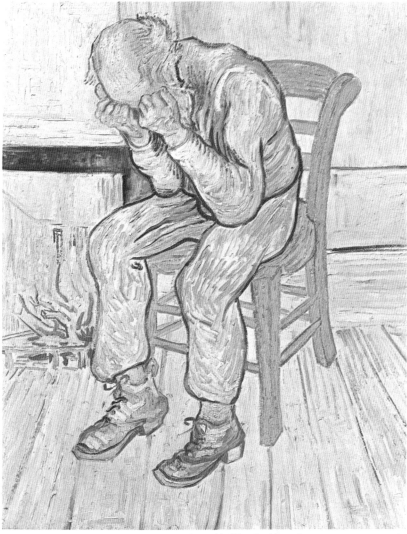

VAN GOGH *On the Threshold of Eternity*. May 1890

After this comes a period of relative security and calm, when van Gogh, under the care of his good doctor Gachet and the hospital nurses, seemed to have attained a certain peace of mind if not actual happiness. The colours in the canvases painted at Auvers-sur-Oise between 23 May and 27 July 1890 are bright and gay, with blues reminiscent of Delft ware and greens predominating. There is often an enchanting fairy-like figure in the pic-ture, picking flowers in the garden, going for a walk or playing the piano; it is Doctor Gachet's daughter. Van Gogh's characteristic technique is still in evidence—dynamic and flamboyant, with spirals and curves and volutes, and his portraits especially are often asymmetrical. The works he produced during these few weeks seem to have acquired a new sense of balance, and of release from anguish and tension; he found something therapeutic

VAN GOGH *Self Portrait with a soft hat*. 1887

VAN GOGH *Self Portrait with bandaged ear*. January 1889

VAN GOGH *Self Portrait at an easel*. September 1889

VAN GOGH *Self Portrait*. 1889

VAN GOGH *The Church at Auvers.* 4 to 8 June 1890

in colour and in the actual act of painting. The most outstanding paintings of this period are *Mademoiselle Gachet in the garden* and *Stubble-fields at Cordeville* (both 1890), *Mademoiselle Gachet at the piano* (1890), *View at Auvers: fields under a stormy sky* (1890), *Auvers Town Hall on the* *fourteenth of July* (1890) and *Landscape at Auvers* (1890). Of his *Church at Auvers*, also painted in 1890, van Gogh wrote to his sister Wil: 'I have got another bigger picture of the village church, a sort of effect where the building looks purplish against a deep plain blue sky, pure cobalt. The stained glass windows show up like patches of ultramarine blue and the roof is purple with touches of orange. In the foreground is grass with flowers and sunny pinkish sand. It is almost the same kind of effect as those studies I did at Nuenen of the old tower and the cemetery, only in this present picture the colour is more sumptuous and expressive.'

Then there is the *Portrait of Doctor Gachet* (1890) 'with the worried expression people have in these days' and the *Self Portrait* (also 1890) with its blue and turquoise colouring and disturbing rather mad expression. This is

VAN GOGH *Cornfield with cypresses*. June 1889

VAN GOGH *Portrait of Doctor Gachet*. June 1890

VAN GOGH *Self Portrait*. May-June 1890

the last self portrait he painted; it seems to foreshadow the artist's tragic end, when he shot himself with a revolver and died two days later on 29 July. An unfinished letter to his brother Théo was found on him after his death: 'Well, I'm risking my life for my work, and I've half lost my reason as a result.'

Van Gogh spoke of his own continual 'search for the infinite'. His art made a deep, lasting impression on succeeding generations of painters as well as on his contemporaries.

He went far beyond the Impressionists in experimenting and investigating the possibilities of line and colour, opening the way for Fauvism and Expressionism and, indeed, for much of contemporary art.

GONZALÈS Eva (Paris 1849-Paris 1883) Her father was the novelist Emmanuel Gonzalès, and she was brought up in a literary and artistic background. Charles Chaplin gave her her first painting lessons, and she was also taught by Gustave Brion, a pupil of Guérin's, before being introduced to Manet by Alfred Stevens and being accepted as his pupil. His taking a woman as a pupil was unusual, and Berthe Morisot was very jealous. Eva Gonzalès attracted attention with the two canvases (*L'Enfant de troupe* and *Portrait of her sister Jeanne*) she exhibited at the 1870 Salon, where Manet also had a portrait of her at her easel. During the war of 1870 Eva Gonzalès lived at Dieppe, where she concentrated on pastels, and her best work was done in this medium. In 1874 she achieved success with *La Nichée* or *Rosy morning*, which was acquired by the State in 1885. In 1879, the year she married the painter Henri Guérard, her canvas *The Box at the Théâtre des Italiens* which had been turned down for the Salon in 1873, was finally accepted. It was a popular subject with Renoir (and incidentally with Mary Cassatt as well). Eva Gonzalès, unlike many of the Impressionists, tends to use sombre, rather dark colouring, and right up to the end of her life she followed the style of her teacher Manet's first manner. In her pastels too, she tends to use clear outlines, with greys and neutral colours predominating, though she often chooses the same subjects as the Impressionists—landscapes, mostly, and portraits, many of them of her sister. In this, she differed from Berthe Morisot, who was more influenced by Renoir and Sisley. The last time she showed at the Salon (1883), she exhibited *The Milliner*, one of her best pastels. Her health never recovered after the birth of a son on 19 April that year, and only a fortnight later she died of an embolism; Manet's death shortly before had much distressed her. In 1885 her husband and her father organised a very successful retrospective exhibition of her work at the Vie Moderne premises in the Place Saint-Georges; the catalogue had a preface by Philippe Burty with Théodore de Banville's poem *Camée* printed before the list of works.

GUILLAUMIN Armand (Paris 1841-Château de Grignon, Orly, 1927) The Guillaumin family had left Paris in 1844 and gone to Moulins to live. In 1856 Guillaumin went back to Paris to learn drawing at the École Municipale under the sculptor

GONZALÈS *The Box at the Théâtre des Italiens. c.* 1873

GUILLAUMIN *Self Portrait. c.* 1875

GUILLAUMIN *Lilacs in the artist's garden*

Caillouet, before becoming an employee of the Paris railway in 1860 and going to live at Montmartre. Not long after, he began attending the Académie Suisse where he met Francisco Oller, Pissarro and also Cézanne, who used to take him now and then to the meetings at the Café Guerbois. In 1863 Guillaumin exhibited along with Cézanne, Edouard Manet and Pissarro at the Salon des Refusés. In 1868 he finally gave up his work with the railways to concentrate on painting. He worked at Ivry, Charenton, Bercy and La Rapée (his painting *Barges at Bercy* dates from 1871). In 1872 he often used to go to Pontoise to see Pissarro. In 1874 he exhibited three works (among them *Sunset at Ivry*, painted about 1873) at the first Impressionist manifestation, and also showed at their exhibitions in 1877, 1880, 1881, 1882 and 1886. In 1877 Pissarro introduced him to Gauguin, and in 1882 he discovered Damiette, near Orsay, where he went to paint regularly for fifteen years. He met Signac in 1883 and then Seurat, and painted with them on the quays, but he did not meet Van Gogh until 1886. Up to 1892 he used to paint in the small villages in the Seine-et-Oise and Essonne districts or else in Paris: *The Park at Issy-les-Moulineaux* (1877), *Charenton bridge* (1878), *View of the Île Saint-Louis* (c. 1881), *Landscape with apple trees* (1884), *Le Pont-Marie* (c. 1883) and *Path to the valley* are examples of his work. In 1891 he received a hundred thousand francs from an option debenture in a Building Society and so was able to travel. He went first to Saint-Palais in 1892, with subsequent visits in 1893 and 1909, and painted *Saint-Palais, the mouth of the Gironde* (1892) and *The Corniche at Saint-Palais* (1893). Between 1893 and 1913 Guillaumin went to Crozant in the Creuse and to Agay in the South of France. He visited the Auvergne (1895, 1898, 1900), the Orne (1893, 1903), the Loing (1896), the Eure (1900), Rouen (1904) and also Holland (1904). In 1907 and again in 1913 he stayed at Le Trayas in the Var, but spent the following winters at Agay. After 1913 he went to Crozant more frequently, spending the winters in the south, and often going to Paris. His work during this period includes: *Storm at Agay* (1895), the *Hamlet of Peschadère* (1895), *View of Agay* (1895), *Mill at Les Bouchardonnes* (1905), *Winter on the banks of the Creuse* (1906), *The Heights above the Creuse* (1918), *Ruins of the Château de Crozant* and *Hoar frost at Crozant*. His work is strongly Impressionist in style and composition, and the colours are very bright, though his winter scenes tend to be more subdued.

JONGKIND Johann-Barthold (Lattrop in Holland 1819-La Côte Saint-André 1891) Jongkind attended the Academy of Drawing at The Hague, where the painter Schelfout taught him how to paint landscapes in water-colours. He visited France for the first time in 1846, when his drawing master gave him an introduction to Eugène Isabey, who took him to Brittany and Normandy. The next years he spent partly in Holland and partly in France, leading a disorderly and dissolute life until 1860. In that year he met Madame Fesser, and under her influence settled down for a time, and his art developed considerably. In 1862 he went to Le Havre, to Sainte-Adresse, and spent the summers of 1863, 1864 and 1865 at Honfleur. There he began painting out of doors, sketching in oils and water-colours with Boudin who had a considerable influence on his development. In return, Jongkind, who was by now painting exceptional watercolours with lively broken brushwork, very soon influenced Boudin as well as Claude Monet. Monet in his reminiscences wrote: 'Jongkind wanted to see our sketches and then asked me to come and work with him. He explained his technique, so completing the teaching I had had from Boudin, and from that time onwards Jongkind was my real teacher; it is to him I owe the real training of my eye.' Edouard Manet called him 'The father of modern landscape.'

In 1873 Jongkind paid his first visit to the Dauphiné and in 1878 went to live with the

GUILLAUMIN *Sunset at Ivry. c.* 1873

JONGKIND *Étretat*. 1865

JONGKIND *The Rue Saint-Séverin*. 1877

Fesser family at the Côte Saint-André, not far from Grenoble. He loved that part of France and remained there until his death, painting more in watercolour than in oils. His sketches along the banks of the Isère and his snow scenes are delightful. He used white body colour to obtain his effects, and he was one of the first artists—even before Monet and Sisley—to capture the iridescent mother-of-pearl effect of light on snow, and to extract from his whites subtle colours and tones. Unfortunately his last years were clouded by outbursts of violent insanity, due to a relapse of his alcoholism; finally on 27 January 1891 he had to be taken to an asylum at Grenoble, and died at the Côte Saint-André on 9 February.

The Department of Drawings at the Louvre has a very fine and representative collection of

JONGKIND *The Beach at Sainte-Adresse.* 1863

Jongkind's watercolours, which includes his *Views of Dutch ports* as well as several *Seascapes* painted in Normandy, at Honfleur and by the Seine estuary. There are also other landscapes of the banks of the Isère, and some of Marseilles and La Ciotat, with *Snow scenes* at the Côte Saint-André. Among his best paintings are: *The Harbour at Honfleur* (1864), *Holland: boats near the mill* (1868) and *The Isère at Grenoble* (1875).

LEBOURG Albert (Montfort-sur-Risle, Eure 1849-Rouen 1928) Lebourg came from a middle-class family and began by studying architecture at Rouen in a private practice. Then, under the influence of the painter Victor Delamarre and Gustave Morin, who was head of the municipal Art School at Rouen, he took up painting instead. An art collector from Algiers called Laperlier then took him back with him in October 1872 and he joined the staff of the School of Drawing attached to the Algiers Fine Arts Society. Apart from one visit to Paris, where he got married on 8 September 1873, Lebourg lived in Algiers until 1877, and there met a painter from Lyons called Seignemartin. Under his influence his painting grew increasingly light and bright, and, some time before Claude

LEBOURG *Snow scene, sunset*

Monet, he started painting series of pictures on the same subject. These include *The Admiralty* (1875), *Arab fantasia* (1876) and *Moorish café* (1877).

On his return to Paris in 1877 Lebourg discovered the Impressionists. After an initial reaction of surprise, he eventually joined their circle and showed at their exhibitions in 1879 and 1880. This did not however prevent his exhibiting at the Artistes Français and at the Nationale when it was first founded in 1890. Lebourg worked mainly in Paris, Rouen and in the Eure district. Like most of the Impressionists, he found ample inspiration in the outskirts of Paris, Sèvres, Suresnes and Bougival. Almost every year, from 1884 to 1888, he also went to the Auvergne, and particularly to Pont-du-Château (Allier), a place he was very fond of. In 1896-1897 he travelled in Holland and then went to London and Switzerland. But his favourite places were still Paris and Rouen; he loved the banks of the

Seine and rendered their soft misty atmosphere and transparent light effects with wonderful subtlety. There are fine examples of Lebourg's work in the Petit-Palais Museum in Paris, including: *Rainy weather, Île de la Cité in Paris* (1900), *The Pont-Neuf* (1906), *The Seine near Rouen*, and in the Jeu de Paume Museum: *Road by the Seine at Neuilly in winter* (1888), *The Harbour at Algiers* (1876) and *The Banks of the Ain* (1897).

LIEBERMANN Max (Berlin 1847-Berlin 1935) Liebermann came from a family of rich Jewish merchants. His father intended him to read philosophy, but he decided instead to study art in Berlin under Karl Steffeck, before going on in 1868 to Weimar to the School of Fine Arts, then considered the stronghold of avant-garde tendencies in art. He was taught painting there by Paul Thumann and Ferdinand Pauwels. After visiting Paris and then

LIEBERMANN *Terrace of the Restaurant Jacob at Nienstedten on the Elbe.* 1902-1903

LIEBERMANN *Self Portrait*

Holland, he went to Düsseldorf where he came across the work of the Hungarian artist Munkacsy. In his painting *The Goose Pluckers* (1871), which Bonnat admired so much in the 1874 Paris Salon but which had previously been the subject of scandal in Germany, when the artist was accused of being 'the apostle of ugliness', Liebermann adopted Munkacsy's sombre realistic manner. He then went to Paris (1873, 1878) and Barbizon, where he met Millet, Daubigny and Corot; then to Holland (1875) where he made a special study of Frans Hals, and to Munich (1878) before finally settling in Berlin in 1884.

Gradually he became interested in open-air painting (see his *Women mending nets*, 1888) and although he did not attempt to use prismatic colours, he did experiment up to a point with divisionism. The painters he admired most were Manet and Degas. Following their example, and also possibly influenced to a certain extent by Joseph Israëls whom he had met in Holland, Liebermann began from 1890 onwards to choose subjects that gave him an opportunity to study light and render movement in painting. He continued, however, to paint rustic scenes, like his *Woman with two*

LIEBERMANN *House on the Wannsee*

LIEBERMANN *Garden with Sunflowers*. 1895

goats (1890), while his *Open-air beer-house at Brannenburg* (1893) gives an excellent impression of sunlight filtering through leaves. In the same style are two later paintings, his *Terrace of the Restaurant Jacob at Nienstedten on the Elbe* (1902-1903) and *Garden on the Wannsee* (1918). In other paintings of polo grounds or race-courses, not unlike Degas, Liebermann excels in the rendering of form in action, skilfully painted in his rapid nervous manner (*Riders on the beach*, 1902).

His many portraits, mostly painted in the last thirty years of his life show his objectivity of approach and prove him to be a true representative of the Berlin tradition. The portraits of *Wilhelm von Bode* (1890), *Alfred von Berger* (1905) and *The Surgeon Ferdinand Sauerbruch* (1932) are examples of his somewhat chilly reserve. Although Liebermann remained firmly set in the tradition of Menzel, he also played a considerable part in the evolution of German painting in the second half of the nineteenth century. He prepared the way for other European influences from Naturalism to Impressionism, which he supported enthusiastically, leading on to movements like Expressionism and Futurism.

MANET Edouard (Paris 1832-Paris 1883). Manet played a fundamental part in the art of his day, but it was also a curious mixture of ambiguity and contradiction. Ambiguity, because in spite of himself he became the leader and spokesman of Impressionism which was in fact a revolutionary movement in art, although he always intended to remain firmly grounded in tradition; and contradiction, because although he claimed to follow in the steps of the Old Masters, such as Raphael, Giorgione and Titian, the Spanish School and Frans Hals, his painting was mostly in the 'modern style' extolled by Baudelaire. Like Courbet, he was theoretically in favour of using light colours, but all his life long he used sombre colouring, blacks and browns and greys that the Impressionists themselves had given up using. He always refused to exhibit with the Impressionists, but after 1871 he began painting out of doors, under the influence of the young artist Claude Monet. Manet, who came from a traditional middle-class background, always hoped to have his pictures accepted at the Salon, but in 1863 he shocked people at the Salon des Refusés, and from that time on, became the butt for general recrimination and criticism; in fact people called his bold 'tachisme' technique nothing but 'a mess'.

MANET *Child with cherries.* 1859

His importance was fundamental, finally, because he became the staunch supporter and propagator of new ideas in art, and the avant-garde painting of the time, in spite of all the adverse criticism. He used to speak with authority during the discussions in the Café Guerbois; he painted with amazing freedom and brilliance; his colour schemes and subjects were beautiful and harmonious, and since he came rather late to the practice of painting out of doors, he helped to influence the technique and development of his Impressionist friends. It is strange to realise, in this connection, that Baudelaire, in an interesting and perceptive article about Constantin Guys and modern painting, did not recognise Manet's supreme importance as a representative of modern art, just as much as Degas was, but in a rather different way.

Édouard Manet's family had decided he was to be a naval officer, but he soon gave up the navy and took up painting instead. In 1850 he began to study in Thomas Couture's studio, and stayed with him till 1856. In 1855 he painted a canvas which his teacher strongly disapproved of, and when all the other students rallied round and gave Manet a standing ovation, Couture was furious. 'My friend,' he said in great indignation, 'If you want to be head of a school, go and start one somewhere else.' Manet completed his training at the Louvre and then travelled extensively abroad, going to Italy (1853), then Holland (1856), Germany and Austria, and finally came back to France to settle.

His *Absinthe drinker* painted in 1858 was turned down for the Salon in the following year. However in that same year, Manet painted his first really famous picture, *Child with cherries*, rather in the style of Murillo and the Spanish school; it was exhibited in 1861 at the Martinet Gallery, 26 Boulevard des Italiens.

In 1862 Manet left his studio in the Rue de Douai and moved to 81 Rue Guyot. From the first of March 1863, and throughout March and April, he exhibited another fourteen paintings, once more at the Martinet Gallery; among them were the *Absinthe drinker, Concert in the Tuileries Gardens* (1860) which caused quite a stir, and *The Old musician* (1862). Manet also showed several paintings which were inspired by a group of Spanish dancers who had made two very successful visits to Paris, in 1861 and 1862; among them were *The Spanish Ballet* (1862) and the famous portrait of *Lola de Valence* (1862) the company's leading ballerina, about whom Baudelaire composed some famous verses, in his *Fleurs du Mal*, comparing her to an unexpectedly lovely and charming black and rose-coloured jewel.

In these verses Baudelaire wanted to show how the Spanish painters, especially Goya, had influenced Manet, in their black and rose-coloured harmonies, when the critics and the public were full of indignation at what they called Manet's 'mixture of red and blue and yellow and black which is just a caricature of colour, not real colour at all'. Not long after, on 1 May 1863 the official Salon opened. That year the Hanging Committee had been particularly strict and a great number of the paintings sent up had been turned down. The Emperor Napoleon III decided therefore that he would found another Salon to be held in the same building, the Palais de l'Industrie, where all the pictures that had been officially turned down for the Salon proper would be exhibited. This was the famous 'Salon des Refusés' which became the first officially recognised show of avant-garde painting. A good many artists took part, including Manet who exhibited three canvases, among which one shown under the title *Le Bain* (no. 363 in the catalogue) or *The foursome*, and now celebrated as *Le Dejeuner sur l'herbe*, which shocked people profoundly. Manet was very much surprised; he had no idea anyone would be upset by his attempts to 'modernise' classical subjects. The picture was inspired by a lost painting of Raphael's, *The Judgment of Paris*, known in an engraving of Marcantonio Raimondi's, and Giorgione's famous *Concert champêtre*, in the Louvre. 'I want to make another version,' Manet wrote, 'and do it in the trans-

MANET *Lola de Valence*. 1862

MANET *Le Déjeuner sur l'herbe.* 1863

parency of the atmosphere.' Eugène Manet, the artist's brother, and Ferdinand Leenhoff, a Dutch sculptor who was later to become his brother-in-law, posed for the two men in the picture, while the lovely nude figure in the foreground was Victorine Meurend, Manet's favourite model from 1862 to 1874. People were shocked both by the subject, which was considered indecent, and by the realistic way the nude figure was rendered, a very different approach from the still fashionable Ingres ideal, and there was a general outcry. Only Antonin Proust and Zacharie Astruc were in favour of the picture.

In 1864 however, two of Manet's paintings *Incident at a bull-fight* and *Christ with angels* were hung at the Salon. The caricaturist Bertail, writing in the *Journal amusant*, taxed them with being 'Spanish toys dressed with black

Ribera sauce, by Monsieur Manet y Courbetos y Zurbaran de las Batignollas'.

There was another scandal at the 1865 Salon, where among other paintings, Manet showed *Olympia*, a nude inspired by a poem by Zacharie Astruc. Again Victorine Meurend was the model. Once more Manet was inspired by old masters; this time his sources were Titian's *Urbino Venus* and on the technical side Goya's *Maja desnuda*. Critics and the public saw the picture as a shameless apology for prostitution, and it was called such names as 'Odalisque with a yellow belly', 'Venus with a cat' and 'a kind of female gorilla'. Only Baudelaire and Zola praised it; Zola even went so far as to declare 'that fate has destined it for the Louvre'. Much later Paul Valéry said in his introduction to the catalogue for the Manet centenary exhibition in the Orangerie:

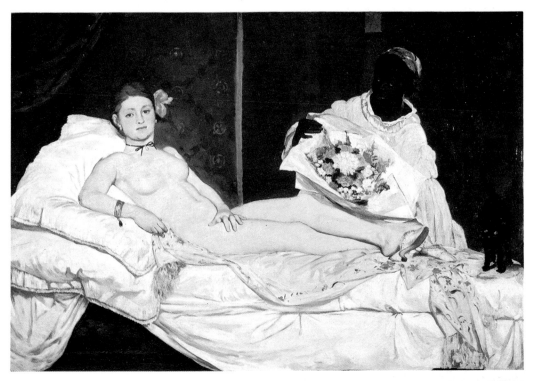

MANET *Olympia*. 1863

MANET *Vase of Peonies. c.* 1864-1865

'Olympia shocks people who react in holy horror; but she triumphs in the end. She is both an idol and a scandal, showing the presence and power of a wretched secret of modern society. She is an empty-headed creature, and the thread of black velvet round her neck cuts her off from her own inner nature. She is the woman whose function calls for tranquil and innocent ignorance of such a thing as modesty; the purity of her perfect outline encloses supreme impurity. She is a bestial creature, a Vestal dedicated to complete nakedness, stirring up all man's barbarous and primitive animal instincts, both hidden and acknowledged.'

In this same year, 1865, Manet went to Spain to look at the paintings that had so much influenced his work. Goya left him cold, but he was enthusiastic about Velazquez. The following year he sent two works to the Salon, *The Fifer* and *The tragic actor*, or *Portrait of*

MANET *Portrait of Berthe Morisot*. 1872

Rouvière as Hamlet. In 1867 he painted *The Execution of the Emperor Maximilian* inspired by Goya's *Tres de Mayo*. He did not exhibit anything at the Salon that year, but instead showed an important collection of some fifty paintings at the Exposition Universelle. On this occasion Zola published his *Édouard Manet: a biophysical and critical study*, and to thank him, the artist painted his *Portrait of Émile Zola* (shown at the 1868 Salon) where an Utamaro print, a photograph of Olympia and the top part of a Goya engraving from Velasquez' *The Drinkers* appear in the background behind the sitter.

During this period, and indeed up to the time of his death, Manet painted some very fine still lifes, such as *Vase of peonies* (*c.* 1864-1865) and *The Salmon* (1866). In the 1869 Salon Manet, who was back in favour there again, sent *Lunch in the studio* and *The Balcony*, with Berthe Morisot in the foreground, Jenny Clauss, a musician who married the painter Pierre Prins, on her left, and further back Antoine Guillemet the landscape artist, with Léon Koëlla-Leenhoff behind.

In August 1872 Manet, who much admired a Frans Hals painting *The Gipsy woman* in the Louvre, paid a visit to Holland. This inspired his painting *Le Bon Bock* which was a great success at the 1873 Salon. The same year he

Manet *Girl in a Garden.* 1880

painted the *Portrait of Nina de Callias* known as *Nina de Villard: lady with fans,* with its combination of various influences—Frans Hals, the great Japanese engravers, the fragmented technique of the Impressionists. Manet was gradually moving nearer to Impressionism and painting out of doors, as can be seen in his *Game of Croquet* and *The Railway,* both painted in 1873. In 1874 he was at Argenteuil, painting with Claude Monet out of doors, and his work then began to show a more lively technique; the colouring became lighter and brighter, though he still occasionally used his favourite rather sombre colours. Among the best examples of this period are: *Boating; Argenteuil, les canotiers,* shown at the 1875 Salon; *Claude Monet painting in his floating studio* and *The Monet family in the garden.*

In September 1875 he paid a short visit to Venice which resulted in the painting *Venice: the Grand Canal.* Three particularly good examples of Manet's late conversion to Impressionism, and its luminous colouring, are *Le Linge* (1875), then two pictures painted in 1878 from the windows of his studio at 4 Rue Saint-Pétersbourg: *Rue Mosnier with flags* (now renamed Rue de Berne) and *Paviors in the Rue Mosnier.* But as we have already seen, Manet was always more of an independent than a real Impressionist, much

more interested in 'modern' painting than working in the open air, which he soon abandoned to concentrate on what was more immediately attractive to his temperament and outlook: for instance, *Nana* (1877), *In the greenhouse* (1878) exhibited at the 1879 Salon, and *At Père Lathuille's,* shown in the 1880 Salon.

In 1880 signs of ataxia appeared. He was living at Bellevue at the time, then he went to Versailles and later to Rueil, where he continued painting in a very personal naturalistic style. Works of this period include: *Corner of the garden at Bellevue; The Walk; Girl in a garden,* all three painted in 1880; *The Bench* (1881) and *The Bar at the Folies-Bergère,* exhibited in 1882.

Paul Colin in his book *Manet* (Paris 1937, p. 139) perfectly expresses how Édouard Manet finally reached a solution 'to the conflicting tendencies at play in his art. He finds out how to resolve two different attitudes by, as it were, painting out of doors in his own home. He gets his models to pose in a greenhouse, under an arbour, or in the uncertain light of a small enclosed Paris garden where a single chestnut tree is enough to shut out the sunlight. In this way he can paint the sort of light effects he is used to, while at the same time intensifying and refining them; this does not interfere with his habits as a painter who likes to work indoors with models posing for hours on end'.

MEIFFREN Y ROIG Eliseo (Barcelona 1859-1940) introduced Impressionism into Catalonia and was one of the artists who contributed to the revival of Spanish landscape painting. He worked for many years in Paris, where he won a bronze medal at the 1900 Exposition Universelle, in Palma in Majorca and in New York.

MEIFFREN Y ROIG *The Lake of Barnyoles*

Most of his paintings show his preference for bright colouring, and his quick lively touch. He has a real sense of atmosphere and loves to paint heavy clouds and stormy light effects.

MONET Claude (Paris 1840-Giverny 1926) On 21 June 1926, only a few months before his death, Claude Monet explained the part he played in the Impressionist movement and in contemporary art generally. 'I have always had an intense dislike of theories. I can only claim credit for having painted direct from nature and trying to record my impressions of the most transient effects. I am distressed that it was because of me that the group was given its name, when most of them are not in the least impressionist.'

The 'father of Impressionism' who used to say: 'we paint just as birds sing' thus explained his attitude to the movement. Impressionism implied an essentially visual approach to painting and was intensely sensitive to the effect of light on form and colour. Someone once said of him: 'Monet is nothing but an eye—but what an eye it is!' He certainly had an exceptional gift for capturing the most fleeting and evanescent effects with astonishing rapidity and skill, and the speed with which he worked meant he could record ephemeral impressions and the subtlest and most varied repercussions of light. Claude Monet translated his feelings and poetic impressions of what one might call 'unreal reality', both in

MONET *Le Déjeuner sur l'herbe.* 1865

Monet *Ladies in the garden.* 1866-1867

success and failure. One day Octave Mirbeau, who had a great admiration for him and wrote some excellent articles about him, admonished him in these words: 'Now come, Monet, once and for all, do be realistic. Do be sensible. Can't you realise there are dreams no reasonable person ought to attempt to put on canvas because it simply can't be done. No one can possibly go beyond the world of the senses—and good heavens! what you see and feel is a big enough and endless enough realm for you to conquer'. No higher praise is possible.

Claude Monet was born in Paris but spent part of his childhood at Le Havre. In 1858 he made the acquaintance of Boudin who encouraged him to paint and to experiment with working in the open air. In 1859 Monet went to Paris to the Académie Suisse where he met Pissarro, and in 1862 moved to Sainte-Adresse to work with Boudin and Jongkind. On his return to Paris he attended Gleyre's studio and there made friends with Bazille, Sisley and Renoir. In 1863 at Easter he persuaded these three to paint with him out of doors at Chailly-en-Bière in the forest of Fontaine-bleau. There he executed his great painting *Le Déjeuner sur l'herbe* during the summer of 1865. This work has since been destroyed, but there is a fragment of it in the Jeu de Paume museum, while a sketch for the painting is in the museum in Moscow. Like Courbet or his friend Bazille, he was absorbed in the problems of painting out of doors. He exhibited a *Portrait of Camille* (who became his wife in 1870) at the 1866 Salon, and finally worked up another large painting, *Ladies in the garden*, which he intended for the 1867 Salon, but it was not accepted. In conception it is very like

Bazille's *Family reunion* (1867). He found inspiration both in Paris and on the Normandy beaches; in 1866 he painted a number of views of Paris such as the *Infanta's garden at the Louvre* and *The Louvre with Saint-Germain l'Auxerrois*, and in 1867 painted by the sea, producing *The shore at Sainte-Adresse* and *Le Havre: the Terrace*. About this time he executed a beautiful snow scene, *The Magpie* (c. 1867-1870) and in 1867 went with Renoir to paint *Les Bains de la Grenouillère at Bougival* with its marvellous effects of light reflected in the waters of the Seine.

In 1870 Monet visited London where he met Pissarro again, and studied the paintings of Constable and Turner. His *Westminster Bridge* (1871) was painted during this visit before he went back to Paris in 1871 by way of Holland (*View of Zaandam*). He was at Argenteuil from 1872 to 1878. This was a particularly prolific period; his vision was extraordinarily keen and his technique, with fragmentation and innumerable little 'com-

MONET *Regatta at Argenteuil. c.* 1872

MONET *The Bas-Bréau Road.* 1865

together with four others and seven pastel sketches, at the first manifestation of the Impressionist group in 1874; its title *Impression, sunrise* gave the movement its name. Examples of this period are: *Quarries at Saint-Denis* (1872) and the following, all painted at Argenteuil: *Regatta at Argenteuil* (c. 1872), *Poppies* (1873), *Railway bridge at Argenteuil* (c. 1873), *Boats at Argenteuil regatta* (1874), *Argenteuil Bridge* (1874), *Le bassin d'Argenteuil* (1875), *Summer* (1874) and *Snow at Argenteuil* (1875). During the same period he did several *Views of the Tuileries* and *Rue Montorgueil with flags* (1878), while his set of paintings of the *Gare Saint-Lazare* dates from 1877, a prelude to his great 'series' masterpieces illustrating the new conception of painting.

ma' brushstrokes, bringing out his subtle sense of colours in juxtaposition, produced the most 'impressionist' of all his works, rivalling photography in pictorial quality and instantaneous effect. During a short visit to Le Havre in 1872 he painted a canvas which he showed,

Monet lived at Vétheuil from the beginning of 1878 until October 1881, and continued to paint rural and riverside scenes, especially along the Seine, with sparkling reflections of light on water. He was also absorbed in the problem of how to render the pearly, iridescent effects of light on snow, in *Vétheuil in*

MONET *The Cart (Road in the snow, Honfleur).* c. 1865

MONET *Snow scene at Vétheuil. c.* 1878-1879

Winter (1878), *The church at Vétheuil: snow scene* (1878-1879), *The Outskirts of Vétheuil in snow* (1879). The winter of 1880 was particularly severe, and this suggested his first series of paintings on one theme that kept recurring like a leitmotiv until about 1893. The whole series was called '*Ice breaking up on the Seine at Vétheuil*' with *Hoar frost, Ice breaking up* and *The Thaw* (1881). One sarcastic critic who saw them wrote about 'the break-up of painting' instead.

In the autumn of 1881 Monet settled at Poissy, and visits to the Normandy coast in 1882 and 1883 produced *The Cliff walk* (1882), *Cliff at Étretat* (1883), *Étretat* (1883) and *Étretat: the lower gate* (1883).

In the same year, 1883, Monet held a one-man exhibition at the Durand-Ruel Gallery, with fifty-six paintings. Towards the end of the year he and Renoir went to stay on the Mediterranean coast, and in 1884 he went back to Bordighera and Mentone on his own (*Bordighera; Cap-Martin, near Mentone*).

In 1885, after an exhibition at the Georges Petit Gallery, Monet went back to Étretat, and in 1886 to Belle-Île-en-Mer, where he met

MONET *View of the Tuileries Gardens.* 1876

MONET *Le Pont de l'Europe, Gare Saint-Lazare.* 1877

MONET *La Gare Saint-Lazare.* 1877

Gustave Geffroy and painted two versions of *The Rocks of Belle-Île*. After that he went to Noirmoutier with Octave Mirbeau who was much impressed by his remarkable feeling for the sea; 'One can say,' he wrote 'that Monet really invented the sea, since he is the only person who has really understood it and painted it with its changing aspects, its vast rhythm and swell, its motion and infinite continually renewed sparkle and sea smell.'

In the spring of 1889 Monet went to Fresselines in the Creuse, well before Guillaumin who lived near there later, at Crozant, from about 1904 onwards. In June 1889 Monet held an exhibition with his friend Rodin, at the Georges Petit Gallery, with sixty-six exhibits. It was his first great success. His friend Octave Mirbeau wrote in his introduction to the catalogue: 'Here Art disappears and vanishes, as it were . . . we are left in the presence of living nature, nature tamed and conquered by this marvellous painter.' He speaks of Monet's vision of 'Nature created anew with its cosmic structure, life subject to the laws of the movement of the spheres,' where 'dreams, with their warm breath of love and spasmodic joy, beat their wings and sing and bind their magic spell.'

Monet at last was not so badly off, and in 1890 he was able to buy the house he had been living in since May 1883 at Giverny on the banks of the Epte. In 1890 and 1891 he began two series of paintings at the same time, one of *Haystacks* and the other of *Poplars on the banks of the Epte*. In 1891 he exhibited twenty-two canvases at the Durand-Ruel Gallery; these included the complete *Haystacks* series of fifteen pictures, sold in the first three days at prices ranging from 3000 to 4000 francs. From 29 February to 10 March 1892 he showed his six *Poplars* canvases at the same Gallery. His aim was, in these two series, to prove that objects (such as haystacks or poplars), when seen from the same position, are transformed by light and reflection in a degree corresponding to their form and colour. In a letter dated 7 October 1890, he wrote to Gustave Geffroy giving an account of his me-

MONET *By the Seine at Vétheuil.* 1880

MONET *La Roche Percée, Etretat.* 1884

thods: 'I really am working terribly hard struggling with a series of different effects (haystacks) but at this time of year the sun sets so quickly that I can't keep up with it. I am getting to be such a slow worker. I feel in despair, but the more I go on, the more I see how necessary it is to work really hard to try and get the effect I want: 'instantaneous' reaction ... getting the same light everywhere; then I am more than ever disgusted with things you can do easily in a moment'.

Monet went on researching and investigating along these lines, and between 1892 and 1895 he undertook a new series, *The Cathedrals*, which consists of about forty canvases of the great west front of Rouen cathedral, painted from a house whose windows overlooked the façade. Monet worked partly on the spot and partly at Giverny from memory. From 10 to 31 May he exhibited fifty pictures at Durand-Ruel's, of which twenty were from his

MONET *Vase of Chrysanthemums*. 1880

MONET *Madame Monet under the willows*. 1880

Cathedrals series. Clemenceau, a great admirer of Monet, wrote an article under the title *The Cathedral Revolution* where he stressed the amazing audacity of the artist in the realm of colour and tone, the wonderful way he conveyed the unchanging structure of the great building through subtly changing light effects and luminous reflections. No artist had ever gone so far in conveying a magical impression of poetry and enchantment.

Monet visited London in 1900-1901 and painted his *Views of the Thames* in fog, completed from memory at Giverny. He paid a second visit in 1904 (*Waterloo Bridge*; *London: the Houses of Parliament*) and this series, consisting of thirty-seven canvases, was shown, again at Durand-Ruel's, from 9 May to 4 June

MONET *Rouen Cathedral,*
West front, in full sunshine. 1894

MONET, *London, the Houses of Parliament.* 1904

1907. In the autumn of 1908 and 1909 he was in Venice, where he was enchanted by the lovely city and its shimmering, changing light effects on sky and water: *The Doge's palace, Venice* (1908), *The Grand Canal, Venice* (1908). In 1912 he held an exhibition consisting of twenty-nine views of Venice, at the Bernheim-Jeune Gallery.

Monet completed this stage of his work by painting a series inspired by the waterlilies in the ponds of his garden at Giverny. Visual reality, perceived and rendered objectively, is here transformed into the poetry of subjective vision, sometimes indeed coming very close to abstract painting. Monet began this last series as early as 1899 and went on working at it until his death in 1926. The *Waterlilies* series consists of a delightful group of paintings where mirage and enchantment, shifting sparkling effects of light, reality and ab-

straction, truth and fantasy, the magic of colour and the endless subtlety of tones are combined. Monet never repeats himself but paints with infinite modulations, like a theme with variations in music. Clemenceau directed that eight of these huge compositions should be hung in the Orangerie in honour of the artist; others can be seen in the Jeu de Paume and Marmottan Museums in Paris, at

MONET *Water-lilies.* 1904

Grenoble, in New York and elsewhere.

So ended the career of a man who was ever alert to the world of sense and never gave up his search, reaching out and discovering its hidden poetry and mystery and enchantment. So he revealed the manifold 'colour harmonies' of the world of Impressionism—the hidden world of the artist, the world of Claude Monet.

MONET *Rouen Cathedral, morning light.* 1894

MONET *Water-lilies.* 1919

MONET *The River in autumn*

MORISOT *Summer day*. 1879

MORISOT *Girl with a cage*. 1885

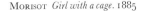

MORISOT *Girl with a cage*. 1885

MORISOT Berthe (Bourges 1841-Paris 1895) Paul Valéry who had married a niece of Berthe Morisot, gives an excellent account of this artist and her Impressionist background in the introduction he wrote to the catalogue for a Retrospective exhibition of her works held at the Orangerie in 1941. 'The special characteristic of Berthe Morisot was the way she lived her painting and painted her life, as if a continual exchange between observation and action, creative energy and light were a necessary natural function simply depending on her ordinary way of living. She would take up and leave her brushes and resume them in the same way as thoughts come into our mind and wander off and then come back again. This gives her work its special charm, with its very close, almost indissoluble relationship between the artist's ideal and the intimate quality of her life. Her sketches and paintings follow the course of her life very closely, and we see her first as a girl, then as a wife and mother. Her paintings taken all together re-

mind one of what a woman's diary would be like if she expressed herself in colour and design instead of in writing.'

Berthe Morisot's work is indeed the 'Diary in paint' of a woman recording her own life and what goes on round her. However, from the stylistic point of view, there is definite development. Her early works were traditionalist, painted very much under the influence of Corot. Her technique became much freer after she had met Edouard Manet; her colours became lighter, and generally more 'Impressionist' after she joined their group, and Renoir particularly had a great influence on her work.

Her father was a high-ranking Civil Servant, and the family were a good deal surprised when Berthe persuaded her sister to take up painting as well. In 1857 the two girls asked the painter Guichart for his advice, and in 1860 he introduced Berthe to Corot who had a great influence on her development. During these years she studied at the Louvre; there she met Fantin-Latour and the engraver Bracquemond, and at the same time she was practising open-air painting. Jongkind encouraged her to attempt landscapes and watercolours as well. Her sister Edma gave up painting in 1868, when she married a naval officer called Pontillon.

Berthe Morisot painted her first landscapes in 1863 at Auvers-sur-Oise, and two of them were accepted for the 1864 Salon. Corot's influence was evident in all her early work (*Lorien Harbour*, 1869).

Berthe met Edouard Manet in 1868; she married Manet's brother Eugène in 1874, and was Manet's model for *The Balcony*. Under his influence she began experimenting with figure and portrait painting (*Portrait of Madame Pontillon*, the artist's sister, pastel, 1871; *The Cradle*, 1873; *Catching butterflies*, 1873, all three in the Jeu de Paume Museum), and also met the Impressionists. Soon after, she joined their group and sent pictures to almost all their exhibitions, starting with the first celebrated one in Nadar's studio in 1874, up to 1886, when her work met with a particularly unfavourable reception from the critics. In 1875 she went to England and stayed at Ramsgate and in the Isle of Wight where she painted a number of seascapes. However she really pre-

MORISOT *Young woman sewing in a garden*. 1881

ferred scenes of modern and especially family life, as Manet had first suggested, and was attracted towards subjects with figures, either singly or in groups. Meanwhile her manner and technique became increasingly Impressionist: *L'Enfant dans les îles* (1875), *Woman at her toilet* (1879), *Question at the looking-glass* (1876), *Eugène Manet and his daughter at Bougival* (1881), *Young woman sewing in a garden* (1881), *Little girl with a doll, after Julie Manet* (1884).

Berthe Morisot went abroad several times, to Italy (1882), Belgium and Holland (1885) and Jersey (1888). She usually spent her winters at Nice and the summer at Mézy near Meulan, where she worked with Renoir; his influence on her work after 1880 is very marked. Typical examples of this period are: *The Cherry tree* (1891), *Hay-making at Mézy* (1891), *The Music lesson* (1892) where the model was Lucie Léon, the pianist at the 'Concerts bleus'; *Girl with a fan* (1893) painted in the Rue Weber with Jeanne Fourmernoir as model; *In the Bois de Boulogne* (1893), *The Violin lesson* (1893) painted in the Rue Weber, with Julie Manet as model; in the background can be seen Manet's portrait of Isabelle Lemonnier; *Julie Manet in white* (1894) and *Gabriel Thomas' children* (1894) both painted in the Rue Weber.

An important exhibition of her work was held from 25 May to 18 June 1892 in the Boussod-Valadon Gallery, with forty-three exhibits. In the following year, 1893, at the end of August and beginning of September, she went to Valvins to see Mallarmé who was a great admirer of her work. In 1894 she visited Brussels and exhibited at the Libre esthétique. In 1896, a year after her death, there was a big posthumous exhibition at the Durand-Ruel Gallery. The exhibits consisted of 191 oil paintings, 61 pastels, 73 water-colours and 64 drawings as well as two pieces of sculpture. Mallarmé, in the introduction he wrote to the exhibition catalogue, called her 'a magician whose work, in the opinion of several important artists she was closely associated with in their struggle to get Impressionism recognised, is quite as good as any of theirs. Her delightful work forms an integral part of the art history of the period.'

NITTIS Giuseppe de (Barletta 1846-St-Germain-en-Laye 1884) He came to Paris as a young man in 1868 and studied at the École des Beaux-Arts under Gérôme. The following year, two of his paintings were accepted for the Salon, *Woman with a parrot* and *Réception intime*. He became successful and fashionable in England, which he visited in 1874, as well as in France. In the same year Degas, whom he knew as well as Manet, persuaded him to exhibit one of his paintings at the first Impressionist exhibition, but Renoir felt the picture was too academic in style and only agreed to have it hung after the exhibition had opened. Nittis decided therefore not to take part in the second Impressionist exhibition and took up a more 'official' line in his work. He enjoyed considerable success and to Degas' intense disgust, he was awarded the Légion d'honneur two years later. In 1882 he and Georges Petit, Durand-Ruel's great rival, founded the Exposition Internationale. His views of Paris and London, usually with elegant female figures in the foreground, enjoyed a considerable success at the time.

NITTIS *La Parfumerie 'Viollet', Boulevard des Capucines*

PIETTE-MONTFOUCAULT Ludovic, better known as Piette (Niort 1826-Paris 1877) was a pupil of Thomas Couture and a fellow-student of Manet's. Piette began to paint with a rather dark palette. He became a close friend of Pissarro, posing for him in 1861; in 1864 Pissarro joined him at his farm at Montfoucault in Brittany; it is here that he took refuge during the war of 1870. In 1875 Piette exhibited at the Salon for the first time, when he showed *The flowering hawthorn*. Pissarro taught him to use lighter brighter colours and to paint out of doors, and in 1877 he joined in the third Impressionist exhibition; several pictures of his were hung after his death at their fourth exhibition in 1879. Among his paintings are *The Grove*, *Riverside Scene*, several *Views of Montfoucault* and *The Hermitage garden at Pontoise*, the latter being a gouache that had formerly belonged to Camille Pissarro and was sold when his belongings were dispersed on 3 December 1928. The Department of Drawings in the Louvre has several of his works including a sketch in oils on paper of *Haymakers resting*, and a gouache dated 10 February 1868, of the *Rue Lepic with the Moulin de la Galette*.

PISSARRO *The Red Roofs.* 1877

PISSARRO Camille (Saint Thomas, Danish West India Islands 1830-Paris 1903) While Claude Monet and Sisley both preferred the ever-changing reflections of water as subjects, Pissarro liked painting dry land. He tends to concentrate less on evanescent colour effects and more on construction and form. He has something of Millet about him in his preference for rural subjects and country life, although he uses a typically fragmented Impressionist technique. Monet, Sisley, Renoir and others among their friends all seem to have put up their easels wherever the fancy took them, if they happened to like the view or the particular light effects. Pissarro on the other hand used to choose his subjects deliberately; he liked painting cultivated fields and villages, country roads leading to grassy meadows, orchards and so on. Like Millet, he took an interest in the men who tilled the ground as well as in the countryside itself, so we often find his pictures include figures of peasants and domestic animals. Zola wrote that 'in his paintings you can hear the earth's deep voices'. Because of his love for the earth he always tended to set his horizons very high up in the picture, just as Millet did, leaving very little room for sky; it may be partly because of this liking for solid not ephemeral things that he attracted Cézanne so much; indeed they often worked together, and Pissarro introduced Cézanne to the Impressionist vision and technique. Pissarro was a convinced socialist, and because of this, tended to make the figures in his pictures peasants, and to paint market scenes. His independence and political convictions make him stand out as a personality among his friends in the group. Staunch supporter of the Impressionist 'revolution', he was the only one to show his work in all eight Impressionist exhibitions, from 1874 to 1886; in fact he used to say 'My own life is bound up with the life of Impressionism'.

Pissarro's father was a French Jew of Portuguese origin. In 1841 Camille left the West Indies for Paris, to study at the Pension Savary where drawing from nature was

PISSARRO *Félix.* 1881

taught—an extremely rare thing at the time. In 1847 he returned to Saint-Thomas and went into his father's business, but in 1852 the attraction of an artist's life became too strong for him and he went off with the Danish artist Fritz Melbye. They went first to Venezuela, but towards the end of 1855 we find him in Paris, as a pupil in Anton Melbye's studio. He was also helped and influenced by Corot, whom he much admired, and by Courbet. In 1857 he met the young painter Claude Monet at the Académie Suisse, painting near Paris. Several of Pissarro's works between 1859 and 1870 were accepted for the Salon, and the

PISSARRO *La Route de Louveciennes*. 1870

Pontoise, 1867; *The Louveciennes road*; *The Stagecoach at Louveciennes*, and the *Versailles road at Louveciennes*, all three painted in 1870.

During the 1870 war Pissarro took refuge in London where he stayed till 1871 and met Claude Monet. Together they studied Turner's painting, and during this period Pissarro's work included: *Snow at Upper Norwood* (1870), *Penge Station, Upper Norwood* (1871) and *Upper Norwood road with a carriage, in overcast weather* (1871).

Pissarro went back to Louveciennes on his return to France in June 1871 and from there

PISSARRO *Self portrait*. 1873

PISSARRO *La Route de Louveciennes*. 1872

critic Castagnary also noticed three paintings of his in the Salon des Refusés in 1863. In 1864 he went to Montfoucault (Mayenne) to stay with his friend Ludovic Piette, and in 1866 went to live at Pontoise, where he often chose the slopes of l'Ermitage as a subject for painting. From 1868 to 1870 he was living at Louveciennes. The paintings executed during this period were still very much influenced by Corot and Daubigny; they include *La Côte de l'Ermitage, Pontoise*, 1867; *La Côte de Jallais*,

PISSARRO *Woman in an Orchard.* 1887

to Pontoise where he lived from 1872 to 1884, although he also had a studio at Montmartre. He and the artist Vignon became friends, and Cézanne also came to paint with him, both at Pontoise and at Auvers-sur-Oise. This was one of the most prolific periods of his career; his works then included: *Route de Louveciennes* (1872), *Le Lavoir, Pontoise* (1872), *Haystack at Pontoise* (1873), *Maison bourgeoise à l'Ermitage, Pontoise* (1873), *Peasant woman pushing a wheel-barrow* (1874), *March sunshine, Pontoise* (1875), *Harvest at Montfoucault* (1876), *Kitchen garden with blossom, in spring, Pontoise* (1877), *Red roofs* (1877), *Resting in the wood, Pontoise* (1878), *Le Fond de l'Ermitage* (1879) and *Landscape at Chaponval* (1880).

After 1881 Pissarro, like Renoir (who also changed style around this time) and Cézanne, began to realise that something was lacking in Impressionism, and that a more solid and structural approach was needed; he moved into a 'constructive' period when his art became simpler and more synthetic. In 1883 Pissarro went to paint at Rouen, particularly round the port, and later went to live at Éragny not far from Gisors (Eure). He was one of the first exhibitors at the Salon des Indépendants, and in 1885 Signac introduced him to Seurat. From that time onwards he attached himself to the Neo-Impressionists' group and practised stippling and pointillisme until about 1890. He and his son Lucien join-

PISSARRO *Winter landscape, Louveciennes. c.* 1870

the technique which no longer satisfied him, and wrote to a friend: 'My dear Van de Velde, I can't stay any longer among the Neo-Impressionists who give up life in favour of a diametrically opposite artistic position. This may suit people who have the right kind of temperament, but it doesn't suit me. I can't

PISSARRO *Chestnut Tree at Louveciennes.* 1870

ed the groups in exhibiting at the eighth and last Impressionist exhibition in 1886, but Camille's technique is noticeably less extreme than that of most of the Neo-Impressionists. Paintings of this period include *The Dieppe train, Éragny* (1887) and *Ile Lacroix, Rouen, in fog* (1888). Towards 1888 or 1890, he gave up

PISSARRO *Landscape at Chaponval.* 1882.

PISSARRO *The Pont-Royal and the Pavillon de Flore.* 1903

bear narrow, so-called scientific theorising. I have made any amount of efforts—I am just speaking for myself here—but I have come to realise how impossible it is to follow my feelings, and in consequence, render any sort of motion in paint; how impossible it is to render the lovely fleeting effects of nature, and to put any sort of individuality into my work; so I have had to give the whole thing up. It was about time too, luckily. I was never really meant for this sort of art, it gives me the feeling of "death the leveller".' He went back to Impressionist technique in the landscapes and rural scenes, painted in bright colours and with powerful light effects, which he painted at Éragny.

In 1892 Durand-Ruel organised a huge

on a series in Rouen: *The Bridges* (1898), *The Cathedral* (1898); at Dieppe: *L'Église Saint-Jacques* (1901) and at Le Havre: *The bridge* (1903).

Each year he spent the summer at Éragny and painted landscapes of the surrounding country and the village, fields and orchards; for instance *Woman in an orchard, autumn morning: garden at Éragny* (1897). He also executed many drawings, watercolours and gouaches of very high quality. Cézanne's words sum him up both as a man and an artist: 'Humble and colossal'.

PISSARRO *Peasant Woman*. 1880

PISSARRO *Young Woman at the window*. 1884

retrospective exhibition of his work, which consolidated his success as a painter. Then after another visit to London, Pissarro began in 1893 to produce series of paintings on single themes: *La Gare Saint-Lazare* (1893), *The Grands Boulevards* (1897), *La Place de la Comédie-Française* (1898), *The Tuileries Gardens and the Carrousel* (1899), *The Louvre and the Seine seen from the Pont-Neuf* (1900), *The Pont-Royal* (1903) and *The Quai Malaquais* (1903), all in Paris. During the same years he also worked

PISSARRO *Boulevard Montmartre, night scene.* 1897

PISSARRO *Boulevard des Italiens, morning sunshone.* 1897

REDON Odilon (Bordeaux 1840-Paris 1916). 'All my originality' Redon wrote in his book *To oneself: a Diary* (1867-1915) 'consists in making the most improbable creatures live like human beings, according to the laws of probability, as far as possible making the logic of what is visible minister to what is invisible.' And again: 'The art of suggestion radiates from the objects towards a dream which can be reached by thought as well; this is found in its fullness in the exciting, stimulating art of music, much more brilliantly and freely than elsewhere. But it is also found in me, through a combination of different connected elements, and through shapes that are transposed and transformed—all things that have no connection whatever with contingency or possibility, but which are logical nevertheless.' And in the same book he continues, taking up his position against certain tendencies he disapproved of in the Impressionists: 'Anything that rises above an object, anything that illuminates or amplifies it, or that raises the human spirit to the realms of mystery and imagination, or to the vague disquieting delights of the indeterminate and the undefined—all this was a closed book to them. Anything symbolic or remotely unexpected or unusual, anything at all enigmatic or difficult to define they avoided; it really scared them. They were like parasites holding on to their objects. They only cared for the purely visual aspect of art, fencing it off from whatever might possibly transcend it, or could illuminate simple ordinary things with the light of spirituality. By this I mean a radiance flooding our spirit, escaping all analysis.' He concludes by speaking of 'Two aspects of truth that will always be both opposite and complementary: on one hand you get substance, reality seen and felt and tangible, without which all concepts must remain abstractions; and on the other hand, imagination, great wide vistas opening out to the sudden unexpectedness of our dreams, lacking which, works of art have no aim or scope whatsoever.'

Redon was born at Bordeaux, and spent part of his childhood at Peyrelebade near Listrac (Gironde). He started drawing lessons at Bordeaux with Stanislas Gorin and later came under the influence of the engraver Rodolphe Bresdin. As he wanted to be a paint-er, he went to Paris and became an un-attached student in Gérôme's studio at the École des Beaux-Arts. In 1878 he went to Holland for the first time. He began by doing pencil drawings and lithographs; one of his earliest drawings is dated 1862 and the last ones between 1895 and 1898: (*Madness, c. 1877*; *Orpheus' head floating on the waters*, 1881; *The smiling spider*, 1881; *Profile of light*, 1881; *Armour*, 1891). Bresdin taught him lithography, and Redon's first attempts at lithographs date from 1878. Between 1879 and 1899, Redon brought out thirteen sets of lithographs, among which the most outstanding are: *Dans le rêve* (1879), *The origins* (1883), *Homage to Goya* (1885), *Night* (1886), *The Temptation of St Anthony* (1st set 1888), *To Gustave Flaubert* (1889), *Les Fleurs du Mal* (1890), *The Temptation of St Anthony* (2nd series

REDON *The Smiling Spider*. 1881

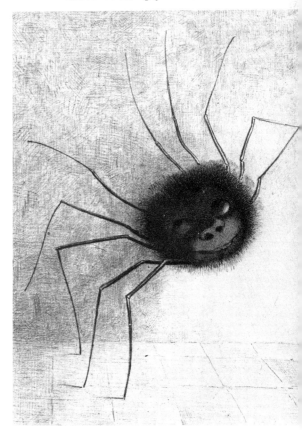

REDON *Flowers in a black vase. c.* 1910

REDON *Bunch of Wild Flowers in a long-necked vase. c.* 1912-1913

1896) and *The Apocalypse* (1899). In 1881 he held an exhibition of drawings and lithographs at *La Vie Moderne* and another in 1882 at the *Gaulois*. In 1886 he took part in the eighth and last Impressionist exhibition and, in the same year, exhibited at the first Salon des Vingt in Brussels. After 1890, Redon's art underwent a fundamental change with his painting *Les Yeux clos*; from that time onwards

light and colour began to appear in his work, and from 1895 predominated. He practically gave up the black and white work he had been doing and devoted himself almost entirely to pastels and oils. In pastel he executed a series of portraits which include *Mme Redon embroidering*, one of the earliest (1880), with several of *Paule Gobillard* (1900) and *Mme Fontaine* (1901). About the same time he produced several religious pictures such as *The Sacred Heart* and *Le Christ à l'épine*.

In 1899, Durand-Ruel organized an exhibition of young painters' work 'in honour of Redon' where the artist himself was represented by pastels only. After 1900, Redon concentrated increasingly on oils. He wrote to his friend Bonger on 2 April 1906: 'There is a

REDON *Buddha. c.* 1905

sort of spell in paint—like witchcraft. It captivates and hinders one when one is working, and every day produces something new to stir and excite one; every day it torments one afresh.' At that time Redon painted pictures like *Apollo's chariot*—a subject both Delacroix and Gustave Moreau had treated previously.

Redon had been much impressed by Gustave Moreau's *Phaeton* and painted several versions of the subject himself, as well as *Pegasus and the Hydra*, between 1907 and 1910. He also painted portraits, landscapes and flower studies as well as working in pastels—always a favourite medium with him. His *Bunch of wild Flowers in a long-necked vase*, dating from 1912-1913, and *Buddha* (*c*. 1905) are among his most successful works. Redon had a strong decorative sense and undertook several schemes of decoration, among them the dining room at the Château de Domecy in Burgundy, and Mme Ernest Chausson's boudoir in Paris. In 1910 and 1911 he decorated the library of Fontfroide Abbey, in the Aude, for Gustave Fayet. In 1906 he exhibited at the Durand-Ruel Gallery and also took part in the International Exhibition in New York. He died in Paris on 6 July 1916.

REGOYOS Dario de (Rivadesella, Oviedo 1857-Barcelona 1913) An Asturian, he was the most outstanding of the Spanish Impressionists. He started in Madrid as a pupil of Carlos de Haes, and after a short stay in Paris, went to Brussels in 1881. There he became involved with a group of artists and writers, among whom were Théo van Rysselberghe, the sculptor Constantin Meunier, Emile Verhaeren and Rodenbach. When he was twenty-three, Regoyos exhibited with the

REGOYOS *The Tona road*

Essor group, and later joined *Les Vingt*, who were even more avant-garde in their outlook, and ˙ took up with the Neo-Impressionists Seurat and Signac. In 1890, 1892 and 1893, he exhibited at the 'Indépendants', after which he went back to Spain where he worked continuously until his death in 1913. Regoyos' clear luminous landscapes with their Impressionist overtones give an unusually attractive idea of Spain (for instance, in *Fumée dans la campagne*).

RENOIR Pierre-Auguste (Limoges 1841-Cagnes 1919) Renoir's particular genius lies in the way he applied Impressionist technique and theory not only to landscape, still life and painting figures out of doors, but also to compositions, nudes and portraits, and applied his own very personal vision to the type of subject chosen by the French eighteenth century painters, Watteau, Boucher and Fragonard. He was, to a far greater extent than Toulouse-Lautrec, the painter *par excellence* of his day, the so-called 'Belle Epoque'. He caught its atmosphere of carefree *joie de vivre*, and fresh

RENOIR *The inn of Mère Anthony.* 1866

RENOIR *Self Portrait.* 1875

uninhibited sense of enjoyment characteristic of middle class circles and above all of the students. He told Albert André 'I know it's very hard to get people to admit a picture can really be great art, and still convey a sense of enjoyment'.

The world he paints glorifies simple pleasures and the happy dreams of youth. He loved the young of all ages; apart from Velazquez and Chardin, he seems to have been one of the very few painters who could convey the subtle appeal of young people and the various aspects of their characters. He also loved all women, from little girls and adolescents, working girls and plump peasant women, to fashionable upper middle class ladies. He had a special gift for painting female nudes with warmth and affection, making the light play on their fresh delicate skin that seemed to come to life under his touch. He painted women bathing, sparkling with pearly, rosy, golden reflections; towards the end of his life

RENOIR *Lise with a sunshade.* 1867

RENOIR *The Duck Pond.* 1873

he painted them ruddy and orange in the sunshine, slender at first, then plump, opulent, sensual but never indecent. When I was a small child, I was fortunate enough to meet Renoir at Cagnes. He was already half paralysed, but I shall never forget his still youthful expression and the affectionate way he looked at me that day. He always preserved something of the wonder of childhood. His art was as straightforward as his look, and he would never have anything to do with complicated methods and theories. 'It is not theories that make a good picture; generally they only serve to cover up a person's inadequacy'. Renoir expressed his ideas in a preface in the form of a letter he wrote to Cennino Cennini's *Book of Art* when it was republished in 1911 by Adolphe Mithouard: 'Whatever may be the secondary reasons for our decline in craftsmanship, I believe the main reason is our lack of ideals. Even the most skilful hand is only the servant of thought, and that is why I am afraid all the efforts people make to turn us into craftsmen like the ones in olden days, can never really succeed. Even if training could manage to produce clever workmen who knew all the skills of their craft, nothing can be done with them if they have no ideals. We seem to have got a long way from Cennino Cennini and painting, but it isn't so really. Painting is a craft just like carpentry and ironwork, and is subject to the same rules.'

Renoir kept this sense of craftsmanship all his life long, particularly where colouring was concerned. One day when Degas was holding forth about how people overdid open-air painting, with special reference to Monet, Ambroise Vollard who was there retorted: 'But Monsieur Degas, doesn't Renoir paint out of doors just like Monet?' 'Renoir can do what he likes,' Degas replied. 'Haven't you ever seen a cat playing with different balls of coloured wool?'

RENOIR *La Grenouillere*. 1868-1869

RENOIR *Sisley and his wife*. 1868

before Monet did, to give up dark colours and use a lighter palette. Renoir exhibited at the Salon fairly regularly, between 1864 and 1870, in spite of some refusals. The artists who chiefly influenced him at this time were Diaz, Delacroix and especially Courbet. Among his

RENOIR *The Seine at Châtou*. 1874

Renoir was born at Limoges but came to Paris with his family when he was still very young, and in 1854 went into a porcelain factory as a china decorator. He very soon gave this up and began painting fans in the eighteenth century tradition to earn a living, and also painted decorative blinds.

In 1862 he put his name down both for the École des Beaux-Arts and for Gleyre's studio simultaneously, and there met Bazille, Monet and Sisley. Not long after, when he was working, as did so many of his contemporaries, in the Forest of Fontainebleau, he made the acquaintance of Diaz who advised him, even

works of this still more or less realist period the following may be mentioned: *The Inn of Mère Anthony* (1866), *Diana the huntress* (refused at the 1867 Salon), *Lise with a sunshade* (1868 Salon) and *Sisley and his wife* (1868). *La*

RENOIR *The Swing.* 1876

RENOIR *The Ball at the Moulin de la Galette.* 1876

RENOIR *Le Pont-Neuf*. 1872

Grenouillère, a canvas which he painted with Claude Monet, already has a feel of Impressionism about it, as has *Barges on the Seine* (1869). After the 1870 war, and up to *c*. 1883, Renoir became increasingly friendly with Monet and began to adopt the Impressionists' technique, stippling and clear

RENOIR *Path in the long grass. c.* 1874-1878

bright colours, as well as painting in the open. He gave up using 'earthy' colours and shades of brown, but unlike most of the Impressionists, still used the odd touch of black. 'The more I paint, the more I like black,' he told Vollard. 'You wonder what to do next; then you put a minute touch of black in, and it looks marvellous.' Renoir's paintings of this so-called Impressionist period are full of life, freshness and gaiety—as he said one day to Albert André: 'What I like is pictures I want to go for a walk in, if they're landscapes, or stroke her breasts or back, if it's a woman', and to Vollard he declared 'I always want to paint people as if they were luscious fruit'. Renoir described his own genius excellently in these two remarks.

During this period, there were scenes painted in Paris such as: *Le Pont-Neuf* (1872) and *Les Grands Boulevards* (1875), then landscapes of Argenteuil painted with Claude Monet, like *The Seine at Argenteuil* (1873-1874), and another beautiful painting of the country near Paris: *Path in the tall grass* (*c*. 1874-1878). In spite of the success of these pictures, neither the public nor the critics really recognised Renoir as being a landscape painter. The critic Philippe Burty even went so far as to write: 'Renoir is generally no good at landscapes. It seems as if he were somehow bewildered by daylight, and he sees bright patches, splashes and rays of light, jets falling from the clouds or arrows flying through leaves and branches. The spectator's eye will never get used to these discs of light splashing on to lawns and paths, even on to people's clothes and faces. The real effect in nature is much too full of movement for anyone to accept the way the artist tries to capture and fix it'. Poor Burty; little did he realise that Renoir's genius lay just in that very ability.

Renoir gave Watteau's 'Fêtes galantes' theme an Impressionist slant in several works of this period, such as *The Henriot family* (*c*. 1871), *Two Women in a park* (1875), *The Arbour* (1876), *The Swing* (1876) and *The Ball at the Moulin de la Galette* (1876) which is one of Renoir's chief masterpieces. This last picture particularly has something of the atmosphere of French eighteenth century painting, with its predominantly pink and blue colouring. All the feminine grace and elegance, the sub-

RENOIR *La fin du Déjeuner*. 1879

RENOIR *Place Clichy*. c. 1880

RENOIR *La Loge*. 1874

joie de vivre and the gaiety are still there—the same things that attracted Raoul Dufy who made a copy of the great picture. Other subjects taken from contemporary life include: *The first outing* (1876), *The end of lunch* (1879),

RENOIR *Girl with a straw hat.* 1878

tiety of whispered conversations and compliments have been brought forward through two centuries, and now appear transformed by the clear light of day; the old melancholy has gone, but the poetry and the dream, the

RENOIR *Portrait of Marthe Bérard.* 1879

RENOIR *Children by the seaside.* 1881

At the Cirque Fernando (1879) and *Place Clichy*, formerly called *Place Pigalle* (c. 1880). We have already mentioned Renoir's very French love of portraits and the nude. One of his masterpieces of this sort is *The theatre box* (1874), definitely reminiscent of a painting, *The Infanta Margarita*, which, in Renoir's day, was attributed to Velazquez. We can see the continued influence of Velazquez' portraits of children in Renoir's child portraits: *Mlle Jeanne Durand-Ruel* (1876), *Mlle Charpentier in blue* (c. 1876), *Portrait of Marthe Bérard* (1879) or *Pink and blue, Portraits of the Mlles Cahen d'Anvers* (1881). The most important of

RENOIR *Boating party.* 1881

Renoir's single or group portraits are: *M. Chocquet* (1876), *Girl with a straw hat* (1878), *Woman reading* (c. 1876), *Young woman with a veil* (c. 1875-1877), *Mme Georges Charpentier*, wife of the publisher (c. 1877), *Mme Charpentier and her children* (1878), and *Full-length portrait of the actress Jeanne Samary* (in the 1879 Salon).

Among Renoir's nudes, one of his first and most important, and one which shocked people very much when shown at the second Impressionist exhibition at the Durand-Ruel Gallery in 1876, was the torso of a *Woman in the sun*, streaming with water and bright light, and full of life and happiness (painted c. 1875-1876). Albert Wolff wrote of this picture in *Le Figaro*: 'Try to explain to M. Renoir that a woman's torso is not a mass of decomposing flesh, with green and purplish patches showing a state of advanced putrefaction in a corpse.' Others are a *Nude* (1880) and *Blond woman bathing* (1881), both full of delicate sensuality. During the summers of 1879 and 1880, Renoir was working by the Seine at Chatou and Croissy (*Boatmen at Chatou*, 1879). Renoir became friendly with a diplomat, Paul Bérard by name, who invited him to stay in Normandy at his country house Wargemont; Renoir paid him several visits (*Rose bushes at Wargemont*, 1879). He also spent several holidays at Berneval. From 1880 onwards he stayed with Mère Fournaise at Croissy, near Bougival, and painted a picture of her outdoor restaurant, calling it *Le Déjeuner des Canotiers* (1881; the *Boating Party*). He exhibited it at the seventh Impressionist exhibition where it was much admired. On the left can be seen Aline Charigot (Renoir's future wife) playing with a little dog, and on the right, facing her, is Caillebotte. In 1883 Renoir painted three pictures in the same spirit: *Dance at Bougival*,

RENOIR *Woman in the sun* c. 1875-1876

RENOIR *Boatmen at Chatou.* 1879

well as his stay in Italy when he studied the great Florentine painters and Raphael; then the influence of Ingres on his return to France, all made him realise the dangers of Impressionism. He felt he was getting into a rut and risked repeating himself, and this worried him. He felt he needed more discipline in his work and a firmer line in composition. He had the courage to go back to study again, and wrote soon after to Vollard: 'I could only really be myself, once I had got rid of Impressionism and gone back to study-

Dance in the country and *The dance in town*. In the spring of 1881 he went to Algeria and returned in March 1882 (*La Ravin de la femme Sauvage, Banana trees, Arab Festival in Algiers, The Casbah*). He also went to Italy in the autumn of 1881, when he painted in Venice and studied in several museums, especially in Florence and Rome. In Palermo, he painted the *Portrait of Richard Wagner*. On his return to France, Renoir worked with Cézanne at l'Estaque near Marseilles; the landscapes he painted at that time were strongly Impressionist in character, with particularly loud colouring. In 1883 he stayed in Guernsey. Between 1883 and 1890, roughly, his style underwent a very great change. After a one-man exhibition at the Durand-Ruel Gallery in 1883, with a catalogue preface by Théodore Duret, Renoir read Cennino Cennini's book. This book, as

RENOIR *Field of bananas.* 1881

Renoir *Portrait of Richard Wagner*. 1882

Renoir *Girl with a rose*. 1886

Renoir *Maternité*. 1885

Renoir *In the Garden*. 1885

RENOIR *The Dance at Bougival.* 1883

RENOIR *Arab Festival, Algiers.* 1881

ing in museums.' He went on: 'Towards 1883, there was a kind of hiatus in my work. I had gone as far as I could with Impressionism, and I had reached the conclusion that I couldn't either draw or paint. In a word, I was stuck.' This next period has been called 'Ingresque' or 'sour'. Shapes were sharply and clearly defined. Bright sparkling colour gave way to deliberately subdued tones, ochre and 'earth' colours, often clashing or 'sour'. Renoir's technique became dry and smooth. His painting *The Umbrellas* (1883) marks the transition between the Impressionism he had relinquished and the beginning of his search for a new style. *Les Grandes Baigneuses* (1883-1884) exhibited at the 1887 Salon, and inspired by one of Girardon's bas-reliefs at Versailles, is characteristic of his new manner, still more

marked in the following works: *L'Après-midi des enfants à Wargemont* (1884), *The Plait* (1886) after Suzanne Valadon, and *Catulle Mendès' daughters at the piano* (1888). Renoir's art continued to develop after these years of study and experiment. The discipline he had practised in going back to drawing, and his deliberately restricted range of colouring led him to a more flexible technique, with form and outline much more emphasised than they had been during his Impressionist phase. His colours became delicately shaded and blended with pearly overtones, so that this period, from about 1890 to 1897, is sometimes known as his 'pearly' period. Renoir was then mostly painting female nudes, with wonderfully iridescent reflections like his *Bather on a rock* (1892) and *Bather asleep* as well as the com-

RENOIR *Catulle Mendès' daughters at the piano.* 1881

posite portrait *The artist's family.* From 1897 onwards he often went to Essoyes and until about 1900 painted landscapes, still lifes and a good many child portraits, among them several of his second son Jean, whom he often painted sitting on the knees of their maid Gabrielle. Gabrielle often figured as a model in subsequent paintings: *Gabrielle and Jean* (1895), *Jean Renoir holding a hoop* (1898), *Jean Renoir as a Pierrot in white* (c. 1902), *Gabrielle wearing jewellery* (1910) and *Gabrielle with a rose* (1911).

Renoir had been suffering from bad rheumatism, and as it was getting worse, he moved to Cagnes in the South of France, where he spent the rest of his life in his villa 'Les Collettes'. There is a kind of luxuriant pantheistic quality about the work of this period, from 1903 to 1919, and a rich sensuality in his painting. The predominating colours are red, pinks, and orange, and various influences, sometimes conflicting, seem to converge in his work. Rubens, Boucher, Fragonard, Ingres and his friend Maillol, the sculptor, all influenced him in different ways. *The Judgement*

RENOIR *Mesdemoiselles Lerolle.* 1890

RENOIR *The artist's family.* 1896

RENOIR *Cagnes Church.* 1905

RENOIR *Jean Renoir holding a hoop.* 1898

RENOIR *The Umbrellas*, 1883

of Paris (1908) is one of the most typical examples of this opulent, sculptural manner. Apart from a number of landscapes with brilliant luminous colours (*The Garden at Les Collettes*, 1909), Renoir painted several female nudes; among the most celebrated are: *La Grande Baigneuse au chapeau* (c. 1904-1906), *Bather wiping her leg* (1905), *Women bathing* (c.

RENOIR *Gabrielle at her looking-glass*. 1913

RENOIR *Les Collettes*. 1914

RENOIR *Self Portrait*. 1910

1915) and *Group of women bathing* (c. 1915). The supreme example of this style is his *Women bathing* or *Nymphs* (c. 1918) with its bold sensuality. The opulent curves of the heavy bodies, and the concentric circles on their bellies, made one critic nickname the picture 'Bibendum' or 'the Michelin Tyres'. This great picture, with its compelling radiance,

RENOIR *Bather wiping her leg.* 1905

RENOIR *Girl with a hat. c. 1900*

light and colour, as well as its poetic quality, is reminiscent of Fragonard's *Baigneuses* and shows how Renoir as he grew old, still preserved his sense of poetry and his love of life, with a continual freshness and youthfulness of approach—delight in life as well as delight in painting.

ROBINSON Theodore (Irasburg, U.S.A., 1852 – New York 1896) During a long stay in France, he began painting in the style of the Barbizon artists, before being converted to Impressionism through Claude Monet. He painted with Monet at Giverny (*Panorama of Giverny*). After his return to New York, he exhibited with the Society of American Artists; his was the first group of Impressionist paintings to have been shown in New York by an American.

RYSSELBERGHE Théo van (Ghent 1862-Saint-Clair, Var 1926) Rysselberghe came from a family of architects. He began studying art in Ghent and then in Brussels. His first paintings were definitely classical in style, but later he overcame his resistance to Neo-

RYSSELBERGHE *The Beach at Cavalaire*

Belgian painters, Rysselberghe among them, reached a very much better understanding of Neo-Impressionism. Not long after this, Rysselberghe, who had become friendly with Seurat, Signac and Cross, began to practise divisionism in his portrait painting (*Portrait of Octave Maus*, 1890) using small dots of different sizes on one canvas. He went on practising this divisionist technique until about 1910, although towards the end of his life he reverted to a more academic style. He exhibited not only with the Vingt but also with the *Libre Esthétique, Art Contemporain* and *Indépendants*, and also sometimes at the official Paris Salon. Rysselberghe was involved with various artistic groups and was a close friend of Verhaeren, whose portrait he painted in 1913. Among his other friends were Maeterlinck, Fénéon, Maurice Denis, André Gide and Copeau. Rysselberghe often went abroad, particularly to Morocco, before finally settling in Paris in 1898. He painted landscapes (*Tea in the garden at Ixelles* gives an excellent idea of his style) and portraits, and also created various decorative schemes for private houses. He had a great influence on the development of Neo-Impressionism in Belgium, more perhaps through his connection with the Groupe des Vingt than by his actual painting. A retrospective exhibition of his works was held in 1927 in Brussels, a year after his death; Maurice Denis wrote the introduction to the catalogue.

Impressionist theories, and at the last Impressionist exhibition in 1886 he broke his walking stick in front of Seurat's picture *La Grand Jatte*. However two years earlier he had been involved in starting an avant-garde group in Brussels, known as Les Vingt, and he was also their Paris correspondent. This group had no special theories; its only object was to get up exhibitions illustrating the newest tendencies in European art. In 1888, the Vingt group invited Signac, Dubois-Pillet and Cross to come and visit them, and as a result several

SARGENT *The Grand Canal, Venice*

SARGENT *Self Portrait*. 1872

The influence of Velazquez and Frans Hals can be clearly seen in his portraits, but there are signs of Impressionism as well. He also experimented with painting out of doors: (*Claude Monet painting on the edge of a wood*. 1888; *Young woman beside a stream*, 1908; *Couple painting out of doors*). In some of his paintings Sargent used strikingly vivid colours and fragmentation, with broad brushstrokes (*View of the Val d'Aosta*, 1908-1910).

SEGANTINI Giovanni (Arco, South Tyrol 1858-Schafberg ob Pontresina, Engadine 1899) Segantini's mother died when he was only five and he had a difficult and unhappy childhood. In 1864 his father sent him to Milan to be looked after by a sister-in-law, but he ran away several times, and finally took refuge with another relative at Borgo Val Sugana. His life continued to be unhappy and restless until 1876, when he returned to Milan, and there attended evening painting classes at the Brera Academy. In 1882 he went to live at Brianza with Luigia Bugatti, and had four children by her. He was able to pursue his career as a painter with the help of a merchant, Vittore Grubicy, and his brother Alberto. Under their influence he gave up the sombre tones he had used in his earlier paintings (*Choir of the church of Sant'Antonio, Milan*, 1878;

SARGENT John Singer (Florence 1856-London 1925) Sargent was the son of an American doctor from Boston. He first studied art in Paris with Carolus Duran, and in 1886 went to London where he soon became a fashionable portrait painter.

SEGANTINI *Girl at the fountain*

The dead hero, 1879) and began to use very brilliant, sparkling, occasionally rather harsh colours with paint thickly applied. There was something pantheistic in his approach to nature, and he often painted scenes of the hard, austere life of the peasants in the mountain valleys, under an intensely blue sky and an implacable sun. (*Hay-making*, 1899; *Husbandman in the Engadine*). His painting *The Angelus in a boat* was awarded a Gold medal by the City of Amsterdam in 1883. In 1886 Segantini went to live at Savognino in the Canton des Grisons, for the sake of its pure clear mountain light and air; later he left and moved to Maloja in the Engadine. For a while he was attracted to symbolism (examples of this period are *The Prisoner Mother*, 1894; *The Goddess of Love*, 1894-1897; *Love at the Fountain of Life*, 1896) but he soon reverted to painting the type of landscape he was famous for, both in Italy and in Germany. He died comparatively young of acute peritonitis in 1899, leaving the last panel of his great *Alpine Triptych: Life, Nature, Death*, which he had hoped to exhibit in Paris in 1900, unfinished; but during his lifetime he painted a large number of mountain landscapes as well as religious and allegorical works.

SÉRUSIER Paul (Paris 1863-Morlaix 1927) Sérusier is, in a sense, the main link between the Pont-Aven and Nabi groups of artists. He started in the Académie Jullian studio, where he used to collect the fees and keep the common purse, and it was not until September 1888 that he met Gauguin at Pont-Aven, through Émile Bernard. The result of this brief encounter was the famous *Talisman du Bois d'Amour*, a landscape painted on a cigar box under Gauguin's direction in 'purple, vermilion, veronese green and other colours used pure and undiluted, with practically no white added, just as they come out of the tube.' When he got back to Paris, Sérusier showed it to his fellow students at the Académie Jullian, Maurice Denis, Bonnard, Vuillard and Roussel, and told them about the new aesthetic as practised at Pont-Aven. They promptly decided to constitute a group of their own. Cazalis, who was something of a Hebrew scholar gave it the name 'nabi' mean-

ing prophet, and Sérusier became its leader. The group developed from its original Impressionism, to adopt a sort of symbolism with neo-platonic leanings. In 1889 Sérusier and Gauguin worked together at Le Pouldu; after Gauguin had left for Tahiti, Sérusier remained for a while in Brittany as he found plenty of atmosphere there and did not feel any need to go elsewhere. The works he painted during this period are brightly coloured (*Night at Le Pouldu*, 1889; *Still life in the studio, c.* 1891); in Gauguin's style, but less forceful (*Portrait of Marie Lagadu*, Paris); more 'anecdotal' (*The wrestlers, Breton Pardon at Châteauneuf-du-Faou*, 1896). Sérusier then went to Germany to visit his pupil Verkade, and from 1895 onwards, travelled in Italy and central Europe. He was strongly attracted by the occult and by medieval thought, as well as by Giotto and Fra Angelico. He went through a period of intellectual doubt only resolved in 1902 at the Benedictine Abbey of Beuron,

SÉRUSIER *Breton Girl knitting.* 1920

SÉRUSIER *Harvest*

SEURAT Georges (Paris 1859-1891) Seurat and his friend Signac reacted against the casual informality of Impressionism, as did Cézanne, but in a very different way. They felt Impressionism was becoming fossilized, so they evolved a new method founded on strictly scientific principles, in order to 'reconstruct' (as they called it) this disintegrating form of art, codify and reorganize it. So Neo-Impressionism came into being, founded on the techniques of divisionism and pointillisme. Seurat felt that Monet's dictum 'We paint just as birds sing' was no longer relevant; instead he wanted to paint according to strict rules and well-founded theories. Having studied books by the physicists Chevreul and N. O. Rood, and the works and writings of Delacroix and Baudelaire, as well as various investigations that had been made into the concept of the Golden Number, he worked out a method that he believed would subject art to strict laws of equilibrium and harmony. He explained the rules to his friends Jules Christophe and Maurice Beaubourg, and in a letter to Beaubourg, dated 28 August 1890, he expounded his theories in full:

where Verkade had been living since his conversion to Catholicism and entering the Benedictine Order. After recovering from his breakdown, Sérusier became more interested in colour harmony than in ideas, and once he was free from Gauguin's influence, was able to develop an individual style. After 1914 he retired to Châteauneuf-du-Faou where he decorated the church, and in 1921 his *A.B.C. of Painting* was published. In this book he asserted that the fundamentals of art were all to be found in the Italian Primitives. He died at Morlaix in 1927. His painting was uneven, poetical and hieratic in style; Charles Chasse, the author of a history of Symbolism, calls him: 'a graceful bridge linking Gauguin's synthetic Symbolism to the rather crude, aggressive synthetism of the Cubists.'

SEURAT *Man painting a boat*. 1883

AESTHETICS

'Art is Harmony. Harmony is the analogy of opposites, the analogy of similarities, of tone, colour, and line considered by taking the dominant under the influence of lighting in

SEURAT *Bathing at Asnières*. 1883-1884

various combinations, cheerful or calm or sad.
    The opposites are:
For *tone* a more ⎰ luminous ⎰ for a
⎱ light one ⎱ darker one
For *colour*: complementary colours, that is, a
certain red and its complementary colour etc.
(red-green; orange-blue; yellow-violet).
For *lines*, those forming a right angle.
Cheerfulness: of *tone*, the luminous dominant;
of *colour*, the warm dominant; of *line*, lines
rising above the horizontal.
Calmness of *tone* is the equality of dark and
light; of *colour*, equality between hot and cold;
of *line*, a horizontal line.
Sadness: in *tone*, the dark dominant; in *colour*,
cold dominant; in *line*, lines going down-
wards.

TECHNIQUE

Having admitted the phenomenon of the
duration of an impression of light on the re-
tina, synthesis is the result. The means of
expression is the optical mixing of tones (loca-
tion; colour of the lighting in question, e.g.

sunlight, oil lamp, gas) that is, of lights and
their reactions (shadows) according to the
laws of contrast in the degrading of irradiation. The frame is to be in the opposite
harmony to that of the tones, colours and lines
of the picture.'
    All Seurat's work, in drawing as well as in
painting, depended on this theory of the laws
of contrast. He was the son of a sheriff's officer
from La Villette, and came from a very devout
and relatively prosperous family. He stayed at
school till he was sixteen and at the same time
attended a municipal art school, under the
sculptor Justin Lequien, who had been
runner-up in the Grand Prix de Rome com-
petition. At the art school, Seurat became
very friendly with Aman-Jean, and later they
both went to the École des Beaux-Arts and
worked under Henri Lehmann who had been
a pupil of Ingres. Seurat also studied in museums, and, as we have already seen, he
became interested in the writings of the
great physicists such as Chevreul and N. O.

Rood. During 1882 and 1883 he spent almost all his time drawing. He had a very original style and his black and white work is lively and expressive, with a sensitive lyrical quality. His *Portrait of the painter Aman-Jean* (1882; exhibited at the 1883 Salon) is one of his masterpieces; Roger Marx reviewed it favourably 'An excellent study in light and shade; a fine drawing; not the sort of thing just anybody could do.' During his brief career, Seurat executed some four hundred drawings in Conté pencil; Signac called them 'the most beautiful drawings by a painter in existence.' It is interesting to notice the likeness between them and some of Millet's work. Among the most outstanding are: *The black bow* (c. 1882); *The Wet-nurse* (c. 1882); *The Sleeper: study for a bathing scene at Asnières* (c. 1884), *Woman fishing: a study for La Grande Jatte* (c. 1885), *At the Café Singer* (1887), *Study for La Parade* (c. 1887) and *Portrait of Paul Signac* (1889-1890). After this Seurat wanted to apply his theories, which he considered absolutely fundamental, to colour.

SEURAT *Study for 'La Grande Jatte'. c.* 1884-1886

But in 1884 the pictures he sent to the Salon were all refused, including his first important large-size painting, *Bathing at Asnières.* It was subsequently exhibited from 15 May to 1 July at the Salon des Indépendants, of which he

SEURAT *Sunday afternoon at the island of La Grande Jatte.* 1886

SEURAT *Portrait of Paul Signac*. 1889-1890

stead at Grandcamp; *Sunset, Grandcamp*. He met Signac at the Salon des Indépendants, and following his advice began to paint like the Impressionists, using pure colours only. Signac also introduced him to Camille Pissarro. It was about this time that Seurat painted his masterpiece *Sunday afternoon at the island of La Grande Jatte*, after doing a number of preparatory sketches and drawings. He showed this picture at the eighth and last Impressionist exhibition, then again at the second Salon des Indépendants, and finally in 1887 at the Exposition des Vingt in Brussels. This large picture, with its perfect composition and balance and its beautiful luminous quality expresses the new theories and methods of the Neo-Impressionists, and brilliantly reveals the harmony of Seurat's art. The perfect balance between heat and cold,

was a founder member, the others being Signac, Redon and Dubois-Pillet. 402 artists took part in the exhibition which was held in some huts put up in the Cour des Tuileries. *Bathing at Asnières* stands half-way between Impressionism and the new Neo-Impressionist technique. Seurat's theory of contrasts was strictly applied, giving the picture an unusual rhythm and static quality, but the brushstrokes are not yet really divided and pointillist technique is not yet used. Signac, who admired the picture, was interested to see that it was painted 'in great flat strokes, sweeping one over the other, with a palette, like Delacroix's, made up of pure colours, but also with some dull earthy ones. The painting is toned down by the use of these earthy ochre tints, and looks a good deal less bright than the average Impressionist picture, that uses only prismatic colours. But his keeping to the laws of contrast, and the methodical separation of the various elements in the picture—light and shade, and the exact balance and proportion of everything, make this a peculiarly harmonious picture.' In 1885 Seurat went to paint at Grandcamp: *Le Bec du Hoc*; *The road-*

SEURAT *Quays at Honfleur (La Maria)*. 1886

light and shade, horizontal and vertical, express the 'calm' of a beautiful sunny day with people walking about and resting in a landscape where nature herself is subject to the laws of harmony and serenity. In fact, in our opinion, it is reminiscent of Raphael's great frescoes in the Vatican, *The School of Athens* and the *Disputation of the Blessed Sacrament*. Once again, Signac understood Seurat's ge-

SEURAT *The Seine at Courbevoie.* 1885

SEURAT *Courbevoie Bridge. c.* 1886

nius when he wrote: 'It seems as if a painter's first care, when he is faced by an empty canvas, should be to decide what curves and arabesques he will put to divide up the surface, and what colours and tones he is going to use to cover it . . . Following Delacroix's advice, he will never start a canvas without having considered how he is going to plan his picture. Guided by tradition and science, he will harmonise the composition as he thinks best, that is, he will adapt the lines (their directions and angles), the light and shade (tones) and the colours (tints) to suit whatever characteristic he wants to predominate.' Seurat went to Honfleur during the summer of 1886 and there painted several seascapes, severe in composition but with delightful colours and shades: *Entrance to the harbour, Honfleur*; *The Hospice and Lighthouse at Honfleur*, and *The Maria, Honfleur*. During the same period he also painted landscapes of the surroundings of Paris: *Bridge at Courbevoie* (*c.* 1886) and *The Seine at the Grande Jatte* (1887). Unlike the Impressionists, Seurat was particularly attracted by large canvases with

SEURAT *La Parade.* 1887-1888

figures, that gave him the opportunity of expressing his theories in paint. His next work consisted of two pictures: *Les Poseuses* (1887-1888)—there are three sketches for it in the Jeu de Paume museum—and *La Parade* (1887-1888), which he showed at the Salon des Indépendants in 1888. In the summer of that year he went to Port-en-Bessin to paint landscapes: *Port-en-Bessin, the Outer Harbour at low tide*; *Port-en-Bessin, the Outer Harbour at high tide*. In 1889 he was at Le Crotoy painting: *Le Crotoy downstream*. He exhibited several landscapes of the channel coast at the 1889 Salon des Indépendants, and then began *Le Chahut* in which he tried to demonstrate his theory of dynamism, according to certain definite rules. In this picture he tries to express gaiety and high spirits by means of lines going upwards, warm colouring and luminous dominants. After a

Seurat *Le Crotoy, downstream.* 1889

Seurat *Port-en-Bessin; the Outer Harbour at high tide.* 1888

SEURAT *Poseuse, profile.* 1887

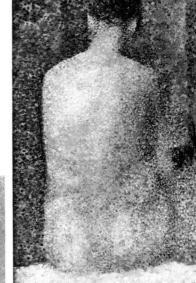

SEURAT *Poseuse, back view.* 1887

SEURAT *Poseuse, front view.* 1887

visit to Gravelines, he spent the winter of 1890-1891 painting *The Circus*, applying the same theories, and this was hung at the Indépendants exhibition in 1891, although still unfinished. The subject called for turbulent dynamism. But Seurat died prematurely, on 29 March 1891, without being able to complete the painting, so it is difficult to judge whether or not it was successful. The Impressionists disapproved of this kind of

painting, based on theory and rules; Pissarro, who practised it himself up to a point, was critical, and Renoir wrote: 'There is something more in painting, something you can't explain, which is the essential element. You come to face nature with all your theories, and nature upsets them all. The fact is that in painting, like all the other arts, there isn't the slightest thing however insignificant that can really be reduced to theory.'

SEURAT *Le Chahut*. 1889-1890

Impressionist lines. His best work probably consists of the landscapes he painted in Bath (1916-1917), with broad sweeping brush-strokes and skilful effects of light and atmosphere.

Sickert's portraits and interiors, and his music-hall pictures are reminiscent of Degas (*Woman washing her hair*, c. 1905-1906). He was made an R.A. in 1924 and a professor in 1926, and both in his teaching and his painting, tried to free British art from academic routine.

Seurat *The Circus*. 1890-1891

SICKERT Walter Richard (Munich 1860-Bath 1942) Sickert came from a family of Danish origin which settled in London about 1868. It was through Whistler that he took up painting seriously, and met Degas on a visit to Paris. In 1885, on the way back from travelling in Europe, with his wife, Ellen (née Cobden) they stopped in Dieppe. He was very much attracted by the countryside, and it was at Dieppe that, through the influence of Boudin and the French Impressionists, he experimented with painting out of doors. Each winter he stayed in London to paint; each summer he used to visit France, and in this way acquired a thorough knowledge of the new tendencies in French art. He tried to make them known in England and in 1893 started the first of his free Painting Schools. In 1895 he went to Venice and in 1899, after his divorce, left England to settle in Dieppe with Jacques-Émile Blanche.

In 1905 he went back to England where in 1910 he founded the Camden Town Group on

Sickert *Ennui*. 1913-1914

SIGNAC Paul (Paris 1863-Paris 1935) It is difficult, with Signac, to separate the theorist from the painter. He started by attaching himself to the Impressionists, but like Seurat, Renoir and Cézanne too up to a point, he realised that Impressionism had reached a dead end. He therefore decided to go back to the start and reduce art to some sort of rules, as he felt Impressionism depended too much on instinct and impulse. Signac was born in the

SIGNAC *Entrance to the Harbour, Marseilles.* 1911

year Delacroix died. He had a very great admiration for Delacroix and in 1899 published his book *From Eugène Delacroix to Neo-Impressionism* which became the charter of the new school. In Chapter IV, *The contribution of the Neo-Impressionists*, Signac wrote: 'One can say that generally speaking, a Neo-Impressionist work is more harmonious than an Impressionist one, one of the reasons being that because of the way contrasts are always observed, there is more harmony in the detail. There is also greater harmony in the general effect, and a kind of "moral harmony" too because the composition is based on aesthetic principles and the language of colours. Impressionism has none of this. Far be it from me to compare the merits of these two generations of painters; the Impressionists were supreme artists who achieved the splendid task they set themselves; the Neo-Impressionists are still in the process of discovery and realise the im-

mense amount of work that remains to be done. It is not a question of talent but of technique, and no lack of respect is implied when we say that the Neo-Impressionist technique assures integrity of colour, luminosity and harmony better than the Impressionists' does. In the same way, we can say that Delacroix's paintings are less luminous than Impressionist paintings.'

Signac began painting in 1882 in Paris and Brittany under the influence of the Impressionists, particularly Monet. In 1883 he started attending the studio of Bin, a Prix de Rome winner, and there met Père Tanguy and Rivière. In 1884 he became one of the founders of the 'Society of Independent Artists' where he exhibited, and made Seurat's acquaintance; he was President of the Society from 1908 till his death. In 1885 he met Pissarro and was involved with a group of literary Symbolists especially Félix Fénéon,

Bessin; 1887 Collioure; 1888 Portrieux, Antwerp, and 1889 Cassis and Antwerp. In 1892 he discovered Saint-Tropez; from then onwards until about 1911 he spent part of each year there, and met Cross and Rysselberghe who were living near by. In 1896 he went to Holland on a visit; in 1898 and 1899 to Genoa, Marseilles and Paris; he went three times to Venice, in 1904, 1905 and 1908, while in 1906 he went to Marseilles and Rotterdam. In 1907 he stayed in Constantinople where he painted a large number of watercolours, and then went to Italy, to Verona and Genoa; in 1911 he went to La Rochelle and Les Sables

SIGNAC *The Seine at Sannois.* 1901

Paul Adam, Kahn and Dujardin, and the 'Revue indépendante'. He had some definitely 'pointilliste' paintings in the eighth and last Impressionist exhibition. Towards 1890 Signac began to paint almost entirely in his studio, working up the enormous number of drawings, sketches and watercolours (incidentally, he was an excellent watercolourist) he had accumulated during his various travels. From 1882-1884 he was at Port-en-

SIGNAC *The Lighthouse at Antibes.* 1909

SIGNAC *The Yellow Sail.* 1904

d'Olonne; in 1913 he settled at Antibes and stayed several years; in 1919 we find him at Sallanches, and from 1921 till his death in 1935, he seems to have visited and painted in practically every part of France as well as the Cotentin, Brittany and La Rochelle. In 1927 Signac brought out a book on Jongkind that contains a 'treatise on watercolour painting', and in the year he died he travelled in Corsica and also went to Barfleur. Among his best-known paintings are: *View of Collioure* (1887),

SIGNAC *Paris, Île de la Cité.* 1912

Portrait de Félix Fénéon sur l'émail rythmique de mesures et d'angles, de tons et de teintes (1890), *Boats in the sun* (1891), *Breeze, Concarneau* (1891), *Marseilles harbour* (1897), *The Popes' Palace, Avignon* (1900), *Venice* (1905), *Constantinople* (1909) and *Antibes, evening* (1914). Among his exquisite watercolours, many of which are still in Mme Ginette Signac's possession, may be mentioned *The Bosphorus, The cliff, Paris, la Cité et le Pont-Neuf* and *La Rochelle*; they are all remarkable for their subtle colouring and light effects.

SISLEY Alfred (Paris 1839 – Moret-sur-Loing 1899) Sisley provides a link between the art of Corot and Boudin, and that of Maurice

Utrillo. As an Impressionist he was, with his delicate sensibility, particularly attracted to subtlety of colour and feeling. His favourite subjects were water, skies, snow and mist effects, which he painted with great sensitivity and skill. He is a typical nature painter, extraordinarily responsive to all her changing moods and quick to notice and record impressions. As he said: 'The work must communicate to the spectator the same emotions and enthusiasm the artist felt when he painted it.'

Sisley was born in Paris of English parents. His father had originally intended him for a business career but he showed no aptitude for it whatsoever; and as he seemed to have a gift for drawing and painting, he went instead to the Atelier Gleyre, where he met Claude Monet, Bazille and Renoir. With them he painted out of doors, and at Easter 1863 went with them to Chailly-en-Bière near Fontainebleau. In 1866, two of his paintings, one of them being *The Chestnut avenue at la Celle-Saint-Cloud*, were hung at the Paris Salon. In 1867 he went to Honfleur, in 1868 and 1870 exhibited again at the Salon, and was in London during the 1870 war. Up to the time of his father's bankruptcy in 1870, Sisley was something of a dilettante, but as he was then married and penniless, he began trying to sell his pictures, and Durand-Ruel, Théodore Duret, Murer the pastry-cook and Doctor Viau bought them for sums ranging from twenty-five to fifty francs apiece. At that time he was influenced a good deal by Courbet and Corot. He loved painting in the Île-de-France, in little villages not far from Paris. Before 1870,

he used to go to Louveciennes and Bougival, and between 1870 and 1875 painted at Voisins and Marly. From 1875 to 1879 he lived at Sèvres and painted in its surroundings, at Meudon and Saint-Cloud. Finally in 1879 he settled near Moret, and then at Moret-sur-Loing in September 1882. He was not a great traveller but he went to London in 1874, to Normandy, where he stopped for a while at Rouen, in 1894, and in 1896 he went to Wales.

From 1870 to 1874 his work was strongly influenced by Corot and Boudin, as one can see in *View of the Canal Saint-Martin* (1870), *A Street at Marly* (1871), *The Square at Argenteuil* (1872), *The road seen from the path to Sèvres* (1873), a subject which Corot had also painted, and *The Louveciennes road in the snow* (1873). Sisley took part in the first Impressionist exhibition in 1874, as well as in

SISLEY *The Flood at Port-Marly.* 1876

SISLEY *The Walk*

SISLEY *La Place d'Argenteuil.* 1872

SISLEY *L'Ile Saint-Denis. c.* 1874

those of 1876, 1877 and 1882. His technique was changing; his palette was brighter and his colours more sparkling (already in 1873 his *Wheat field* showed signs of this). His subjects were water: *The Flood at Port-Marly* (1876), *Boat during the flood, on the Seine at Suresnes* (1877), or misty effects: *Fog* (1874) and the

SISLEY *Boats at the Lock, Bougival.* 1873

SISLEY *Fog.* 1874

SISLEY *Moret by the Loing.* 1892

subtle pearly effect of snow: *Snow at Louveciennes* (1874 and 1878). The following, painted towards the end of his life, may be mentioned: *Saint-Mammès* (1885) with the river Loing in the foreground; the picture is full of light and painted with lively, sweeping brushstrokes; *The bridge at Moret, thunderstorm* (1887), *Moret, by the Loing* (1892) and *The Loing canal* (1892). Unlike Pissarro who was more solid and down-to-earth, Sisley is the painter of imponderables and fleeting evanescent impressions. Everything he does has an unusual delicacy of touch, suggesting the poetry of a sensitive and artistic nature.

SISLEY *Snow at Louveciennes*. 1878

SLEVOGT Max (Landshut 1868 – Neukastel 1932) Slevogt began at the Munich Academy as a pupil of Wilhelm von Diez, and went on to Paris where he attended the Académie Jullian, and copied a number of Old Masters in the Paris museums. He settled in Berlin, and from 1917 onwards taught at the Academy. Like Lovis Corinth, who was ten years his senior, he represents what might be called Berlin Impressionism—that is, he took over from the French Impressionists, whose works he had been able to see in Berlin on two occasions, their fresh bright colouring, without adopting the more extreme aspects of their technique such as fragmenting colours (*Corner of a garden in the sun*, 1921). Slevogt was a great music-lover, being especially fond of Mozart and Wagner. He enjoyed painting

SLEVOGT *View of a Forest*. 1904

SLEVOGT *Corner of a garden in the sun*. 1921

SLEVOGT *Hunter on a hillside.* 1903

scenes of contemporary life and was particularly attracted by the theatre, while his portraits are reminiscent of Manet whom he much admired (*The Portuguese singer Francisco D'Andrade in the part of Don Juan*). He was a talented book illustrator with a real gift of imagination and a typically German fluency of line.

English Impressionists, and in many ways his attitude is very like that of the French Neo-Impressionists, but towards the end of his life he reverted to painting more in the style of Constable, with broad brush-strokes, and contrasts of clouds and sunshine (*Richmond Castle*,

STEER *Portrait of Mrs. Hammersley.* 1907

STEER Philip Wilson (Birkenhead 1860-1942) Steer was the son of a drawing teacher, and studied at an art school in Gloucester before attending the Académie Jullian and the École des Beaux-Arts in Paris. He was much influenced by both Whistler and Monet, and exhibited his work mostly at the New English Art Club which he and his friend Sickert founded in 1886. His sunny landscapes, worked with a palette knife, established his reputation, although he also painted portraits and still lifes (*Girls running*; *The pier at Walberswick*). He is one of the most important of the

1903). However his last watercolours are more in the manner of Turner, with increasingly diffused colouring and poetic imagination.

THOMA Hans (Bernau 1839-Karlsruhe 1924) Thoma was of humble origin but the Duke of Baden took him under his protection, so he was able to study painting, first at Karlsruhe with Schirmer, and later at Düsseldorf. In 1868 he was able to go to Paris and work under Courbet, who had a great influence on him (for example, in *Portrait of the artist's sister*

THOMA *The Glade*

and *Mountains near Carrara*, 1886). At first Thoma's work was not particularly well received, but in 1889 an exhibition of his paintings at Munich marked the breakthrough for his art. Many critics wrote of him as one of the outstanding German artists of the period, but his mythological and allegorical paintings rather in the style of Böcklin do not much appeal to present-day taste, and seem to us formal and uninteresting. His most attractive work consists of landscapes; here one sees his deep love and understanding of nature, especially of trees, and a sense of poetry lacking in his other works. Several of his landscapes, such as *Waldwiese* (1879) and *Valley in the Taunus district*, show his keen observation of atmosphere and light.

TOULOUSE-LAUTREC Henri de (Albi 1864-Malromé, Gironde 1901) 'I have tried to paint things as they are, not idealised,' Toulouse-Lautrec said when he was still only seventeen. Right up to the time of his death, this clearsighted self-knowledge was typical of his attitude to life and to painting. His profoundly human and yet uncompromisingly truthful approach to his models—to prostitutes for instance—is characteristic of all his work. He is an extraordinarily perceptive painter; nothing about a person escapes him, whether it be his outward appearance and behaviour or his mannerisms, his habits, attitudes and gestures, in fact all the person's particular characteristics, whether inherited or acquired. His period pieces and scenes of contemporary life, as well as his actual portraits, are always strikingly convincing and true to life. He realised that a portrait, if it is to be not only a good likeness but also true psychologically, must not just be a kind of glorified photograph with the sitter posing self-consciously and revealing nothing of his true self. A really good portrait must be an exploration in depth, both physical and psychological, of the model, an impression caught at the moment the person is least expecting it, so that he reveals his true character and not just the side he wants people to see, which is so often deceptive. The artist needs a keen eye and very great skill; he ought as well to be thoroughly imbued with the atmosphere or

character he is attempting to paint. With this in view Lautrec always made a large number of preliminary sketches and drawings. Yvette Guilbert noticed him doing this, and at first thought he was taking her off, but she soon realised instead he was attempting to convey her remarkable talent as a comic actress.

In this connection a comparison springs to mind with the great caricaturist Sem, a contemporary of Lautrec's. He had done a large number of caricatures in the papers of the Prince of Wales (later Edward VII), who very often went to Paris. One day he did a sketch of nothing but a circle and a cigar; no hair, no eyes, no ears, no mouth, no nose. But everyone in Paris recognized the extraordinary likeness to the Prince. We find something of this spirit of synthesis, concentrating on the essential, leaving out unnecessary detail, but underlining what is typical, in Lautrec's vigorous and witty portraits. For example, there is the nouveau-riche couple in the second row on the left in one of the decorations Lautrec did for

TOULOUSE-LAUTREC *Count de Toulouse-Lautrec driving his Four-in-hand at Nice*. 1881

La Goulue: *La Goulue and double-jointed Valentin dancing*. The woman is wearing a grotesque hat, with a feather boa tightly wound round her neck; her extremely common-looking husband evidently wants to go one better than the Prince of Wales, who started the fashion of wearing a cornflower in his

TOULOUSE-LAUTREC *Aristide Bruant at the Ambassadeurs.*
1892

colour-washes and their 'cloisonniste' technique. And like all the painters of his generation, he was influenced by the Japanese, with their taste for simplifying things and their bold composition.

Henri was born at Albi, and was the son of Count Alphonse de Toulouse-Lautrec-Maufra and Adèle Tapié de Céleyran; he was thus descended from the Counts of Toulouse. He was always a delicate child and two accidents he had as a boy, in 1878 and 1879, left him with both legs broken; this arrested his growth and he remained a stunted dwarf all his life. He started drawing about this time, and went on to paint mostly horses and carriages—for instance his painting *The Count de Toulouse-Lautrec driving his four-in-hand at Nice* (1881), obviously influenced by the ani-

TOULOUSE-LAUTREC *The Englishman at the Moulin Rouge*

buttonhole, so he is wearing a whole bunch of cornflowers. Just this small detail pinpoints the man's character. Lautrec constantly does this, producing the maximum effect with the minimum of resources. He remained independent and did not belong to any school of painting, but took what he wanted from various groups—from the Impressionists, the use of pure colours and brush-strokes in juxtaposition; from the Symbolists, their flat

TOULOUSE-LAUTREC *Woman at her window.* 1893

thing for him; for instance *The woman with gloves, Honorine P.* (*c.* 1890-1891) and *Woman in Père Forrest's garden* (1891). But one can hardly call these backgrounds 'out of doors', they are really more like stage sets, with all Lautrec's attention concentrated on the characters. As he said: 'Only the figure matters; the landscape is merely an accessory and ought not to be anything more. A pure landscape painter is inhuman; the only point of landscape is to help understand the person's character better.'

Lautrec was now becoming the painter of 'la belle époque', the Naughty Nineties that the film 'Moulin Rouge' has brought back into fashion. His subjects were the artificial,

TOULOUSE-LOUTREC *Jardin de Paris: Jane Avril.* 1893

mal painter Princeteau; landscapes and portraits (*An Ecclesiastic*, 1881; the *Countess de Toulouse-Lautrec with a cup*, 1883). In 1882 Lautrec decided to take up painting seriously, and went to live in Paris. He studied first with Bonnat and then in Cormon's studio where he met Van Gogh and was much attracted to his way of painting. He also admired Degas and Renoir. Towards 1885 he began going to the Mirliton, Aristide Bruant's famous cabaret, and did drawings of the best-known of the songs (*À Batignolles; Belleville; À Saint-Lazare*). He also painted one of his most celebrated posters, *Aristide Bruant at the Ambassadeurs* (1892), and did a whole series of paintings inspired by the famous singer: *Gueule de bois or the Drinker* (1888-1889), *À la Mic* (1891), *Alfred la Guigne* (1894), with their shrewd criticism of contemporary life and conditions. He also painted portraits, such as *Mlle Dihau at the piano* (1890) and *Augusta* (1890), and occasionally got his models to pose out of doors, in Père Forrest's garden at Montmartre, an unusual

TOULOUSE-LAUTREC *Alfred la Guigne.* 1894

animated night life of circuses and bars, cabaret and music-hall—particularly the famous Moulin-Rouge—the world of the French Can-can, theatres and brothels with stage and music-hall personalities such as Jane Avril, la Goulue and double-jointed Valentin, Marcelle Lender and Cha-U-Kao the female clown, Miss May Belfort and Yvette Guilbert. *At the Cirque Fernando: the Equestrian* (1888) and *Au Bal du Moulin de la Galette* (1889) are ex-

TOULOUSE-LAUTREC *Starting the Quadrille*. 1892

TOULOUSE-LAUTREC *Jane Avril dancing*. 1892

Toulouse-Lautrec *Panel for La Goulue's stand; La Goulue and Valentin le Désossé dancing.* 1895

Toulouse-Lautrec *The Clowness Cha-U-Kao.* 1895

Toulouse-Lautrec *Yvette Guilbert taking a curtain call.* 1894

Toulouse-Lautrec *Portrait of Madame Lucy.* 1896

Toulouse-Lautrec *In the parlour at the Rue des Moulins.* 1894

Toulouse-Lautrec *Woman putting on her stocking.* 1894

Toulouse-Lautrec *'Chocolat' dancing in Achille's Bar.* 1896

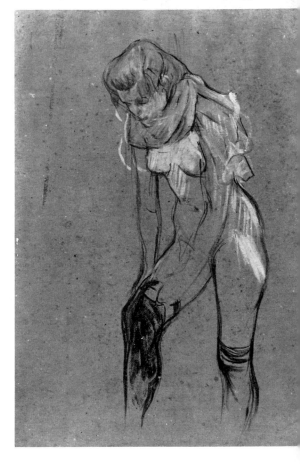

TOULOUSE-LAUTREC *The English girl at the Star, Le Havre.*
1889

amples. Lautrec showed this last picture at the Salon des Indépendants, his first exhibit there. Among other paintings of this period are: *Starting the Quadrille* (1892), *Dance at the Moulin-Rouge* (1890), *At the Moulin-Rouge* (1892), *M. Boileau at the café* (1893), *At the café: the anaemic cashier* (1898), *Japanese divan* (poster, 1892), *Jane Avril dancing* (c. 1892), *Jane Avril leaving the Moulin-Rouge* (1892), *Jane Avril at the Jardin de Paris* (poster, 1893) and *Yvette*

Guilbert (1894) whom he drew and painted several times, *La Goulue and double-jointed Valentin* and *Dance of La Goulue, or the Almées* with the photographer Paul Sescau at the piano, and Maurice Guibert, Doctor Tapié de Céleyran the artist's cousin, Oscar Wilde, Lautrec himself (back view) and Félix Fénéon in profile, all in the front row. These two large panels, now in the Jeu de Paume museum, were painted as decorations for La Goulue's stand at the Foire du Trône. Other examples of his work are: *Doctor Tapié de Céleyran* (1894), *Oscar Wilde* (1895), *May Belfort* (1895), *Marcelle Lender dancing Chilpéric's boléro* (1895-1896), *Cha-U-Kao seated* (colour lithograph, 1896), *'Chocolat' dancing in Achille's Bar* (drawing, 1896) and *Mme Poupoule at her toilet* (1898).

From 1892 onwards Toulouse-Lautrec's favourite subject was prostitution and most of his models were prostitutes. 'Ordinary models are always so stiff and stuffy,' he said 'but prostitutes are alive.' In 1894 he even went to board in a brothel in the Rue des Moulins, and while there produced a set of studies for his series of lithographs *Elles* which came out in 1896; examples of these are *Woman putting on her stocking* and *Woman in a brothel* (*c.* 1894), and a large picture that sums up all he had seen there: *In the parlour at the Rue des Moulins* (1894). But Lautrec's health was getting very frail. His heavy drinking did not improve things, and at the beginning of 1899 his health became so much worse that he had to go into a nursing home; while there he worked at a

TOULOUSE-LAUTRÉC *At the Races*. 1899

series of fine lithographs, *The Circus*. In May he was able to leave, and lived partly in Paris, partly in Bordeaux, mostly painting portraits; one of the most striking is *The English girl at the Star, Le Havre* dated 1899. His last, unfinished work was *Examination at the Faculty of Medicine* (1901, now in the Museum at Albi); its disturbing quality reminds one of Georges Rouault's work.

Lautrec died on 9 September 1901 at the age of thirty-seven, in the great family house at Malromé in the Gironde. His mother presented all the paintings and sketches he had left in his studio to the city of Albi, to found a Toulouse-Lautrec museum in the old Bishops' palace of La Berbie.

The art historian Roger Marx was one of the first to appreciate Lautrec's remarkable talent; he wrote an article about him in *Art Nouveau* at the time of an exhibition of his works at the Boussod-Valadon Gallery in 1893. 'It is a long time,' he wrote 'since we have come across such a gifted artist as M. Toulouse-Lautrec, with his penetrating analysis of character and extreme simplicity of technique. He is not attached to a school nor does he belong to a clique, but became independent very early, so as to be able to be really himself.' Lautrec was not in any sense a caricaturist, as his art is far above that level; he was not even a satirist. The brutal sincerity of his work and emphatic approach may appear painful and hurt people's feelings, but his is the response of an oversensitive wounded nature; he did not rebel against harshness and injustice, but tried instead to penetrate the poignant secret of the human soul.

TWACHTMAN John Henry (Cincinnati 1853-Gloucester, U.S.A. 1902) Twachtman is the most interesting of the American painters to be influenced by French Impressionism. It was he who conceived the idea in 1898 of founding a group, 'Ten American Painters', as official representatives of Impressionism in the United States. The group consisted of Frank Benson, Joseph de Camp, Thomas Dewing, Childe Hassam, Willard Metcalfe, Robert Reid, Edward E. Simmsons, Edmund Tarbell and J. Alden Weir, as well as Twachtman himself. Among his most remarkable

works are several winter scenes (*Pond in the snow*, now in the Chicago Art Institute) which show great sensitiveness and delicacy in rendering the pearly iridescence of snow, rather as Sisley and Monet did.

UHDE Fritz Karl Hermann von (Wolkenburg 1848-Munich 1911) He was originally destined for an army career, and served for ten years in a Saxon cavalry regiment. He studied painting in Munich and then in Paris with Munkacsy, whose influence helped to direct Uhde towards painting religious pictures. These were popular both in France and Germany. Uhde's originality consists in the fact that his sacred figures are not presented in the usual conventional way, but quite simply form part of the modern world (*Jesus with the peasants*.) In 1880, Uhde met Liebermann in Munich, and it was his influence that made him gradually give up the bituminous paint of

UHDE *Jesus with the peasants*

his early canvases and adopt the bright clear colours of 'open-air' painting (*The Bavarian drummers*, 1883). He is rather too fond of 'anecdotal' painting (*The Children's room*, 1889) but several of his pictures, sensitively and delicately painted, well convey the effect of sunlight filtering through leaves (*Old Brewery at Dachau*, 1888; *Young Girls in the garden*, 1906).

UHDE *Young girls in the garden.* 1906

VIGNON *Landscape at Auvers*

VIGNON Victor (Villers-Cotterets 1847-
Meulan 1909) Corot helped Vignon with advice at the beginning of his career, and he was
also influenced by Monet. Vignon loved
painting from nature and out in the country.
He belonged to the Impressionist group and
exhibited with them, and his clear colouring
and fondness for painting out of doors are
typically Impressionist. He worked chiefly in
the Auvers district, Chaponval and Nesles-la-
Vallée (e.g. *Landscape at Auvers*). His painting
is traditional in its care for composition and
sense of volume, while his love for quiet landscapes and clear skies is often reminiscent of
Pissarro.

ZANDOMENEGHI Federico (Venice 1841-Paris 1917) was the son and pupil of the sculptor Pietro Zandomeneghi. From about 1862-1866 he worked in Florence, and in Venice from 1866-1874, before going to Paris where he joined the Impressionists' group and exhibited at the Salon des Indépendants. His subjects include Paris café and street scenes (*By the Seine, Square d'Auvers, Paris*) as well as portraits. Diego Martelli, whose portrait he painted, was also painted by Degas, with whose work Zandomeneghi's has a certain affinity.

ZORN Anders (Utmeland, near Mora 1860-Mora 1920) Zorn is the most important Swedish painter of the late nineteenth century. He was the illegitimate son of a Bavarian brewer who had gone to work in Sweden, and a peasant girl from Dalecarlie. In 1875 he began to attend the Art Academy in Stockholm, where he concentrated chiefly on drawing and watercolour painting. In 1881 after going to Paris, he travelled extensively; he went twice to Spain and Portugal, in 1881-1882 and 1884 he went to London (1882-1885), to Hungary (1885-1886), to Turkey and then Greece with his young wife, then once more to Spain, and finally to Algiers.

In 1887 we find him working with the small international colony of artists at St. Ives in Cornwall. He was particularly interested in studying the effects of light on water (*Seascape, St. Ives, Cornwall*, 1887-1888, watercolour; *Seascape, c.* 1887, watercolour). In 1888 his first large painting *St. Ives, Cornwall: fishermen*, which had been hung in the Paris Salon, was bought by the state for the Luxembourg museum. In 1896 Zorn settled at Mora and founded a museum there to house his own paintings, but continued to travel in Europe and in the United States. A retrospective exhibition of his works was held at the Durand-Ruel Gallery in Paris in 1906.

He was a versatile artist, executing oil paintings and drawings, lithographs and engravings, but his particular gift was for watercolours. He also painted a number of portraits, that recall the style of Monet and Degas (*Portrait of Antonin Proust*, 1888). But if one should wish to compare him to a French Impressionist, he is really closer to Renoir than to anyone else, and like him, was especially interested in painting female nudes, preferably by the side of water. Like Renoir, he attempted to capture the reflections of light on pearly flesh (*On the rocks: sea nymph*, 1894; *Summer night*, 1891). During the last ten years of his life he tended to give up this type of painting, and his pictures became much more like those of Corinth.

ZORN *A Fisherman.* 1888

The Defenders
of Impressionism

AROSA Gustave (second half of the nine-teenth century) is chiefly known as having been Paul Gauguin's patron. He was a banker by profession as well as being a great lover of the arts, particularly interested in Pissarro's work. In 1870 Paul Gauguin, who had just finished doing his national service in the navy, came back to Paris; Arosa welcomed him and found him a job at the Bertin Bank, where Gauguin worked for twelve years before fi-nally deciding, in 1883, to take up painting. It was at the bank that Gauguin met Schuffe-necker who also worked there and used to paint in his spare time; he and Gauguin soon became close friends.

Arosa had a great number of artist friends, and assembled a fine collection of paintings. He deserves mention here for having en-couraged Gauguin to take up painting and fostered his late vocation as an artist.

ASTRUC Zacharie (1835-1907) The fa-mous name Olympia comes from one of Astruc's poems: 'When tired of dreaming, fair Olympia sleeps . . .' Astruc was an art critic as well as a painter and sculptor, and took part in the first Impressionist exhibition, but he is chiefly known as a patron of Manet, who painted his portrait in 1864. In 1860, in *Le Salon intime* he gave an idea of what the si-tuation in art was at the time: 'The new school is gradually emerging. It has to build on ruins; the future depends entirely on the rising generation.' In Monet's *Concert in the Tuileries Gardens*, painted at about this time, several of the bystanders can be recognized; they in-clude Astruc walking with Eugène Manet, the composer Offenbach, Baudelaire and Théo-phile Gautier.

Three years later Zacharie Astruc took up the cudgels on behalf of the Salon des Refusés and founded a daily paper *The 1863 Salon* just for the duration of the exhibition. It was he who wrote the catalogue introduction for the 1867 Manet exhibition, which was arranged to coincide with the great Exposition Uni-verselle—'The vital thing for the artist is being able to show his works, because after people have looked at them for a while, they begin to get used to what had formerly shocked them. Then gradually people begin to understand

the artist and to accept him.' He did not care for Renoir as much as for Manet, but he did write a perceptive comment on *Lise with a sunshade* (1867): 'This is an attractive fi-gure . . . a charming painting, . . . skilful exe-cution, delicate colouring, clear composition,

MANET *Portrait of Zacharie Astruc.* 1864

excellent light effects . . .'

In his picture of *The Batignolles Studio* (1870) Fantin-Latour painted a group consisting of the German artist Schölderer, Renoir, Zola, Claude Monet, Edmond Maître and his friend Bazille all gathered round Manet, who was in the process of painting the portrait of Zacharie Astruc seated by the artist.

AURIER Albert (1865-1892) was a young symbolist writer, who belonged to the 'Impressionist and Synthetist group'. He was originally Editor of the *Moderniste*, an avant-garde review in which Gauguin published his *Notes on the art of the Exposition Universelle*, thus taking the opportunity of censuring official art.

Émile Bernard had often spoken very en-thusiastically to Aurier about van Gogh, so Aurier decided to write the first article to appear about the painter's work. It was pub-lished in January 1890 in the first number of the Symbolist review *Le Mercure de France.*

It was a brilliant article. Aurier called it *The Loners: Vincent van Gogh* and in it he stressed the naïve veracity and absolute sincerity of van Gogh's art, combining with a deep love of nature. 'He is a kind of drunken giant, an exuberant mind, a terrible mad genius.' For him van Gogh was not only a great painter, he was also 'a dreamer, an ardent believer, an idealist, living in Utopia, in a world of visions and imagination.' He went on to consider van Gogh's technique, emphasizing the violence of his approach, the power of his design and finally his dazzling colouring. Aurier's article attracted a great deal of attention, and as a result he was asked to undertake the regular Arts feature in the *Revue Indépendante.*

Again on Émile Bernard's suggestion, in 1891 Aurier wrote another article in the *Mercure de France*, this time entitled *Symbolism in painting: Paul Gauguin.* This too was a resounding success. Aurier regarded Gauguin as the leader of the Symbolist movement in art, and found in his 'masterly and disturbing work, an artist of genius with the soul of an aboriginal.' By now Aurier had become the official theorist of the new movement, and this article was written as a manifesto for Symbolist art. The work of art, he declared, 'must be "ideist", symbolist, synthetic, subjective and decorative.' It must also possess 'the transcendental power to move us, which is so precious and so important; the power to stir the soul and make it thrill with emotion at the moving drama of abstractions.'

Aurier again added to his reputation, in April 1892, by publishing an important article on the Symbolists, with special reference to Redon, Bonnard and Gauguin. He again emphasizes the influence of Gauguin 'the undoubted originator of this movement in art, whose work is marked by a profoundly philosophical and intensely idealist approach.' He also mentions van Gogh with his 'feverish questioning'; Odilon Redon, another 'bringer of good tidings', and finally the part played by the Impressionist and Post-Impressionist movements, with Degas, Cézanne, Monet 'that sun-worshipper', Sisley, Pissarro, Renoir and Seurat as his examples.

BARNES Albert Coombs (1872-1951) Doctor Barnes was one of the most astonishing of American self-made men, and a great art-collector. He was extremely intelligent and began by studying medicine and chemistry, and then worked in a pharmaceutical laboratory. In 1902 he, with the German Hermann Hille, put a new strong antiseptic on the market, and made his fortune. He had always been very much interested in art, so he decided to go to Europe and visit museums and

RENOIR *La Sortie du Conservatoire. c.* 1877

art galleries. He went to London, Berlin and Paris where he met Leo and Gertrude Stein; they introduced him to the paintings of Cézanne and Renoir, and also to the works of Matisse, Picasso, Braque, Juan Gris and Léger. One of the first Impressionist pictures he bought was a Renoir.

In 1912 he only bought one painting by Cézanne, but over the years he acquired another fourteen of his as well as works by Renoir, Sisley, Monet, Gauguin and van Gogh, including his *Roulin the postman*, as well as pastels by Degas, *Nude on a blue divan* by Toulouse-Lautrec, and some very fine pictures by Matisse and Picasso.

By the end of the 1914 war he had already made an important collection of paintings which he was very proud of; he even attempted to dabble in art criticism, and wrote an article on 'How to judge painting'. He emphasized that nothing can take the place of prolonged looking at original works for acquiring a real knowledge and understanding of art. He also wrote two studies, *The Art of Renoir* (1935) and *The Art of Cézanne* (1939); at that time he owned something like a hundred of their works. In 1920 Barnes conceived the idea of setting up a foundation named after himself. This was finally opened in 1924, in Merion, Pennsylvania, and houses his art collection, one of the finest in the world.

BAUDELAIRE Charles (1821-1867) The author of *Les Fleurs du Mal* also wrote many important works in the field of art criticism, in which he reveals his keen sense of appreciation and his receptivity to visual impressions. It often happened, he wrote, that he 'appreciated a picture only because of the fund of ideas and reflections it can supply me with.'

His first two *Salons* articles date from 1845 and 1846, while the last two are 1855 and 1859. He asserts that 'if criticism is to justify its existence at all, it must be biased and passionate and involved; it must have a definite point of view—the one that gives the widest horizon.' He had the greatest admiration for Delacroix as the artist with 'an indefinable *sui generis* quality that somehow expresses the melancholy of the period', and that made of him an original and unusual

artist. In his famous poem *Les Phares* he mentioned him in one breath with Rubens, Leonardo da Vinci, Rembrandt and Michelangelo. Fantin-Latour, in his great painting *Tribute to Delacroix* (1864) showed the poet among various militant writers and artists grouped round Delacroix's self-portrait.

He admired Daumier whose drawing has an 'absolute relevance', adding that his caricatures are 'astounding in their comprehensiveness'. In the work of his friend Constantin Guys he finds 'the real waywardness of life.' His remarks about Boudin proved prophetic; while in Courbet he sees 'a powerful

Courbet *Portrait of Baudelaire. c.* 1848

workman, a fierce but steady will.' Courbet painted Baudelaire's portrait in about 1848, and also put him into *The Painter's Studio*. Baudelaire praised Corot for his 'infallible precision in harmony' and upheld his 'unfinished' look against his critics. He praised Jongkind and his friend Manet whom he supported with unfailing loyalty. He recognised Manet's particular 'temperament' and was full of admiration for him as an artist: 'He has a decided taste for modern life, a keen imagination, boldness and sensitivity.' As Valéry has pointed out, Manet's success can be connected with his encounter with poetry.

Baudelaire particularly liked Manet's early paintings, but he did not really understand him and criticized him for certain apparent weaknesses in his work.

Baudelaire's sustained interest in art, with his sensitivity and poetic feeling, assure him an established, if unconventional place in the history of art criticism.

BELLIO Georges de (1828-1894) Doctor de Bellio was a rich Romanian. He studied in Paris and then stayed on indefinitely. He was a friend and counsellor of the Impressionists, and helped them when things were difficult; he was also one of the first people to encourage them by buying their paintings. He acquired various pictures by Renoir, Sisley, Pissarro and Monet, including the famous *Impression, sunrise*, which at the time seemed to have no market value.

Bellio was a vigorous champion too of the Impressionist cause and defended it before his friends, who included a good many critics and men of letters. He went to the 'Impressionist dinners' at the Café Riche from 1890 to 1894, the year he died.

Théodore Duret tells us how he rented an empty shop in the Rue Alfred-Stevens just opposite where he lived, and used it to house all the 'objets d'art' and pictures he had collected. He used to take anyone who would care to follow him to see them and would try to convince them of the merits of the artists, especially Monet whom he particularly admired. Incidentally, several times he helped to tide him over difficult patches in his life.

Bellio played an important part in the art world of his time by his warm, open-hearted generosity and his friendly encouragement of artists.

BERNHEIM JEUNE Alexandre Bernheim, better known as (1839-1915) The Bernheim Jeune Gallery, one of the earliest art galleries in France, going back to the eighteenth century, was founded in Besançon by Joseph Bernheim. In 1863 his son Alexandre settled down in Paris at 8 Rue Laffitte. He became friends with Courbet and showed his works, as well as those of Corot. The gallery grew rapidly and towards 1900, moved to larger premises at 25 Boulevard de la Madeleine. For the next twenty-five years exhibitions were held there regularly, with Bonnard, Vuillard, Cézanne, van Gogh, Renoir and Matisse all showing their works. In 1924 the gallery moved again, to its present quarters at 83 Faubourg Saint-Honoré and 27 Avenue Matignon.

From 1892 onwards the Bernheims were involved in most of the large public auctions in Paris, such as the art sales held by Charpentier, Natanson, Roger Marx and Octave Mirbeau. The Bernheim Gallery also started a publishing department for books dealing with the documentary, biographical and critical history of outstanding modern artists. Monographs were published on Manet, Courbet, van Gogh, Lautrec and Renoir, as well as larger books on Degas, Matisse, and Vlaminck; the complete drawings of Seurat, Renoir's paintings, with 800 illustrations, and finally the authoritative *Bulletin de la vie artistique*.

Grigorescu *Portrait of Doctor de Bellio. c.* 1877

RONDEL *Portrait of Alexandre Bernheim*

BLANCHE *Portrait of Francis Poulenc*. 18 July 1930

BLANCHE Jacques-Émile (1861-1942) was a painter and novelist as well as an art critic. He became involved in artistic circles in Paris and got to know the Impressionists, who taught him to appreciate landscapes painted out of doors. He enjoyed good society and met many of the important writers of the day; he painted portraits of Stéphane Mallarmé, André Gide, Paul Valéry, Marcel Proust, Paul Claudel, Jean Giraudoux, James Joyce, Jean Cocteau and Max Jacob, among many others, with a fresh and sensitive approach.

Among his writings are *Propos de peintre de David à Degas* and *La Pêche aux souvenirs* which has some delightful anecdotes about Renoir. Blanche often went to stay at Offranville near Dieppe, and met Renoir whom he was very fond of. 'One doesn't realise all his qualities at first—he seems so uncouth when one first meets him,' he said. 'But he is full of common sense and very unassuming, and just goes on painting these marvellous pictures, that in years to come will turn people's heads with excitement, as quietly and steadily as if nothing else mattered.' He tells us that Renoir used to paint landscapes as a relaxation: 'It was an odd sort of painting, like something done in pastels, with hatching and a kind of multi-coloured trellis with the reds overflowing on to the blues and greens.'

BONNAT Léon (1833-1922) Léon Bonnat was born at Bayonne on 20 June 1833, and began to study art, first in Spain at the Madrid Academy and then in Italy, before finally attending Léon Cogniet's studio in Paris. He first painted historical works and later became an official portrait painter. His sitters included

BONNAT *Portrait of Jules Ferry.* 1888

DEGAS *Portrait of Léon Bonnat.* 1862

many important people of the period, such as Victor Hugo, Jules Ferry, Thiers and the younger Dumas.

He taught at the École des Beaux-Arts and in 1855 met Degas. Among his famous pupils were Gustave Caillebotte and especially Toulouse-Lautrec. Lautrec went to study with Bonnat in 1882, recommended by Henri Rachou and introduced by René Princeteau the animal painter, as he wanted to show his willingness to learn, but the experiment was not a success and only lasted a few months. Bonnat thought his drawing was 'atrocious'; all he wanted was academic painting and he strongly disapproved of personal interpret-

ations. Lautrec therefore left and went to work with Cormon.

Bonnat was a great collector and patron of the arts, and in Bayonne there is a museum named after him containing the art collections he bequeathed to the city.

BURTY Philippe (1830-1890) Burty was one of the few critics to show approval of the Impressionist painters at the time of their first exhibition in 1874. He understood the spirit underlying the movement; 'in technique, conveying the broad light of the open air; in feeling, the distinctness of first impressions.'

A year later Renoir, Monet and Sisley were in financial difficulties, so they decided to hold a sale of their works at the Hôtel Drouot, on 24 March 1875. Burty said, in his introduction to the catalogue: 'The paintings express light effects, and colours in opposition, masses and silhouettes in a high-handed way, without bothering about pleasing short-sighted spectators.'

In 1880 Burty brought out a novel *Grave*

Imprudence, telling the life story of an Impressionist painter, with his various adventures and love affairs, the hero being a mixture of Monet, Renoir and Manet. The author described the beginnings of Impressionism and how the group used to meet in cafés; one of the characters is an art critic, the author himself expressing his own views. In one place the hero of the book 'noticed that the formula varied *ad infinitum* according to place, season, atmospheric tension and setting, in fact to endless local or psychological causes. But it always demanded clear rapid execution of the impression of the moment, based on complete control of the medium.'

CAILLEBOTTE Gustave (1848-1894), a rich young bachelor, was a naval engineer by profession, but was also a talented painter. He is chiefly remembered as a friend and patron

CAILLEBOTTE *Self Portrait*

of the Impressionists. He first met Monet, then Renoir, and soon became their friend and benefactor; he used to help them by buying their paintings, among them Renoir's *The Swing* and *Dance at the Moulin de la Galette*.

In 1876, at the time of their second exhibition, he joined the group himself. He then made a will, bequeathing his entire collection

CAILLEBOTTE *Sailing boats at Argenteuil. c.* 1888

of paintings, which included many important Impressionist works, to the State, on condition it should be handed over to the Louvre. He appointed Renoir as his executor, and declared: 'I will that out of my estate, the necessary sum should be made available so as to hold an exhibition, in 1878, of the painters known as the intransigents or Impressionists, under the best possible conditions.'

Caillebotte managed to enthuse his friends, and a third exhibition was organised in the spring of 1877. Soon after it was closed, he took a very active part in the second auction of Impressionist works, and in 1879 offered to help again with arrangements for the fourth exhibition, which opened on 10 April. That same evening he sent a note to Monet saying: 'We are saved! By five o'clock we had already taken over 400 francs. Two years ago it was less than 350, on the opening day.'

The sixth exhibition was held in April 1881, but Caillebotte was not involved. In a letter to Pissarro he explained the differences he had had with Degas, who seemed to him to be upsetting the whole group. However, being extremely persevering, he pressed on and towards the end of 1881 he agreed to organize a fresh exhibition. His plan succeeded and on 1 March 1882, the exhibition opened at 251 Rue Saint-Honoré. Several months earlier Renoir had portrayed his friend in the *Déjeuner des canotiers* where he appears as the young man astride a chair, among the assembled crowd.

After eight years working together, the Impressionists had at last managed to form a really representative homogeneous group of painters.

When Caillebotte died in 1894, the Government did not feel able to accept the whole of his collection, which consisted of sixty-five pictures. There was a great deal of discussion and conferring, and controversy in the press, before an arrangement could be reached; and finally only thirty-eight pictures went to the Luxembourg museum (8 Monets, 7 by Pissarro, 6 by Renoir, 6 Sisleys, 2 each by Manet and Cézanne, and 7 by Degas). It was not until 1928 that they found their proper place in the Louvre.

CAMONDO Isaac de (1851-1911) was a rich collector, who paid the fabulous sum of 43,000 francs for Sisley's painting *The Flood at Port-Marly* at the sale of the Tavernier collection, on 6 March 1900. Actually Sisley's pictures did reach very high sale prices, less than a year after his death in January 1899. Cézanne's pictures had also become very fashionable, and when the Chocquet collection was sold and the thirty-two paintings fetched a total of 51,000 francs between them,

Camondo had to bid 6,200 francs for Cézanne's *La Maison du pendu*, the highest price in the sale.

Count de Camondo died on 7 April 1911 and his collection of paintings went to the Louvre three years later. Apart from works by Delacroix, Corot, Boudin, Manet, Degas, Renoir, Cézanne, Pissarro, Sisley, van Gogh and Toulouse-Lautrec, it included fourteen pictures by Monet representing his different

CÉZANNE *La Maison du Pendu*. 1873

periods, and ten by Manet, including *Lola de Valence* and *The Fifer*.

CAROLUS-DURAN Charles-Émile Durand, known as (1838-1917) Carolus-Duran was born at Lille on 4 July 1838, and became a painter, musician, sculptor and writer. He was much influenced by Courbet and particularly admired his *After dinner at Ornans* which he had seen in the Lille Museum. He travelled in Italy and visited Rome, Venice, Florence, Naples and Pompei, and also went to Spain.

In 1868, when he was back from his travels, he made a name for himself in Paris as a society painter; his portraits of *Madame Feydeau* (1869), *Madame de Lancey* (1876) and *The Lady with a glove* (1869) are among the best known of his works.

He was appointed a member of the Institut in 1902 and then became head of the French portrait; he was much impressed by Carolus-Duran's successful career.

CASSIRER Paul (1871-1926) and Bruno (1872-1941) About the turn of the century, the German publishing firm of Cassirer became celebrated for publicizing Impressionism in Germany. It was also interested in Neo-Impressionism and the artists claiming to belong to Art Nouveau, a movement which found its expression mainly in the field of applied arts, particularly architectural and interior decoration, typography and graphic art.

Towards 1898 the two cousins Paul and Bruno reopened a Salon in Berlin which had been closed since 1892. There Impressionist artists like Max Slevogt, Lovis Corinth and Max Liebermann could exhibit their works, thus declaring their opposition to academic art and their close links with the 'Sezession' group.

Paul and Bruno Cassirer commissioned the

CAROLUS-DURAN *Lady with a glove.* 1869

GROSSMANN *Portrait of Paul Cassirer*

Academy in Rome. During the summer of 1876, Manet met Carolus-Duran at Montgeron at the country house of Hoschedé, the well-known art collector, and painted his

ORLIK *Portrait of Bruno Cassirer*

turn of Cézanne, Gauguin and Lautrec. Between 1901 and 1907, Paul Cassirer organised one-man-shows of Courbet, Delacroix, Renoir and van Gogh, which had great repercussions in the contemporary art world. In 1906 there was an exhibition of paintings by Manet and Monet from the collection of the singer Faure who had been collecting Impressionist pictures since 1874. Then in December 1929 there was held an extraordinarily large and comprehensive exhibition entitled 'A Century of French drawings', which included works by artists of the Barbizon school, Impressionists and Post-Impressionists.

In 1902 Bruno founded the famous review *Kunst und Künstler*; the best contemporary German art critics contributed articles, Meier-Graefe among them, and the editor was Karl Scheffler. He published important articles on Neo-Impressionist and Post-Impressionist art.

The firm of Cassirer also won an extremely high reputation with their art publications, especially their illustrated books. Among others, they published Antonin Proust's book on *Manet*, in about 1917, and *The Impressionists* by Théodore Duret; about 1930 they brought out Vollard's *Degas and Renoir* and Jedlicka's book on *Toulouse-Lautrec*.

Belgian painter and architect Henry van de Velde to plan and decorate their gallery. He was in close touch with the avant-garde group in Brussels, Les Vingt, and this turned out to be important as Les Vingt had connections with the French Impressionists Monet, Renoir and especially Seurat.

One of the first exhibitions organised by the two Cassirers was of Degas' work, followed by one of Raffaelli's. Shortly before 1900 the firm was reorganised, Bruno taking over the general publishing side of the business and Paul being in charge of the gallery and of art publications.

On the various occasions when the Berlin 'Sezession' group held their exhibitions at Paul Cassirer's gallery, several rooms were put at the disposal of French artists. Pissarro, Renoir and Vuillard were represented in 1900, and the following year van Gogh, Guillaumin and Monet. In 1903 it was the

CASTAGNARY Jules-Antoine (1831-1888) Castagnary's commentaries on the *Salons* range from 1857 to 1879. The first ones praise Corot and his 'infinite charm', the 'breadth, sobriety and sincerity' of Millet, and Courbet's excellence, as 'the only painter of our time'.

In 1863 he was admiring Jongkind, 'an artist to his fingertips' as he called him, 'I find in him a rare and genuine sensitivity. With him, everything lies in the impression.' Castagnary's appreciation of Jongkind, as a forerunner of Impressionism, led him on to support the movement itself. He did not care for Manet. He thought he 'lacked conviction and sincerity', finding in him 'more imagination than observation; he is more eccentric than powerful.' However by 1875 he had come to recognize his importance as a leader; he admitted his undoubted influence on other artists, and could not fail to realise the important place he would eventually take in the history of contemporary art: 'Anyone who should want to write about the development or the deviations of French nineteenth century art will have to reckon with Manet.' Castagnary was a strong supporter of naturalism, and from 1863 onwards we find him using the actual term. 'The naturalist school,' he explains, 'believes that art is the expression of life in all its forms and all its various stages of development: its one and only aim is to imitate nature in its most intense and most powerful aspects; it is truth and knowledge balancing each other.' In his *Salon* for 1866, he is full of praise for Monet, who had only just joined the naturalists' group; two years later, it was the turn of Renoir, Bazille and Pissarro.

In 1868, he spoke well of Renoir, but still with certain reservations; ten years later, he was enthusiastic about him, mentioning his 'vigorous witty approach, his delightful grace and sprightliness, and the richness of his palette . . . as for his observation, it is as sharp as his execution is free and spontaneous.'

RENOIR *Portrait of Madame Charpentier.* 1876-1877

CHARPENTIER Georges (1846-1905) In 1871 Georges Charpentier inherited the publishing firm of Charpentier from his father. The firm had always enjoyed an excellent reputation, and among the authors it published were Victor Hugo, Alexandre Dumas senior, Musset and Balzac. Georges Charpentier followed in his father's footsteps, publishing the best authors, including Zola and Alphonse Daudet. He got to know Renoir about 1876 and was always an ardent supporter of his.

Renoir was a regular visitor at Madame Charpentier's drawing room, and there he met the most famous writers, artists, politicians and musicians of the day. There he also got to know Juliette Adam, and the actress Jeanne Samary, whose portrait he painted several times. Madame Charpentier commissioned Renoir to paint five portraits of the various members of her family as well as of herself, and in 1878 he painted the famous picture *Madame Charpentier and her children*.

In the spring of 1879, Charpentier began publishing a weekly, *La Vie Moderne*, devoted to the artistic and literary as well as the society life of the period. Edmond Renoir used to write for it, and contributed an article on his brother.

Charpentier left behind him a collection of paintings when he died in 1905; apart from a number of pastels, it included two Renoirs, two Monets and a Cézanne.

CHOCQUET Victor (1821-1898) Victor Chocquet was an ordinary Customs inspector, but was also a dedicated art collector, and spent a large part of his salary on buying Impressionist pictures. 'A delightfully crazy creature' said Renoir, 'who starved himself to buy pictures he liked.' His first purchases were some watercolours by Delacroix whom he very much admired, and a painting by Manet, *The Spray of White Peonies*.

On 24 March 1875, he met Renoir at the Hôtel Drouot, at the famous sale the painter had organised together with Monet, Sisley and Berthe Morisot. That same evening he wrote to Renoir to congratulate him on his painting, and to ask him to do a portrait of Madame Chocquet. Renoir accepted, and he also painted the gentle thoughtful face of the collector himself. At the sale Chocquet bought one of Monet's views of Argenteuil.

Renoir took him to Père Tanguy's shop, to show him some of Cézanne's work. He bought one of the paintings straight away, exclaiming: 'How good that will look between a Delacroix and a Courbet!' Not long after-

MANET *Spray of White Peonies. c.* 1864

CÉZANNE *Portrait of Victor Chocquet.* 1877

wards he met Cézanne himself and from that time onwards, became, according to Duret, 'a kind of apostle' of Cézanne's work. Cézanne painted a portrait of him in 1875 and another in 1885.

On the occasion of the second Impressionist exhibition at the Durand-Ruel gallery in 1876, Chocquet lent a landscape by Manet, a picture by Pissarro and six by Renoir. Théodore Duret tells how on this occasion, Chocquet ' approached any visitors he knew, and also many others, to try and convert them to his own convictions and get them to share in the pleasure and admiration he felt.'

In 1899, after the death of Madame Chocquet who had inherited her husband's collection, eleven canvases by Monet and Renoir were auctioned, as well as five by Manet, one each by Pissarro and Sisley, and no less than thirty-one by Cézanne. Up to then his pictures had fetched very little, but ever since this sale, prices began to rise until they reached the vast sums we now know.

COURTAULD Samuel (1876-1947) Samuel came from a family of industrialists. He was intelligent and discriminating and so became one of the first people to make Impressionism known and accepted in England.

With the aim of promoting the movement, he gave a large sum to the Tate Gallery to enable it to enlarge its collection of nineteenth century French paintings. His wife encouraged him; and having seen and admired the paintings in the Lane Bequest, in 1922 he began acquiring his own collection of Impressionist and Post-Impressionist pictures. Among his first acquisitions were Renoir's *Woman at her toilet* and a painting by Toulouse-Lautrec. After only a year's collecting he had managed to buy two Cézannes, a Gauguin, a Manet, a Daumier and some bronzes by Degas. In 1924 he bought two Renoirs, *The First Outing* and *La Place Clichy*, and the follow-

RENOIR *The First Outing*. 1876

now divided between the Tate Gallery, the National Gallery and the Courtauld Institute in London.

DALE Chester (1883-1962) was a great art lover. He was specially attracted to nineteenth and twentieth century French painting, and his first wife Maud Dale, herself a painter and art critic, encouraged him in his taste. His close connection with the Georges

RENOIR *Little Girl with a watering-can*. 1876

ing year Renoir's *Theatre box* and *Courbevoie bridge* by Seurat. In 1926 he increased his purchases and acquired several more pictures by Seurat and Degas, Henri Rousseau's *l'Octroi*, *The Bar at the Folies-Bergère* by Manet and one of the versions of Cézanne's *Card Players*. Twenty years later, his collection, which covered the period from Delacroix to Picasso, was unique in England. It contained a marvellous and tastefully chosen range of paintings including Corot, Boudin, Van Gogh, Bonnard, Utrillo, Vuillard, Derain, Dufy; and among his favourite painters, nine Degas, seven Monet, seven Renoir, ten Cézanne and twelve Seurat. His collection is

Petit gallery, which specialised in Impressionist and Post-Impressionist paintings, meant he was able to follow the art market and big sales in Europe and America. His collection includes examples of almost all the great Impressionists; there are several Monets and an important group of paintings by Mary Cassatt, Berthe Morisot, Sisley and Pissarro, while perhaps the most outstanding are Degas' *Four dancers* (*c.* 1899) and Renoir's *Little girl with a watering-can*.

Post-Impressionism is represented by several Cézannes, including a fine *Still Life*, van Gogh's *La Mousmée*, and paintings by Gauguin, Toulouse-Lautrec and the Douanier Rousseau.

Dale left his collection to the National Gallery of Art in Washington.

DESBOUTIN   Marcellin (1823-1902) was a writer, painter—he took part in the second Impressionist exhibition—and above all, a remarkably good engraver, whose exceptional skill can be seen in a number of dry point portraits. He studied first in 1847 with

MANET *Portrait of Desboutin.* 1875

Thomas Couture. In 1850 he left France and bought a villa in Florence, where he lived for the next twenty years. In 1873 he went back to Paris; he was a colourful personality and lived a bohemian life, being often seen at the Café Guerbois.

Manet portrayed him in 1875 in his picture called *The Artist*. He became friendly with Degas, who put him into his picture *The Absinthe Drinkers* together with the actress Ellen Andrée sitting outside the Nouvelle-Athènes, a café he often patronized and where he used to invite his friends.

In 1880 he went to live in Nice. He continued painting there, and several pictures of his children date from that period.

DURAND-RUEL   Paul (1831-1922) When his father died in 1855, Paul Durand-Ruel inherited a stationer's shop which also supplied artists' materials. He was a friend of Corot, Millet, Théodore Rousseau, Diaz, Daubigny and Boudin, and helped them both financially and with moral support. He held exhibitions of the Barbizon painters in his gallery, first at 1 Rue de la Paix, and after 1867, at 16 Rue Laffitte, and tried to sell their works. 'A real art dealer,' he wrote, 'must also be a discriminating art lover. He must be ready if necessary to sacrifice his immediate interests to his artistic convictions, choosing rather to resist speculators than take part in their dealings.'

It was about 1870 that he first began to help the Impressionists, and when war broke out that year he transferred all his pictures to London, where he met Monet and Pissarro. He opened a gallery in New Bond Street where he held exhibitions to show works by Pissarro, Sisley, Monet, Renoir, Degas and Manet. He also did the same thing in Brussels.

In 1872 he went back to Paris, where he was the first art-dealer whom painters, whose work had been refused at the Salon (*les refusés*), could count on to help them. He bought a large number of pictures, and so acquired twenty-three of Monet's paintings for 35,000 francs. In 1876, he organised the second exhibition of the *refusés* group in his gallery in the Rue Le Peletier, so setting himself up in opposition to the official Salon. A few years later he

RENOIR *Portrait of Paul Durand-Ruel.* 1910

found himself in financial difficulties and had to suspend his purchases as there were so few buyers.

On 13 March 1886 he left for New York to organise an exhibition of modern French painting at the National Academy of Design. The exhibition opened on 25 May when Manet, Monet, Degas, Renoir, Pissarro and Sisley received official recognition. His success there decided him to open a gallery in New York in 1887. Later he organised exhibitions in Berlin, Venice and Stockholm, and again in London. From November 1890 until May 1891 he brought out in Paris a periodical entitled *L'Art dans les Deux Mondes*, containing articles on the Impressionists written by the outstanding critics of the day.

In Paris he organised a Gauguin exhibition in 1893, one of Odilon Redon's works in the following year, and a Toulouse-Lautrec exhibition in 1902. When he was about eighty, he wrote his reminiscences, which give a vivid

The Durand-Ruel Gallery, Rue des Petits-Champs. 1845

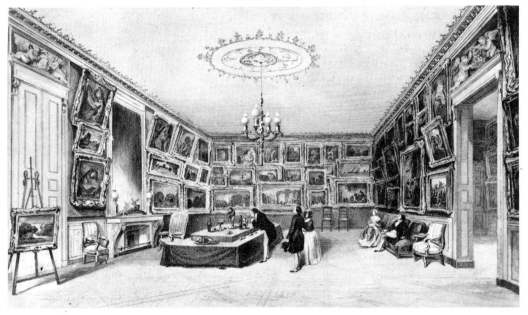

account of the difficulties of an art dealer. When he died in 1922, the last survivor of the great Impressionist generation, Monet, wrote to his son Joseph: 'I shall never forget all that my friends and I owe to your father, in a very special way.'

DURANTY Louis Edmond (1833-1880) was the illegitimate son of the author Prosper Mérimée. He is chiefly known as a fervent supporter of Impressionism. He was a friend of both painters and authors, and figures in Fantin-Latour's picture *Homage to Delacroix*, together with Manet and Baudelaire. In 1856 Duranty founded a review which he called *Réalisme* with the aim of refuting writers with romantic leanings; it included a regular feature *Notes on art* where he addressed painters in these words: 'In classical times they painted what they saw; now *you* paint what you see.'

Quite near the beginning of his career as a critic, Duranty wrote several enthusiastic articles in *La Gazette des Beaux-Arts*, comparing the Impressionists to the Venetian school as well as to Constable, and emphasizing the likeness between contemporary literature and painting. He praised the work of the Impressionist artists, considering them to be the 'primitives' of a great new renaissance of the arts.

After paying tribute to Courbet, Corot, Boudin and above all Manet, whom he looked on as forerunners of the movement, he went on to speak enthusiastically of Monet, Degas, Renoir, Sisley, Pissarro and Berthe Morisot. The great discovery of the Impressionists, he continued 'lies in their having realized that strong light makes tones lose their colour, and that sunlight reflected by objects tends, by its very brightness, to restore them to that luminous unity which merges all seven prismatic colours into one single colourless beam—that is, light.'

Duranty made Manet's acquaintance and soon a close friendship developed between the two. Later he wrote: 'In every exhibition, a couple of hundred steps away, and going through one room after another, there is only one picture that stands out among all the others, and that is always by Manet.'

At the Café Guerbois Duranty met Degas,

DEGAS *Portrait of Duranty*. 1879

and the two became close friends. Their ideas about the social and literary aspect of painting coincided, and Duranty wrote of Degas: 'he is an artist of unusual intelligence and, unlike most of his colleagues, is really interested in ideas. There was no rhyme or reason in his active mind; it was always in a state of effervescence and that is why some called him the inventor of the social chiaroscuro'.

On the occasion of the group's fourth exhibition, Duranty wrote an article praising all the exhibitors, particularly Monet and Pissarro, as well as Degas and his circle. It was about this time that Degas painted Duranty's portrait in distemper and in 1880 Huysmans commented on this famous work: 'There he is sitting at his table among his books and engravings. His shrewd humorous expression, his keen searching look, the way he laughs into his pipe are all conjured up by this picture, that gives an extraordinarily vivid impression of a strange and memorable character.'

Only nine days after the opening of the fifth exhibition, Duranty died suddenly.

DURET Théodore (1838-1927) Théodore Duret was a politician as well as being a writer and art critic, and was one of the first supporters of Impressionism. In 1867 he expressed a very unfavourable opinion of Manet, as well as of Sisley and Monet, but it was not long before he revised his first impressions. Manet painted his portrait in 1868 at the time when they both used to go regularly to the Café Guerbois, and in *Le Salon de 1870* he wrote an enthusiastic article about Manet: 'We stop in front of Monsieur Manet's canvases,' he wrote, 'because their compelling originality and inventiveness attract us.' And again 'We only look at a picture so as to experience it, and to receive some impression or emotion when we look at it.'

MANET *Portrait of Thédore Duret.* 1868

After the fall of the Commune, Duret went to England. In London he met Pissarro, and was full of enthusiasm for his recent paintings: 'In some ways Pissarro is a realist. Any landscape he paints must be a portrait of an existing part of the world.' From England he went to the United States and then continued his journey round the world by visiting Japan, China and India. He was back in France by 1873, and could then speak from experience: 'The Japanese are the original and most perfect Impressionists.' In December of the same year he wrote to Pissarro: 'You have a very real and deep feeling for nature, and your technique is powerful, so that there is a really satisfying stability about your work.'

In 1878 Duret published a brochure under the title *The Impressionist Painters*, with a preface containing 'some good little home truths addressed to the public' where he takes up the cudgels on behalf of his painter friends. He felt they had been laughed at quite enough. In the first chapter, which contains the explanation of the point of departure and raison d'être of the Impressionists, Duret reminds his readers that the Impressionists were the successors of Corot, Courbet and Manet, and were also greatly influenced by Japanese art. There follow short accounts of Monet, Sisley, Pissarro, Renoir and Berthe Morisot, and the final chapter ends with a prophecy: 'We will never alter our original opinion. But you people have made a mistake, and you *will* alter yours!'

This 1878 brochure was considerably enlarged in 1906 when it was reprinted as *l'Histoire des Peintres Impressionnistes* with the names of Cézanne and Guillaumin added.

FÉNÉON Félix (1861-1944) The name of Félix Fénéon is especially connected with the Neo-Impressionist movement, a term he invented in 1886. He became editor of *La Revue indépendante* in 1886 and chose his contributors from among supporters of 'dying naturalism and dawning Symbolism.' On the one side were Zola, Huysmans and Edmond de Goncourt, and on the other, Mallarmé and Moréas, heading a group of Symbolist poets. Several small exhibitions were organised in

Seurat and Pissarro, and was also friendly with Bonnard and Vuillard, the Nabis group and with Toulouse-Lautrec who put him into one of his pictures, a panel for *Decoration of La Goulue's stand at the Foire du Trône*, together with Oscar Wilde. In 1890 Signac, in his *Portrait of Félix Fénéon* put his new artistic theories into practice very skilfully in bringing out his sitter's appearance and character.

GACHET Paul (1828-1909) Gachet was an enthusiastic art lover, painter and engraver specializing in etching, as well as being a doctor of medicine. He admired the Impressionists and knew several of them well, and as he often went to the Café Guerbois, also met Pissarro and Guillaumin.

After the 1870 war he lived with his wife and two children at Auvers-sur-Oise, where he set up a studio in his house, on a hill overlooking the Oise valley, sharing it with his friends Pissarro, Monet, Renoir and Guillau-

Van Gogh *Portrait of Doctor Gachet.* 15 May 1890

the editor's office, with works by Manet, Pissarro, Berthe Morisot, Van Gogh, Seurat and Signac. Fénéon was a loyal supporter of the group of artists which had founded the *Société des Indépendants* under Seurat.

In 1886 Fénéon brought out a brochure called *The Impressionists*. Its aim was to expound the theory of Neo-Impressionism, as he felt that Impressionism had now been superseded by the new ideas of Seurat, the inventor of divisionism.

Fénéon was a contributor to the Symbolist review *Vogue*, and also wrote several important articles for the Brussels publication, *L'Art Moderne* in which he clearly defined the tenets and technique of Neo-Impressionism. He later became a sub-editor on the *Revue Blanche* and in 1900 organised a Seurat retrospective exhibition in connection with the review. At the end of the First World War, he became artistic director of the Bernheim-Jeune Gallery. He was a special friend of Signac, min. He had Cézanne staying with him for two years (1873-1874) and it was in Gachet's house that Cézanne painted *La Maison du pendu*, a turning point in his development as an artist. He also painted the second version of *A Modern Olympia* there, as a kind of parody of Manet's original *Olympia*.

On 21 May 1890 van Gogh went to Auvers on his brother Théo's advice to see Doctor Gachet professionally. The doctor reassured him and told him his illness was not as serious as he had feared. Gachet was very sympathetic and understanding, and he also very much admired van Gogh's painting. His encouragement produced in van Gogh a great rush of creative activity. It was about this time that he painted *Mademoiselle Gachet at the piano*, the famous *Town Hall* and *Auvers church*, and also painted the doctor's portrait. Gachet however had to put up with van Gogh's increasingly violent moods and fits of anger; and it was obvious that his illness was getting very much worse. On 29 July van Gogh shot himself in the chest and died. Gachet said of the paintings he left behind: 'It is irrelevant to speak of his love of art: instead you must speak of his faith, even to the point of martyrdom.' That very day Doctor Gachet made a quick pencil sketch of van Gogh on his deathbed.

Among the most important works of art belonging to the collection of Paul Gachet and now in the Louvre, we should mention Renoir's *A model*, Monet's *The Chrysanthemums*, Cézanne's *A Modern Olympia* and *The house of Doctor Gachet*, Pissarro's *The Road to Louveciennes*, Sisley's *Le Canal Saint-Martin*, and finally van Gogh's *Portrait of Doctor Gachet*, *The Church at Auvers* and the *Self-portrait* of 1890.

GAUDIBERT (second half of the nineteenth century) When Monet was still living at Le Havre, wretched and poverty-stricken, he was asked to take part in an International Maritime exhibition held in that town in 1868. On that occasion Gaudibert, who was to become his patron, commissioned him to paint a portrait of his wife, and this he did at Étretat.

In spite of having won a silver medal at the exhibition at Le Havre, Monet did not suc-

MONET *Portrait of Madame Gaudibert.* 1868

ceed in selling a single picture, and when it came to the last day of the exhibition, several of his creditors tried to seize the pictures to pay his debts. Boudin tells us that the pictures were finally bought by Gaudibert for eighty francs each. Gaudibert realised something of Monet's distress and guaranteed him a small annuity to ensure he got some peace of mind and a certain amount of encouragement in his work.

While living at Fécamp, in September 1868, Manet wrote to Bazille: 'Here I am surrounded by all the things I love. I spend my time in the open air and on the beach . . . of course, I am working hard and I believe that this year I will produce some really serious works. Thanks to this gentleman from Le Havre who helped me, I am now perfectly serene and carefree'.

GEFFROY Gustave (1855-1926) Gustave Geffroy's *History of Impressionism*, published in 1894, and Lecomte's *History* (1892) are the first two general accounts of the Impressionist movement. Both were written to defend the painters in the face of lively opposition, and aimed at converting the public to a better understanding of their work.

Geoffroy was a well-known art critic, with a special interest in Corot and his experiments with light, that in some ways anticipated Impressionism. In an article on Corot as 'painter of woman' he shows how the artist confronts his model as if standing before a landscape, and paints 'her body and clothes as he paints fields and trees and clouds. It is unusual to find a Corot landscape without any human figures.' In 1890 he wrote of Pissarro's work, in *La Vie artistique*: 'no artistic effort is more worthy of respect and more deserving of high praise'; he also much admired Manet, and wrote of *Olympia* that her 'flesh was like flowing light spreading out like a river, from the roots of her hair to the tips of her toes.' He was a great friend of Monet, and in his book *Claude Monet: his life, his times and his work* summed up his artistic achievement in these words: 'No one has been as intent as he was to portray every aspect of nature perfectly on his canvas, and no one has ever surpassed him in breadth, spaciousness or harmony.' Monet, he felt, had found the means of 'summing up all the poetry of the universe in a span.'

Both Cézanne and Eugène Carrière painted portraits of Gustave Geffroy, and there is also a bust of him by Rodin.

RODIN *Bust of Gustave Geffroy.* 1905

GLEYRE Charles (1806-1874) was of Swiss origin, born at Chevilly in the Canton of Vaud. As a young man he travelled in the East and in Italy, and in 1838 settled in Paris, joined the staff of the École des Beaux-Arts, and opened a studio which was attended in 1862 by Monet, Bazille, Sisley and Renoir. The Ecole des Beaux-Arts used to provide free art classes, but as there was no proper system of teaching, a number of the instructors started private courses where pupils could have regular classes and practice, under the teacher of their choice.

Monet began attending Gleyre's studio on the advice of the painter Toulmouche. One day, when the pupils were drawing nude studies from life, Monet's teacher remarked to him: 'Not bad really, but it's too much like the model. You must remember, young man, that when you're painting a figure, you must always bear classical models in mind. Nature is all very well as a subject for study, but it has no intrinsic interest. Nothing really matters but style.' Monet was disgusted. Renoir too refused to paint in an academic style. One day his instructor said 'I suppose you're just painting to enjoy yourself?' 'Well, yes,' Renoir answered, 'I certainly wouldn't paint at all if I didn't enjoy it.' But in spite of minor disagreements most of Gleyre's pupils had a great respect for their master.

In 1864, as his eyesight was deteriorating, Gleyre closed his studio and discontinued his art classes.

GONCOURT Edmond de (1822-1896) and Jules de (1830-1870) Both Goncourt brothers loved painting and they had many artistic and literary tastes in common. They were both writers belonging to the realist school, and believed in portraying 'real life' and working 'from nature'; very soon they developed their own style which they called 'artistic writing'.

They preferred Gavarni (who painted their portrait in 1853) to Daumier, and Gustave Moreau to Manet. They were particularly interested in French eighteenth-century art and wrote monographs on Watteau, Chardin and Fragonard, with the idea of making them generally better known and appreciated; they also helped to popularize Japanese art, which in its turn greatly influenced Impressionism. Artists became enthusiastic about Oriental art

GAVARNI *Portrait of the Goncourt brothers.* 1853

which they had seen at the 1867 Exposition Universelle.

We have special reason to be grateful to the Goncourt brothers for the detailed account of the contemporary world of art in their novel *Manette Salomon*, published in 1866. It tells the life story of a painter in the mid-nineteenth century. The hero, Coriolis, sets out to 'capture the modern aspect of landscape' and 'this new indication of the beauty of a period, an era, an aspect of humanity.' This helps us to understand why Degas admired the Goncourts so much; in fact they help to explain what he was really seeking in his work from 1868 onwards. The dancer on the stage, the music-hall singer, the laundress and the milliner are all manifestations of modern life, that the Goncourts kept urging as a suitable subject for art. Edmond wrote of Degas in his *Journal*: 'Of all the people I have seen so far he is the best at rendering the essence of modern life.'

After his brother's premature death, Edmond went on with the *Journal* they had started writing together, and in it he wrote of Monet: 'One thing specially strikes me—that is, the influence of Jongkind. All the best modern landscape painting is derived from him, borrowing his skies, atmosphere and backgrounds.' In 1869 Monet had gone to live on the banks of the Seine, and Edmond looking back to those days wrote of 'Bougival, the home of modern French landscape where every bend of the river and every willow tree reminds us of some art exhibition.'

HOSCHEDÉ Ernest (1837-1891) The financier Hoschedé was one of the earliest admirers of Impressionist painting. He was the owner of a large Paris department store. He greatly admired the new school of painters and collected a large number of their works, as well as extending hospitality to them in his country house at Montgeron on the outskirts of Paris. In 1876 Manet spent the summer with him; Sisley and Monet both stayed at Montgeron and Hoschedé bought several landscapes that Monet had painted during his visit.

In January 1874 Hoschedé held an auction sale consisting of six Pissarros, three Monets, three Sisleys and two Degas, when the prices fetched were very encouraging. Duret wrote at that time to Pissarro telling him the Hoschedé sale had helped them more than any number of one-man shows.

In June 1878 Hoschedé went bankrupt and the Court ruled that all his pictures should be sold. His collection of five Manets, nine Pissarros, twelve Monets, thirteen Sisleys and nine Renoirs was put up to auction, but this sale was a disaster. Prices had never been so low, the only painting to reach a good sum being Manet's *Woman with a parrot* which went for 700 francs.

Manet *Woman with a Parrot.* 1868

HUYSMANS Joris-Karl (1848-1907) At one time the author Huysmans belonged to the naturalist movement and was a disciple of Zola; later he condemned that movement, having turned to Symbolism, as can be seen in his book *À Rebours*. He was a restless soul, discontented with writing, which he felt had reached 'a dead end', and he finally found comfort in religion. His last two novels *The Cathedral* (1898) and *The Oblate* (1907) show the increasing attraction he felt for mysticism. He was also interested in modern art and poetry, particularly Baudelaire and Verlaine; he enjoyed the poems of Mallarmé whom he often met about 1884 over Impressionists' dinners.

In 1883 Huysmans brought out his *Modern Art*, a collection of articles on the Paris Salons from 1879 to 1881 and the Impressionist exhibitions between 1880 and 1882. He never really understood Impressionism and was much more attracted to 'extraordinary and unique' painters such as Gustave Moreau and Odilon Redon.

In 1879 however he praised the work of Degas and his friends Forain, Mary Cassatt, Raffaelli and Zandomeneghi, as having a real feeling for contemporary life. 'M. Degas,' he wrote 'is a past master in the art of rendering what one might call a civilised complexion,' and by 1881 Huysmans was firmly in favour of the Impressionist painters. 'M. Pissarro,' he wrote, 'has a true artistic temperament. He is a wonderful colourist, and may well be counted among the boldest and most remarkable of our modern artists.' He considered Manet an original and striking painter, approved of Monet's treatment of light and out-of-door subjects; as for Renoir, he thought he had much improved; his recent paintings were more consistent and more truly modern than anything he had done before. 'He is the painter of young women *par excellence*, he renders the bloom of their skin, the soft smoothness of their bodies, their bright eyes and their ele-

ROUAULT *Portrait of Huysmans*

fracted and reflected by creatures and objects.' Contrary to academic tradition, the Impressionist 'sees perspective as made up of innumerable minute touches by a constantly changing quality in the air, never stationary but in continual motion.'

SKARBINA *Portrait of Jules Laforgue.* 1885

gant dresses, in a gay sunny atmosphere.' On Gauguin he wrote that 'among contemporary painters of the nude, no one is more vigorous or more convincing.'

LAFORGUE Jules (1860-1887) Jules Laforgue was a Symbolist poet, born in Montevideo but of Breton parents. He studied in Paris and in 1881 went to Germany as tutor to the Empress. He wrote *Les Complaintes* and also, on the occasion of an exhibition of Impressionist art in Berlin in 1883, published a remarkable 'physiological and aesthetic explanation of Impressionism' which was reprinted in 1903 in *Les Mélanges posthumes*.

Konrad Fiedler's theory of 'pure visuality' had a considerable influence on Laforgue, and the poet wrote: 'The Impressionist is a modern painter who has succeeded in renewing his vision; he sees reality in a living atmosphere of disintegrated forms, endlessly re-

LANE Sir Hugh Percy (1875-1915) was known as a great English collector of modern paintings well before Samuel Courtauld.

He spent some time working with a picture dealer, and in 1898 decided to launch out and open a gallery of his own. He had a flair for discovering new talent and a real love of art, so it was not long before he made his fortune. By 1905 he was recognised as the leading authority on Impressionist painting in England, and an ardent supporter of the Impressionist cause.

His first purchases were two pictures by

MANET *Concert in the Tuileries Gardens.* 1860

Manet, *Concert in the Tuileries* and the *Portrait of Eva Gonzalès*, for which he gave 100,000 and 150,000 francs respectively; *Spring at Louveciennes* by Pissarro and Renoir's *The Umbrellas*. During the following seven years he continued to buy large numbers of pictures, including works by Boudin, Corot, Courbet, Daubigny, Jongkind, Théodore Rousseau, Degas and Vuillard. He died tragically in the wreck of the Lusitania in 1915.

It was not until 1917 that the splendid collection of thirty-nine paintings which he bequeathed to the nation were hung in the National Gallery, being the first Impressionist and Post-Impressionist works to be added to their collection.

MALLARMÉ Stéphane (1842-1898)

Mallarmé was a Symbolist writer, who aimed at comprehending the essence of things and expressing it by means of a new language, 'speaking then,' as René Ghil puts it, 'like a high priest of symbols.'

After spending some time in London, Mallarmé was appointed professor at the Imperial College at Tournon and did not reach Paris until May 1871. In 1875 Mallarmé's translation of Edgar Allan Poe's *The Raven* was published, with woodcuts by Manet. An etching by Gauguin represents the author in profile, with the raven behind him.

Manet's *Portrait of Stéphane Mallarmé* (1876) is a most remarkable picture, illustrating the communion of two great souls united by their common love of art. For many years Mallarmé kept this picture hanging in his Paris dining room at 89 Rue de Rome.

In September 1876 he brought out an article in a London magazine, entitled 'The Impressionists and Édouard Manet'. He spoke of Manet as the apostle of the new school of painting, paid tribute to Zola's criticism and showed keen appreciation of the art of Monet, Sisley and Pissarro. There followed sympathetic accounts of Degas, Berthe Morisot and Renoir, but Cézanne was only just mentioned in passing. This article was his most important contribution to art criticism until the catalogue preface he wrote for an exhibition of Berthe Morisot's paintings.

His influence was greatest from 1884 onwards, when he started the Tuesday gatherings in his flat, attended by numerous writers and artists. Between 1890 and 1894 he also went regularly to the Impressionist dinners that were held every month at the Café Riche.

His article 'The Hanging Committee and M. Manet', published on 12 April 1874 in *La Renaissance artistique et littéraire* made a great stir. The author began: 'The time for the Salon is not far off now, and everyone who is at all interested has been astonished to hear quite suddenly that the Hanging Committee have refused two out of three of the pictures sent by M. Manet.' He went on: 'People will be very much disappointed not to be able to study such an exceptionally gifted artist more thoroughly.' After this, Mallarmé and Manet saw each other every day.

MANET *Portrait of Stéphane Mallarmé.* 1876

There were articles on Berthe Morisot and Edouard Manet in his collection of essays *A few medallions and full-length portraits.* The Berthe Morisot article was used as a preface to the catalogue of a one-man show of her paintings in the Durand-Ruel Gallery from 5 to 23

March 1896, a year after Mallarmé's death. The pages about Manet are typical of Mallarmé's poetic imagination: 'The artlessness of a satyr in a putty-coloured coat; fair hair and beard, hair getting thin and greying . . . and in the studio, a sort of bewildered fury that used to hurl him towards his empty canvas, as if he had never painted anything before.'

MANTZ Paul (1821-1895) Paul Mantz was an art critic who wrote regular commentaries on the *Salons* each year from 1845 to 1891. He was extremely outspoken in his opinions, saying he did not care for Ingres or Couture or Vernet, but liked Corot, Théodore Rousseau and Delacroix. Other favourites of his were Michelangelo and Watteau. His article 'The 1865 Salon', which came out in the *Gazette des Beaux-Arts*, deals with Monet. He notes how Monet had attracted attention by his boldness, his main quality being his 'harmonious colour schemes with matching tones'; he then went on: 'He has broken with academic methods and fashionable refinements, but responds to the unspoilt charm of nature in a quite simple uncomplicated way, and then registers his impressions in all their intensity and freshness.'

MARX Roger (1859-1913) was an art critic and collector, and the author of *Masters of yesterday and today* (1914) which was not published until after his death, and contained a chapter on Monet's series of *Waterlilies* paintings. He imagines the paintings decorating a drawing-room and declares (prophetically, as it so happened) that 'if they were stretched end to end along the walls, covering the sides of the room continuously until they merged into one, they would give the impression of an endless unity, an ocean without shores and without horizon.' And still in this poetic vein, he speaks of 'this sanctuary of meditation and stillness, in the midst of a pool full of flowers.'

Marx was a great admirer of Gauguin's, and in 1891 in *Le Voltaire* he wrote an enthusiastic article on his work, commenting on

Renoir. In 1904 he published a work on Lautrec, Gauguin, Neo-Impressionism and Japanese prints, and in the same year, in Stuttgart, he brought out his first *General History of Art*, where all the Impressionists are individually and favourably mentioned. *The Impressionists*, published in 1906, contains chapters on Manet, van Gogh, Pissarro and Cézanne.

MIRBEAU Octave (1848-1917)

Octave Mirbeau wrote realistic novels, such as *A Housemaid's Diary*, but was also a fervent supporter of Impressionism.

In 1891 he got to know Pissarro, and wrote of him: 'He knows why he paints and what he paints, and speaks as a technician and a philosopher. And he also has a broad and consistent idea of the social rôle of the artist.'

CARRIÈRE *Portrait of Roger Marx*

RODIN *Octave Mirbeau*. 1895

his 'supreme power of vision and expression' 'giving the example of an unusual decorative talent, united to a brilliant intelligence.'

For the 1900 Centenary Exhibition, he collected together a large number of paintings by artists not all yet generally recognized—sixteen Manet, seven Degas, fourteen Monet, eleven Renoir, eight Sisley, seven Pissarro, as well as works by Cézanne, Gauguin, Redon, Seurat and Berthe Morisot. The public thus had an excellent opportunity of judging the progress made in French painting over the last hundred years.

MEIER-GRAEFE Julius (1867-1935)

Meier-Graefe, a German art critic, was the author of a number of publications on Impressionism which helped to make the movement known in Germany. In 1902 in Berlin he published a book on *Manet and his circle* with studies of Monet, Pissarro, Cézanne and

In the same year he wrote an enthusiastic article in favour of auctioning thirty of Gauguin's pictures. They fetched thirty thousand francs in the sale, which made it possible for Gauguin to go to Tahiti.

In an article in the review *l'Art dans les Deux Mondes* published by Durand-Ruel, Mirbeau expressed the opinion that of all painters, Monet was perhaps the one who appealed most to poets. He spoke of his 'incomparable genius' and the 'delightful intellectual surprises' awaiting anyone 'wandering with him through the nature he has created anew'.

As for Pissarro, he declared that 'the artist's eye, as well as his thought, discovers the greatness of things, their tones and their harmony.' Mirbeau believed that Pissarro was one of the first artists to understand and introduce that great 'happening' of contemporary painting: that is, light.

MONFREID Georges Daniel de (1856-1929) was a painter, and after meeting Gauguin at the beginning of 1889, he became a regular member of his group. He helped Gauguin in his financial difficulties and bought several of his paintings, as well as lending him his studio so that he could go on working.

Monfreid exhibited three paintings at Volpini's at the same time as Gauguin, Schuffenecker and Émile Bernard. He became a member of the Nabis group, and exhibited at the Salon des Indépendants in March 1891.

He and Gauguin kept up a long correspondence during the time the artist was in Tahiti, and Monfreid undertook the difficult task of looking after Gauguin's affairs in Paris for him during his absence.

MOORE George (1852-1933) In 1873 a young Irishman, George Moore, arrived in Paris to study painting under Cabanel. He spent a short time at the Jullian academy, but after a few years gave up art to devote himself

MONFREID *Self Portrait.* 1902

MANET *George Moore at the Café de la Nouvelle-Athènes. c.* 1879

entirely to writing. He soon became a familiar figure among the Impressionists and went regularly to the Nouvelle-Athènes, of which he has given a vivid description in his *Reminiscences of Impressionist Painters*. There he met Degas and Manet, joining in their conversations and being captivated by Manet, who in 1879 or thereabouts did a delightful sketch of Moore sitting at a table in the famous Parisian Café. In his book, Moore speaks of Manet's delicate features and his outspoken way of talking; he was inclined to hold forth rather, when he was excited. He spoke of Degas' lively wit and penetrating intelligence, coupled with a rather aloof, supercilious and sarcastic manner. Pissarro, he said, 'reminded him of Abraham. He had a very sweet nature; he was much more reserved than the others, a good listener who said very little, except now and then to show his approval of various ideas that came up in the long café conversations.' Moore was struck by Renoir's dislike of the nineteenth century; he was however impressed by his devotion to what he called his 'craft'.

Moore also wrote *Confessions of a young man*, published in 1888, which was full of lively anecdotes about Impressionist painters, especially Manet and Degas. There is also an interesting account of Monet, Sisley, Pissarro and the decline of Impressionism in his book *Modern Painting*, and his recollections of Degas come into *Impressions and Opinions*. The reminiscences of his young days in Paris spent among artists give a frank and vivid account of life among the Impressionist painters.

MANET *Le Bon Bock*. 1872

MOREAU-NÉLATON Étienne (1859-1927) was the biographer of Corot, Jongkind and Daubigny. He brought out a book called *Manet by himself* with accounts of the artist's vocation, his professional training, his disappointments at the Salon and his passion for Spain; then his friendship with Baudelaire and Zola, Durand-Ruel's first purchases of his works and the success of his painting *Le Bon Bock* (*The Glass of Beer*), followed by his being awarded the Légion d'honneur; in short, all the outstanding events in his often difficult life, right up to the time of his recognition after his death. 'Thanks be to this creator of visions of peace and calm' the author exclaims in the last few lines of the book.

In 1907 Moreau-Nélaton bequeathed his fine collection of paintings to the State. It comprised a group of nineteenth century paintings and drawings by Delacroix, Ingres, Corot, Courbet, Boudin, Jongkind, Manet, Pissarro, Sisley, Berthe Morisot and Monet.

MOROSOV Ivan (1870-1921) was a Russian art collector of discriminating taste. The Impressionists and Post-Impressionists were his special favourites and he had a fine collection of their paintings bought over a period of about ten years. He and his compatriot Serge Shchukin are chiefly responsible for the wonderful collections of Impressionist art in the Hermitage Museum in Leningrad and the Pushkin museum in Moscow.

Morosov particularly admired Cézanne and owned eighteen of his pictures, including *Still life with a sugar basin* and the *Road in front of the montagne Sainte-Victoire*. In his collection there were also paintings by Monet, Renoir's

RENOIR *Portrait of Jeanne Samary*. 1877

Woman with a fan and *Child with a whip*, several good Gauguins and van Goghs, among them the famous *Prisoners' round*.

MURER Eugène (1845-1906) Eugène Meunier better known as Murer, owned a tea-room at 95 Boulevard Voltaire with a restaurant attached, where Guillaumin, Renoir, Sisley, Pissarro, Monet and Père Tanguy were among his regular customers. They used to give Murer pictures now and then to thank him for the meals he offered them, and he also acquired a good number of their paintings in the regular way. He commissioned Renoir, for instance, to paint portraits of himself, his son Paul and his half-sister

Maria. An article Paul Alexis wrote in 1887 mentions Murer's collection as including eight Cézannes, twenty-five Pissarros, ten Monets, twenty-eight Sisleys, twenty-two Guillaumins and sixteen Renoirs including his *Portrait of Sisley*, *Confidences* and *l'Ingénue*.

About 1883 he left Paris and went to Rouen

RENOIR *Confidence*. 1878

where he opened the 'Hôtel du Dauphin et d'Espagne'; near the front door there was a poster informing customers that an Impressionist exhibition, including thirty paintings by Renoir, was being held inside.

Towards the end of his life Eugène Murer took up painting and also wrote several novels. His first one-man show of 172 canvases was held in 1895, and the second, at Vollard's, in 1898. His art collection was sold by private treaty and dispersed after his death in 1906.

NADAR Tournachon Félix, better known as (1820-1910). Nadar was a well-known photographer, writer and designer, who was much involved in the literary and artistic life of the period.

In the nineteenth century a general change and renewal occurred in the field of vision, largely due to the discovery of photography. People, and artists especially, began to see things differently: light became the overruling principle and motion appeared under a completely new aspect.

DAUMIER *Nadar raising Photography to the height of an art*

With Nadar, photography became an art, just as much as painting, and his portraits of Baudelaire, Delacroix, Courbet, Corot, Constantin Guys, Daumier, Manet and Monet, among many other famous men, are invaluable as historical documents.

In 1869 he began to go regularly to the Café Guerbois to meet his friends, the future Impressionists. Later he was very generous to them, among other things lending them the studios in his large second-floor flat in the Boulevard des Capucines, for their first exhibition. This ran from 15 April to 15 May 1874, and all thirty painters whose work had been turned down for the Salon now exhibited their paintings—165 canvases. The exhibition proved well worth while both financially and artistically.

NATANSON Alexandre (1867-1936) and Thadée (1868-1951) The Natanson brothers were close friends of the Nabis and Toulouse-Lautrec, and founded the *Revue Blanche* together in 1891. The contributors to the review, which was definitely left-wing and anti-bourgeois in outlook, included Tristan

TOULOUSE-LAUTREC *La revue blanche.* 1895

Bernard, Jules Renard, Félix Fénéon, Romain Carolus and Paul Leclercq.

In 1895, when the *Revue Blanche* moved its

offices to the Rue Laffitte, Vuillard, Bonnard and then Toulouse-Lautrec, who played a specially active part, joined the group.

Alexandre Natanson married the actress Marie Mellot, and Lautrec designed one of his first posters, *La Gitane*, for her. Thadée married Missia Godebski, a cultivated and musical woman; Lautrec was devoted to her, and used her as his model for the *Revue Blanche* poster in 1895. Thadée Natanson's *Reminiscences* are a valuable source of information for the last ten years of Lautrec's life.

PROUST Antonin (1832-1905) In 1846 Antonin Proust met Manet while attending

MANET *Portrait of Antonin Proust.* 1880

drawing classes at the Collège Rollin near the Panthéon, and became one of his greatest friends. In 1850 Manet took him to Thomas Couture's studio, and later on Proust in his *Reminiscences* recalls the uneasy tension be-

tween Manet and his teacher. Manet and Proust often met at the Café Guerbois, and went together to visit Delacroix in 1857.

Manet painted his friend's portrait which was hung in the fifth Impressionist exhibition. On 14 November 1881 Gambetta appointed Proust as Minister for Fine Arts; one of his first actions was to acquire a series of Courbet paintings for the State.

VAN GOGH *Portrait of Alexander Reid.* 1886-1888

REID Alexander, lived in the second half of the nineteenth century, and Great Britain owes him a debt of gratitude for his strenuous advocacy of contemporary French painting. His father was a well-known goldsmith in Glasgow, who set up as an art dealer in a small way in the eighties, and in 1886 sent his son to Paris to learn the business. He was articled to the firm of Boussod-Valadon (formerly

Goupil), one of the most influential art galleries in Paris, where Théo van Gogh, Vincent's brother, was also working. This soon gave him the opportunity of meeting avantgarde artists and getting to know their work. He painted a little himself and through Théo, became a friend of Vincent van Gogh who shared his enthusiasm for Monticelli.

Van Gogh painted two portraits of Reid, one in 1886 and another in 1887, but it was not long before the two men quarrelled over Vincent's proposal of a suicide pact which Reid rejected, thus breaking up the friendship. He then went back to Glasgow and in 1891 opened an art gallery there, appropriately named 'Société des Beaux-Arts'. He had brought back from Paris a substantial collection of paintings by Monticelli, artists of the Barbizon school, Corot, Courbet, Daumier, Boudin, Degas and van Gogh. Soon after, he moved to London and in 1892 held an exhibition of paintings by the great French Impressionists at Collie's gallery.

RIVIÈRE Georges, who lived in the second half of the nineteenth century, was father-in-law to Cézanne's son and a good friend to the Impressionists, particularly to Renoir.

In 1877 he published four numbers of an art review called *l'Impressionniste*, timed to coincide with the third Impressionist exhibition. He wrote most of the articles himself, defending the new school of painting and replying to unfavourable criticism.

He explained that his friends took the name 'Impressionist' to let the public know there would be no *genre* painting and no historical, biblical or oriental pictures in the exhibition. 'What distinguishes Impressionists from other painters,' he wrote, 'is the way they deal with a subject for its tonalities and not just for the subject itself.' He then went on to give an account of the personalities and distinguishing traits of the various artists—Renoir's happy, witty nature; Monet's penetration, and the supreme technique of Degas who 'never exaggerates but always obtains his effects by being faithful to nature', the epic quality of Pissarro, and Sisley's great delicacy of composition and treatment. As for Cézanne, he

wrote: 'his landscapes have a compelling majesty, and his beautiful still lifes have a deep solemn quality of truth.'

In his painting *Le Moulin de la Galette* (1876) Renoir has put his friend Rivière in among the

RENOIR *Georges Rivière and Margot in the studio.* 1876

crowd in the popular dance hall at Montmartre, and he also painted his portrait with Margot, in 1876.

ROUART Henri (1833-1912) Henri Rouart was an engineer, a painter and art collector whose name will always be connected with that of Degas. He and Degas were

ROUART *The Terrace. c.* 1880

at school together in Paris at the lycée Louis-le-Grand, always remained firm friends, and during the 1870 war they were in the same artillery regiment.

In 1874, when the Impressionists decided to turn themselves into the 'Société Anonyme des artistes peintres, sculpteurs et graveurs', Degas had the idea of also getting some less controversial painters as members, whose works would not be so objectionable to the public. So from 1874 to 1881, Rouart showed his pictures at the various group exhibitions. After his death, his large collection of Impressionist paintings was sold, between 9 and 18 December 1912. Among other works it comprised five Cézannes, five each by Manet and Monet, five Pissarros and three Renoirs.

Rouart's son Ernest married the daughter of Berthe Morisot and Eugène Manet.

SILVESTRE Armand (1837-1901) Armand Silvestre was an art critic, and in his reminiscences *Au pays des souvenirs* he recalled the gatherings at the Café Guerbois he so often went to, and the authors and artists he knew

there, Manet and Zola, Desboutin, Duranty, Degas and Fantin-Latour.

In 1873, Durand-Ruel decided to draw up a complete catalogue of the works in his gallery, and asked Armand Silvestre to write the preface. Silvestre took the opportunity to praise the new painting, and described three of the great landscape painters in some detail. 'M. Monet, the most skilful and the most daring; M. Sisley, the most timid but the most harmonious, and M. Pissarro, the most genuine and the most unaffected. All these artists show the influence of Japanese art especially when they paint springtime, golden evenings and apple blossom, a river laden with passing boats and the sky streaked by light wreaths of mist.'

In 1876 at the time of the second Impressionist exhibition, Silvestre summed up the work of these Impressionist innovators who 'will most certainly find a place in the history of contemporary art.' He praised their concern for 'accuracy' and 'elemental harmonies', Pissarro's 'delightfully delicate blues', Degas with his 'truthful studies of life behind the scenes', and Renoir who paints 'flesh in deliciously rosy tints.'

SHCHUKIN Serge was an importer of oriental fabrics, who became an generous patron of the arts. With his unusual discrimination and taste and his large fortune, he was able to buy a great many Impressionist paintings by Monet, Sisley, Renoir and Pissarro; he also enjoyed the Neo-Impressionists, and

After the Russian Revolution Shchukin went to live in Paris and was often seen at art exhibitions. He was no longer a rich man, but he had the satisfaction of knowing he had assembled one of the finest collections of modern French painting in existence. In 1949 it was divided between the Pushkin Museum and the Hermitage.

MATISSE *Portrait of Shchukin*

bought paintings by Cézanne, including *Shrove Tuesday* and *The Lady in blue*, Gauguin, and van Gogh. In fact he was one of the first to appreciate their individuality and genius. He also recognized Henri Rousseau's talent, and commissioned several pictures from Matisse, including *Dance and Music* which he wanted to decorate the walls of the splendid Troubetzkoi Palace in Moscow which he owned. It must have been extraordinarily beautiful, its walls hung with pictures by Matisse and Puvis de Chavannes, Whistler and Carrière.

TABARANT Adolphe (1863-1950) Adolphe Tabarant's writings are of very great importance in the history of the Impressionist movement. He wrote a number of books on Manet, whom he admired enormously; one of the best-known being *Manet and his works* (1947) which gives a detailed day by day account of the poet's life, together with a description of his works, taken individually. His *Catalographic History*, published in 1931, lists all Manet's work with exemplary perseverance and dedication; his *Unpublished correspondence of Edouard Manet* includes the letters he wrote during the siege of Paris and those written during a journey in Spain.

Tabarant also wrote a *Biography of Pissarro* (1924) and a study on *Artistic life at the time of Baudelaire* (1942) in which he gives an account of early Impressionism. He wrote poetry as well as being an art historian, and among his other works, produced a series of verses on van Gogh, Gauguin and Renoir.

TANGUY Julien, known as le Père (1825-1894) started life as a plasterer and then worked on the railways before 1870; later he was a travelling salesman of painters' materials, and in this way met Pissarro, Monet and Renoir when they were working outside Paris. As a militant partisan of the Commune of 1871, he was arrested by the Versailles army and sent to a concentration camp at Satory. He was then court-martialled and narrowly escaped death through the intervention of Degas' friend Rouart.

After returning to Paris, he opened a shop for supplying artists' materials at 14 Rue Clauzel, and from 1873 onwards was an enthusiastic supporter of the Impressionists—

'The School' as he called them. He gave them canvases and paints and they gave him pictures in exchange. In this way he accumulated a large number of paintings by van Gogh, Monet, Sisley, Pissarro, Cézanne and Gauguin, but he had the greatest difficulty in selling them even though the prices he asked were ridiculously low.

VAN GOGH *Portrait of Père Tanguy*. 1886

Pissarro introduced him to Cézanne, and from 1877 to 1893 his shop was the only place in Paris where Cézanne's work could be seen. Van Gogh's friends took him to see Père Tanguy, and the two became close friends. Tanguy bought van Gogh's paintings to help him, and eventually came to admire his paintings as much as he did Cézanne's.

Van Gogh's *Portrait of Père Tanguy* shows him as a man of the people, wearing a Breton hat, with wide powerful shoulders and a stubborn-looking face. In the background of the picture can be seen some Japanese prints hanging on the wall.

After Tanguy's death in 1894, an auction of his pictures was held. There were six Gauguins, one Monet, three Pissarros, one Seurat, two Sisleys, two van Goghs and six Cézannes.

THORÉ-BÜRGER (1807-1868) Théophile Thoré was an author and critic. In 1849, when he was in exile for eleven years, he took the name of William Bürger. From 1844 to 1848 he wrote a series of reviews on the *Salons* and resumed them after his return to Paris in 1860, the second series running from 1861 to 1868.

Bürger is generally acknowledged as the leading realist art critic of the period, who saw art as an expression of man's love of nature and of the harmony of his surroundings. 'Art' he wrote 'arises from the impression nature produces on man, and by the reflection of the outside world in the microcosm, in the small world we carry within ourselves.' He believed 'the ideal consists not in the subject, but in the way it is painted,' and was deeply involved in the upheaval in the world of art during the Second Empire, which culminated in 1863 in the *Salon des Refusés*. He felt that naturalism, combined with a sense of humanity, could well take the place of 'old hat classical and mythological stuff' that the official Salon favoured. He was a close friend of Théodore Rousseau, whom he considered the greatest landscape painter of his time, and also much admired Corot. Other painters he approved of were Courbet and Manet, then at the beginning of his career. In his *Salons* articles of 1866 and 1878 he drew particular attention to exhibits by Manet, Degas, Renoir, Monet, Bazille and Pissarro. He was especially struck by Monet's 'opulent' style of painting and picked out his portrait of *Camille* as outstanding. 'It was time for the Salon to open' he wrote in 1866, 'and there was Camille, coming in from picking violets, with her long grass-green train and her velvet jacket. Now Camille is immortal; she is called the *Woman in a green dress*.' At the same Salon he also noticed a landscape of Monet's, *The way to Barbizon* (Forest of Fontainebleau) and 'the evening sun lighting up the great trees.' 'When someone is really a painter' he com-

MONET · *Woman with a Green Dress*. 1866

mented, 'he can do anything he likes.' He was struck too by Renoir, who was beginning to show his true character in *Lise* (1867), where Bürger noticed particularly his treatment of contrasting tonalities and his use of colour in shadows: 'her white gauze dress lightly

shaded with green from the reflection of the leaves, and her head and neck in delicate subdued light under her sunshade.' 'We may be surprised at the natural effect of the picture because we are so used to depicting nature in conventional colours, but,' he went on rather cautiously, 'surely colour depends on the surrounding atmosphere?' Here Bürger is anticipating Impressionist theory and ideas.

TSCHUDI Hugo von (1851-1911) He was director of the National Gallery at Berlin, and is chiefly known, together with Liebermann and Meier-Graefe, for having introduced contemporary French painting into Germany, especially Manet and the Impressionists. In 1899 he had several Impressionist paintings hung in the gallery, including Manet's *In the greenhouse* and *Conversation* by Degas; as well as pictures by Renoir, Pissarro, Monet and Sisley, and a landscape by Cézanne. There was a great public outcry

Portrait of Hugo von Tschudi

at the time, and the Emperor William II then announced that he would be visiting the gallery, as he wanted to see for himself what all the fuss was about. Von Tschudi was prepared to take the consequences of what he foresaw might be a stormy interview, but at the last moment he took the precaution of withdrawing the Cézanne, as in 1874 the artist had been labelled an 'anarchist painter'. The Emperor, as expected, did not care for the Impressionist pictures and had them removed from the first floor gallery where they were, and relegated to the second floor.

However von Tschudi pluckily continued to defend modern French painting in spite of violent opposition.

VOLLARD Ambroise (1865–1939)
Ambroise Vollard was born in the Island of Réunion, and as a young man went to Paris to study law. He then became assistant to a picture dealer, and in 1893 opened a gallery of his own in Rue Laffitte. He began buying pictures by Cézanne, whose 'magic' name he had heard through Pissarro, and finally acquired about two hundred canvases for which he paid something between eighty and ninety thousand francs.

In the autumn of 1895 he organised his first exhibition containing nothing but Cézanne's works, with fifty paintings on view. There was a general outcry, and he had to withdraw the pictures from his shop window because of public opposition. However several real art-lovers like Auguste Pellerin and Count Isaac de Camondo encouraged him, and Vollard became a celebrity almost overnight, and the centre of the art world in Paris. Gertrude Stein's first visit to his gallery in 1904 made an unforgettable impression on her. 'It is an incredible place,' she wrote, 'not a bit like an ordinary picture gallery. When you go in you see several pictures face to the wall, in a corner a pile of canvases accumulated all one on top of the other, and in the middle of the room a great tall black man with a melancholy expression; this was Vollard.'

All his friends painted his portrait: Cézanne, Renoir twice, in 1908 and 1917, Bonnard and Picasso.

In 1896 he wrote to Gauguin, then in Tahiti, suggesting an arrangement by which he would undertake to buy any pictures he painted. Gauguin agreed, and Vollard thus became dealer for both Cézanne and Gau-

RENOIR *Portrait of Vollard*. 1908

guin. In 1901 he arranged the first Picasso exhibition, three years later the first of Matisse, and in the same year he exhibited 150 of van Dongen's paintings. Between 1905 and 1906 he contracted to buy all Derain and Vlaminck's pictures.

He was not only an art dealer; he also wrote several books, including *Reminiscences of an art dealer* and a book on Cézanne. He was an ardent bibliophile and had something like thirty books illustrated by the foremost artists of the day; these include Verlaine's *Parallèle-*

ment with lithographs by Bonnard, and *La Maison Tellier* by Guy de Maupassant with monotypes by Degas.

CÉZANNE *Portrait of Ambroise Vollard.* 1899

ZOLA Émile (1840-1902) Émile Zola spent his youth in Aix-en-Provence where his father was an engineer. He and Cézanne were at school together and became friends, and the two met again in Paris in 1861 when Zola went there to live. About 1866 he started going to the Café Guerbois and met the group of painters who later developed into the Impressionists.

Zola was a critic for *l'Événement* and published an article there defending Manet. In 1866 he wrote a series of articles on the Salon of that year, in which he attacked the Hanging Committee violently: 'I admit quite calmly that I intend to admire M. Manet,' he wrote, 'and today I am showing it by publicly shaking hands with the artist whom some of his fellow-artists have just sent away and refused admission to the Salon.' He went on:

'Monsieur Manet's place is waiting for him at the Louvre, as it would for any artist with a strong and original temperament like his.' Writing about realism in connection with the same 1866 Salon, he said the word meant nothing to him: 'I declare that for me, reality

MANET *Portrait of Émile Zola.* 1868

must depend on character.' According to him the artist must 'be absolutely devoted, body and soul . . . he must have the kind of character that will take nature boldly in both hands and put it straight down in front of us, just as he sees it.' These articles caused such an uproar among the paper's readers that Zola had to discontinue them.

On the occasion of the Manet exhibition held in connection with the 1867 Exposition Universelle, Zola published *A new method in painting: Monsieur Edouard Manet* in which he explains that Manet's art is compounded of accuracy and simplicity. Manet had to start right at the beginning with exact observation, as some of his colleagues were so incredibly stupid. Zola was determined to get his message across; knowing that what he called 'a complete education' was needed before genius could be accepted, he pressed on with his campaign to defend the Impressionists, and wrote another series of articles paying tribute to Monet, Renoir and Pissarro. His writings are directed against authors and painters who refuse to move with the times, and against critics who reject anything new, in the name of arbitrary rules or even from sheer laziness. His violent attacks really only depended on his wish to safeguard his naturalistic ideas, and about 1868, he began to have serious doubts about the painters he had been defending. By 1880 he was opposing the whole theory of Impressionism, and in 1886 quarrelled with Cézanne over the publication of his novel *L'Œuvre*.

In spite of this, we have to recognize that between 1866 and 1868, Zola was one of the few who showed real understanding of Manet at a time when almost everyone else was against him.

The Verdict of the Sale-room

'Get this into your head, no one really knows anything about it. There's only one indicator for telling the value of paintings and that is the sale-room.'

This sounds like blasphemy. You wonder who can have said such a thing—an auctioneer perhaps or an art dealer, or a financier who doesn't know any better. No; actually it was Renoir who said it and when he says 'value' he really does mean aesthetic value, not value in monetary terms. Some people may object and say Renoir was just trying to be funny; after all, he did enjoy paradoxical statements. They are wrong though to protest, because Renoir, in recognizing the competence of the Hôtel Drouot, is merely being shrewed and sensible. If he had left the verdict to contemporary critics, and depended on what official mandarins and arbiters of taste had said at the time, he and his Impressionist friends would have come off very badly and lost their case. The sale-room public thought otherwise, although the Impressionists did have to appeal more than once before the final verdict was reached in their favour.

1870-1880: Contempt

We have taken 1870 as the starting point for our study. We could of course have chosen 1865 or 1874, but 1870 seemed best for several reasons. Most of the future Impressionists were in their thirties: Cézanne and Sisley were thirty-one, Monet thirty and Renoir twenty-nine. Pissarro, Manet and Degas were thirty-nine, thirty-eight and thirty-six respectively, all about the age when they might reasonably expect to be making a living from their painting. But one cannot say that collectors were exactly falling over each other to buy their works.

Since the *Olympia* scandal at the 1865 Salon, Manet has earned a solid reputation with the public—a reputation for playing practical jokes. He sold his canvases for relatively large sums—for instance in 1870 the critic Théodore Duret paid him 1200 francs (£864)[1] for a minor work, *Le Toréro saluant*—but he sold very few. Degas had a slightly better reputation, and in 1869 he felt able to refuse a contract that would have meant an annual sum of 12,000 francs (£8,682). Pissarro, who was then considered to be a disciple of Corot, did succeed in selling a few

---

1 The figures in brackets are the approximate 1978 sterling equivalents of the prices stated in French francs, dollars or guineas. They do not necessarily represent today's sale-room values.

paintings, but on the other hand Sisley and Renoir were very hard up, while Monet was almost starving and had not enough to buy the paints he needed. In September 1869 he wrote: 'I am in despair. I have just sold a still life which means I've been able to work a little—but as usual now I am stuck for lack of paints.'

Fortunately Durand-Ruel appeared at the crucial moment, and in 1871 bought his first Monet. He then took an interest in Pissarro, Degas, Manet and Renoir. It is true he did not pay vast sums: from 400 to 3000 francs (£265 to £2005) for Manets, 800 francs (£531) for Degas, 300 francs (£200) for Monets, 200 francs (£133) for Pissarro, Renoir and Sisley. But as he wrote in his *Memoirs*: 'No one else would have been so generous, because after I had to stop buying, they had to let other people have them at a hundred francs, and then fifty or even less.' Paul Durand-Ruel was not exaggerating. It was quite true that when he was in serious financial difficulties and had to reduce his purchases of Impressionist pictures, the artists had to let their paintings go elsewhere at ridiculously low prices. The sale they got up in 1875 was a disaster, and the same could be said of the Hoschedé sale in 1878, when a Manet could be bought for 315 francs (£212), a Monet for 60 francs (£41), a Renoir for 31 francs (£21), a Sisley for 21 francs (£14) and a Pissarro for 7 francs (£5).

1880-1892: Hope

At the end of 1879 the Impressionists' financial position seemed to be hopeless, but a year or two later things were looking up and there was cause for guarded optimism. There were several reasons for this.

First, the great success of Renoir's *Portrait of Mme. Charpentier and her children* in the 1879 Salon. The success did perhaps depend more on Mme. Charpentier being so well-known as the wife of a fashionable publisher, than on Renoir's talent. But the fact remains he was paid 1500 francs (£1035) for the portrait, and became a popular painter among the well-to-do.

The next reason is the financial help afforded to Durand-Ruel by the manager of the bank l'Union générale, so that he was able to resume buying from the Impressionists. He still paid roughly the same prices as in 1874, but the artists now knew they could count on regular payments. Unfortunately this did not last long, as the Union générale went bankrupt in 1882 and Durand-Ruel was back in his usual financial muddle.

In 1883 he did however manage to get up several one-man shows devoted to Impressionist painters. Renoir's was only moderately successful, Monet's was disappointing, while Pissarro's and Sisley's were complete failures.

Manet died in 1883. He came from a prosperous background but died a poor man, and the accumulation of canvases he left in his studio had to be sold to pay his debts. The much-esteemed critic in the *Figaro*, Albert Wolff, prophesied that the sale (to be held in February 1884) would be a complete failure, but the results surpassed all hopes, and although *Olympia* had to be withdrawn as it did not reach the reserve of 10,000 francs (£7285), the total for the sale was 116,637 francs (£84,728). Eighty-nine paintings, forty-one studies and forty pastels were sold, as well as a number of drawings.

Gradually the Impressionists began to make their mark. An unmistakable sign was when Georges Petit, the recognised art dealer for academic painters, began to admit them to his magnificent gallery; in 1885 Monet exhibited there with considerable success. In the following year Petit managed to sell several Monets, some for as much as 1200 francs (£864). From 1886 to 1890 Monet was increasingly successful, and in 1890 he was actually able to buy the house at Giverny he had been renting. The following year he exhibited his series of *Haystack* paintings, at the Durand-Ruel Gallery, and only three days after the opening they were all sold. Prices ranged from 3000 (£2278) to 4000 francs (£3032).

The same thing happened with Renoir. In 1885 his *Mme. Charpentier and her children* was shown at Georges Petit's, and in 1892, when his one-man show at Durand-Ruel's opened, the occasion, according to Frantz Jourdain, 'was little short of an apotheosis'. The Government actually commissioned a picture from him.

Also in 1892, and again in Durand-Ruel's gallery, a Pissarro exhibition was a very great success, with a large number of pictures sold at between 1500 and 6000 francs (£1126 and £4508). Only Sisley was ignored and of course the two 'accursed ones' as people called them, Cézanne and van Gogh. By the time van Gogh died in 1890 he had only managed to sell one of his paintings at a reasonable price, his *Red vines at Arles*, which the sister of a Belgian artist friend of van Gogh's bought for 400 francs (£292) only a few months before his suicide.

1892-1899: The break-through of the rear-guard

After 1892 Monet, Renoir, Degas and Pissarro had all more or less established a reputation and as time went by, their rating slowly but surely improved. But what is more remarkable about the period 1892-1899, is that works by hitherto neglected Impressionists such as Sisley, Cézanne and van Gogh now began to fetch respectable prices. These two points, the discovery of neglected artists and consolidation of those already known are what we need to remember about this period.

It is not very easy to give a scale showing the increase in prices for Monet, Renoir, Degas and Pissarro although one can of course pick out of a few record prices; but while these figures often show a rise in prices, they can only reflect the exceptionally high quality of the paintings sold. It would perhaps be better to follow the prices of a few pictures sold in 1892 and again in 1899. But as so few 1892 prices are available, we have had to go further back to make our comparison; here are two examples:

> *The Harbour at Honfleur* by Monet
> 28 January 1881　　72 francs (£52)
> 1 July 1899　　2550 francs (£1926)
> 　　　　Increase: 3603%

> *The Toilet* by Renoir
> 24 March 1874　　140 francs (£96)
> 19 March 1894　　4900 francs (£3690)
> 　　　　Increase: 3744%

Thus since the earlier 'period of neglect', the value of certain paintings by Monet and Renoir increased by over thirty-five times.

And the fact that the collectors were actually discovering painters so far neglected is made clear by some of the prices realised in the sale rooms. In 1897 two works by Sisley, *The Road to Louveciennes, snow scene* and *The Flood*, were sold respectively for 4600 francs (£3482) and 3100 francs (£2326); in 1899 *Thawing snow in the forest of Fontainebleau* by Cézanne fetched 6750 francs (£5087); and in 1900 the *Hollyhocks* by van Gogh found a buyer at 1100 francs (£829).

1899-1930: Ups and downs of fame

The death of Sisley in 1899 marks the beginning of a very great increase in the prices paid for Impressionist pictures, so this date can be taken as the starting-point of a period of real triumph for the Impressionists, after the failures and neglect of previous years.

It seems only right that prices for Sisley's works should have been among the first to go up. A year after his death, his *Flood at Port-Marly* was knocked down to the Count de Camondo for 43,000 francs (£32,415), which would have been quite inconceivable four years previously.

We can obtain a pretty good idea of what to expect if we follow the prices given for some of Sisley's paintings which were sold in the few years immediately preceding his death and then re-sold a few years later. For instance, between March 1894 and December 1905, his *View of the Thames at Hampton Court* increased in value by 449%; between April 1894 and May 1900, the *Road to Les Sablons* increased by 525%, and between February 1897 and March 1900, *First snow at Veneux-Nadon* by 344%. So in less than ten years, prices of Sisley's paintings have gone up between four and six times.

The year 1899 was a good one for most of the Impressionists. When Count Armand Doria's collection was dispersed in May of that year, Renoir's *La Pensée* was knocked down at 22,000 francs (£20,861); Renoir was believed to have sold it to Doria originally, less than twenty years earlier, for 150 francs (£103). At the same sale, *The Photographer* by Degas fetched 22,850 francs (£17,169).

To their contemporaries, these 'absurd' prices were merely symptoms of collective madness, and they were sure it would all end in a great crash. This was actually what Renoir thought himself. Writing to a friend in 1903, he said: 'I am quite disgusted with painting. These ridiculous inflated prices have made everyone crazy, and everyone is selling.' Looking back, these 'inflated prices' do seem 'ridiculous' to us, but not in the sense Renoir intended, when we compare them with prices in about 1930. For after 1899, Impressionist prices went up and up. Records were broken one after another. On the eve of the outbreak of war in 1914, it was not only the 'safe investments' like Degas, Monet and Renoir, that had reached fantastic prices, but even the 'accursed' ones ('les maudits') like Cézanne and van Gogh had become so-called 'expensive painters'. But let the prices speak for themselves. In 1912, *Dancers at the bar* by Degas fetched 435,000 francs (£381,921); the following year a *Still life* by van Gogh went for 35,200 francs (£22,464) and Cézanne's *Boy in a red waistcoat* reached 56,000 francs (£35,784).

Once war was over, the upward trend resumed and reached its highest point between 1925 and 1930. In 1925 the Gangnat collection was dispersed, and the hundred and sixty Renoirs, mostly of his later period and not considered to be his best work, went for more than ten million francs (£1,580,643). Also in 1925, a Cézanne was sold for 528,000 francs (£83,926) and in 1932 a van Gogh fetched 361,000 francs (£45,090). But these record prices—and this cannot be too

Auction of Cézanne's 'Boy with a red waistcoat' at Sotheby's, London

often repeated—have only a relative value. It is really much better, if we want to gauge the rise in prices between 1899 and 1930, only to take those pictures for which we have price records during the whole of the period. We will choose one of Degas' pastels, a painting by Monet and one by Pissarro.

> *Portrait of Jacques de Nittis as a child* by Degas:
>> 1085% increase between March 1900 and December 1932.
> *Parasol pines, cap d'Antibes* by Monet:
>> 180% increase between May 1897 and December 1932.
> *Cornfields at Champagniat* by Pissarro:
>> 41% increase between 1902 and 1934.

This last figure is much less significant than the first two, as the year 1934 is really too late for the comparison to be valid. In fact since about 1930-32, the price of Impressionist paintings had been going down, not as a result of changing tastes, but because of an economic and financial disaster: the Wall Street crash in 1929.

1932-1940: Recovery

The financial crisis, which began in the United States on that 'black Thursday' in October 1929 spread to France: share prices plummetted. People wondered about Impressionist pictures and how their prices would react, after the unprecedented rise of the last twenty years.

The reaction was disappointing, as we can see from the drop in prices obtained for several Renoirs, as compared with the 1925 peak and the Gangnat sale prices:

		Variation between Gangnat sale price and present price
1933	*Girls' head*, 1913	−69%
1936	*Bronze Cupid*, 1913	−78%
1939	*The road at Cagnes*, 1907	−77%
	Roses and small landscape, 1911	−61%
	Nude wiping herself, 1912	−45%
	Girl leaning on her elbows, 1911	−31%
	Woman with a red hat, 1908	−7%
	Woman reading, 1919	−2.5%

It would seem at first from these figures that the crisis had seriously affected the art market and Impressionist values. We must not however make hasty judgements. We cannot take these percentages by themselves as indications of the overall price curve. There are two reasons for this; first, the Gangnat sale prices tended to be somewhat inflated; and secondly, the Renoirs in the Gangnat collection, on account of their generally rather indifferent quality, seem to have been particularly vulnerable to fluctuations in the market. It is easy to confirm the seriousness of the shock of the financial crisis on Impressionist prices by referring to some other examples.

Let us take Toulouse-Lautrec. One of his works, *The Clown at the Fernando Circus* dropped by 38% between June 1926 and February 1932, while another, *Woman taking off her shift*, lost 65% between June 1928 and June 1931. One of van Gogh's paintings dropped by 35% between 1933 and 1937, and finally, Sisley's *Pont de Moret in autumn*, after reaching 130,000 francs (£14,280) in December 1929, went for only 150,500 francs (£13,624) in February 1939, showing a drop of about 4.6%.

It is obvious from these figures that on the eve of the Second World War, values of Impressionist pictures had not yet fully recovered from the blow they suffered in the financial crisis of 1929.

From 1952 to the present day

When Mme. Walter gave 33,000,000 francs (£130,302) for a still life of Cézanne's at the Cognacq sale in May 1952, it set off the rush of rising Impressionist prices. The Cognacq sale was spectacular; but ever since 1948 what then seemed fabulous prices had been paid for Impressionist paintings. For instance, in 1948, Renoir's *Girl reading* had fetched 9,050,000 francs (£59,695). But the increase in prices after 1952 was nothing less than spectacular.

To mention a few records: in 1964 Cézanne's *Grandes Baigneuses* was sold for 10,800,000 francs (£500,000); in 1967, Monet's *The Terrace at Sainte-Adresse* for 10,200,000 francs (56,000 guineas) in 1968; Renoir's *Le Pont des Arts* reached 10,800,000 francs (£1,550,000); and in 1970 Cézanne's *Portrait of Louis-Auguste Cézanne* was bought by the Metropolitan Museum of New York for a price believed to be in the region of 10,000,000 francs (£2,005,891).

Leaving these record figures obtained for first class paintings, let us now go on to consider one or two pictures whose prices we can follow over the course of several years even though they are less important. The first period chosen as reference is between 1925-1932 which marks the height of the first great boom in Impressionist painting. We have taken two pictures by Manet which were sold in 1932 and came up for auction again in 1973:

Sale of 'The Terrace at Sainte-Adresse' by Claude Monet at Christie's, London

The Pyramids at Port-Coton (Belle-Île)
6 May 1932   220 guineas (£2550)
27 March 1973   68,000 guineas (£133,511)
an increase of 5134%

Antibes, Rue des Jardins de la Salis
15 December 1932 205,000 francs (£25,385)
27 March 1973   95,000 guineas (£186,595)
an increase of 635%

Another example: *Le Pont des Arts* which so far is the Renoir to have reached the highest price in the sale room ($1,550,000, that is about £1,733,090) had been sold in 1932 for 133,000 francs (£16,528); that is, its value increased by 10,400%.

It would be a mistake to imagine that because of this spectacular increase in the value of *Le Pont des Arts* compared with the prices paid for the two Monets, Renoirs had gone up in value much more than Monets had. The fact is that really first-class works, particularly those of 'museum quality' like *Le Pont des Arts* have gone up in value very much more than paintings of moderate quality. We can see this by comparing the rise in the *Pont des Arts* with that in the prices of other Renoir paintings. We may compare for instance, the prices fetched by several pictures that came up in the Gangnat sale, when they appeared again in the sale room from 1966 onwards:

		Percentage increase in relation to the Gangnat sale price
1966	*The Hut*, 1917	+917%
	Cagnes, 1909	+830%
	Walk in the Collettes garden	+1393%
	White roses, 1907	+697%
	Women squatting, 1913	+930%
	Olive trees at Cagnes, 1909	+877%
1969	*Head of a blonde*, 1908	+1210%
1972	*Seated woman*, 1913	+784%
	Studies of a head and still life	+554%

Of course, compared with the performance of *Pont des Arts*, these seem relatively modest; but the fact remains that in less than fifty years, the value of all these Renoirs has gone up by something between seven and fourteen times their 1925 value. And in 1925, people were horrified at the 'ridiculous' and 'scandalous' prices being paid.

In order to obtain a more complete idea of how Impressionist prices have moved over the years, let us now take the period 1870-1880 which we settled on originally as the starting point of our study. We may again take *Le Pont des Arts* as our first example, as it was bought by Paul Durand-Ruel in 1872—incidentally the first Renoir he ever bought:

In 1872 the picture was bought for 200 francs (£136)

In 1968 it was sold for $1,550,000 (£1,733,090)

an increase of about 1,270,000%

So in a hundred years, the price of the picture was multiplied by 12,700.

As a second example, we will take a painting by Sisley *Flood on the road to Saint-Germain*. In 1880 this picture was bought by Durand-Ruel for 300 francs (£200). In 1969 it was sold for 151,002 francs (£150,000), an increase of about 75,000%.

One must bear in mind that over a hundred years, Sisleys have increased in value proportionately less than Renoir, Monet, Cézanne or van Gogh. On the other hand, *Flood on the road to Saint-Germain* is a picture of extremely high quality without quite being a masterpiece, and the increase in its value gives quite a good idea of the general movement in Impressionist prices. A price increase of 75,000% in less than a hundred years must thus be considered normal.

What would the Impressionist painters themselves have thought if one had told them their paintings would reach such astronomic prices fifty or sixty years after their death? One wonders if they would have agreed with van Gogh who said to his sister, only a few months before his death: 'Although the other day someone gave more than half a million for Millet's *Angélus*, don't go and think that all that many more people understand what there is in Millet's mind.' And Renoir told his son Jean, towards the end of his life: 'Now it is no longer a picture people hang on the wall, it's securities. Why not hang up a share in the Suez canal instead?'

The Impressionist Exhibitions

FIRST EXHIBITION 15 April to 15 May 1874, in the studios of the photographer Nadar, 35 Boulevard des Capucines. Thirty artists represented: Astruc, Attendu, Béliard, Boudin, Bracquemond, Brandon, Bureau, Cals, Cézanne, Colin, Debras, Degas, Guillaumin, Latouche, Lepic, Lépine, Levert, Meyer, de Molins, Monet, Berthe Morisot, Mulot-Durivage, de Nittis, A. Ottin, L.-A. Ottin, Pissarro, Renoir, Robert, Rouart, Sisley.

SECOND EXHIBITION April 1876, Galerie Durand-Ruel, 11 Rue le Peletier. Twenty artists: Bazille (he died in 1870 but had belonged to the group), Béliard, Bureau, Cals, Caillebotte, Degas, Desboutin, François, Legros, Lepic, Levert, J.-B. Millet, Monet, Berthe Morisot, L.-A. Ottin, Pissarro, Renoir, Rouart, Sisley, Tillot.

THIRD EXHIBITION April 1877, 6 Rue Le Peletier. Eighteen artists: Caillebotte, Cals, Cézanne, Cordey, Degas, Guillaumin, Jacques François, Lamy, Levert, Maureau, Monet, Berthe Morisot, Piette, Pissarro, Renoir, Rouart, Sisley, Tillot.

FOURTH EXHIBITION 10 April to 11 May 1879, 28 Avenue de l'Opéra. Sixteen artists: Bracquemond, Mme Bracquemond, Caillebotte, Cals, Mary Cassatt, Degas, Forain, Gauguin, Lebourg, Monet, Piette, Pissarro, Rouart, Henry Somm, Tillot, Zandomeneghi.

FIFTH EXHIBITION 1 to 30 April 1880, 10 Rue des Pyramides. Eighteen artists: Bracquemond, Mme Bracquemond, Caillebotte, Mary Cassatt, Degas, Forain, Gauguin, Guillaumin, Lebourg, Levert, Berthe Morisot, Pissarro, Raffaelli, Rouart, Tillot, E. Vidal, Vignon, Zandomeneghi.

SIXTH EXHIBITION 2 April to 1 May 1881, 35 Boulevard des Capucines, in an annex of the Nadar studios. Thirteen artists: Mary Cassatt, Degas, Forain, Gauguin, Guillaumin, Berthe Morisot, Pissarro, Raffaelli, Rouart, Tillot, E. Vidal, Vignon, Zandomeneghi.

SEVENTH EXHIBITION March 1882, 251 Faubourg Saint-Honoré, at Durand-Ruel's gallery. Nine artists: Caillebotte, Gauguin, Guillaumin, Monet, Berthe Morisot, Pissarro, Renoir, Sisley, Vignon.

EIGHTH EXHIBITION 15 May to 15 June 1886, at 1 Rue Laffitte. Seventeen artists participated: Mme Bracquemond, Mary Cassatt, Degas, Forain, Gauguin, Guillaumin, Berthe Morisot, Camille Pissarro, Lucien Pissarro, O. Redon, Rouart, Schuffenecker, Seurat, Signac, Tillot, Vignon, Zandomeneghi.

The great Retrospective Exhibitions

BAZILLE *Exhibition for the centenary of Frédéric Bazille*. Musée Fabre, Montpellier, May to June, 1941.
Exhibition organized in aid of the Musée Fabre, Montpellier, by the Wildenstein Gallery, Paris, in the summer of 1950.
Frédéric Bazille Exhibition. Musée Fabre, Montpellier, October 1959.

BOUDIN *Exhibition of the works of Eugène Boudin*. École nationale des Beaux-Arts, Paris, 1899.
Eugène Boudin Exhibition. Galerie Schmit, Paris, 1965.
Eugène Boudin retrospective exhibition. Hirschl and Adler Galleries Inc., New York, 1966.

CASSATT *Mary Cassatt Exhibition*. Museum of Art, Baltimore, 1941.
Mary Cassatt Exhibition. Wildenstein Galleries, New York, 1947.
Mary Cassatt, painter and engraver. American Cultural Center, Paris, November 1959 to January 1960.

CÉZANNE *Cézanne Exhibition*. Musée de l'Orangerie, Paris, Spring 1936.
Paul Cézanne Exhibition. Kunsthalle, Basle, August to October 1936.
Paul Cézanne Exhibition. Museum of Art, San Francisco, September to October 1937.
Paul Cézanne Exhibition. Société des artistes indépendants, Grand Palais, Paris, March to April 1939.
Tribute to Paul Cézanne. Wildenstein and Co., London, July 1939.
Cézanne Exhibition. Wildenstein Galleries, New York, March to April 1947.

Cézanne Exhibition. Art Institute of Chicago and Metropolitan Museum of Art, New York, 1952.
Hommage à Cézanne. Musée de l'Orangerie, Paris, June to October 1954.
Cézanne Exhibition. Tate Gallery, London, summer to December 1954.
Cézanne Exhibition. London, summer 1954.
Paul Cézanne Exhibition. Gemeentemuseum, The Hague, June to July 1956.
Cézanne Exhibition. Kunsthaus, Zürich, August to October 1956.
Cézanne Exhibition. Wallraf-Richartz-Museum, Cologne, December 1956 to January 1957.
Cézanne Exhibition. Wildenstein Galleries, New York, November to December 1959.
Cézanne Watercolors. Knoedler Galleries, New York, April 1963.

DEGAS *Exposition Degas*. Galerie Georges Petit, Paris, April 1924.
Edgar Degas, das plastische Werk. Berlin, May 1926; Munich, July to August 1926; Dresden, September 1926.
Degas, Portraitist and Sculptor. Musée de l'Orangerie, Paris, 1931.
Degas Exhibition. Philadelphia Museum of Art, 1936.
Degas Exhibition. Musée de l'Orangerie, Paris, March to April 1937.
Degas, Painter of Movement. André Weill Gallery, Paris, 1939.
Edgar Degas, Skulpturer og Monotypier. Ny Carlsberg Glyptotek, Copenhagen, 1948.
Degas Exhibition. Wildenstein Galleries, New York, 1949.
The Complete Collection of Sculptures by Edgar Degas. Marlborough Galleries, London, 1951.
Edgar Degas, Original Wax Sculptures. Knoedler Galleries, New York, 1955.
Etchings by Edgar Degas. University of Chicago, May to June 1964.
Works from the Louvre Museum. Paintings, pastels, drawings, sculptures. Musée de l'Orangerie, Paris, 1969.

GAUGUIN *Gauguin Retrospective*. Autumn Salon, Paris, 1906.
Centenary Exhibition. Musée de l'Orangerie, Paris, 1949.

Gauguin Exhibition. Wildenstein Galleries, New York, 1956.

Gauguin Exhibition. National Museum of Modern Art, Tokyo, 1969; National Museum of Modern Art, Kyoto, 1969.

VAN GOGH *The Life and Work of van Gogh* (in connection with the International Exhibition). Nouveaux Musées, quai de Tokyo, Paris, 1937.

Vincent van Gogh Exhibition. London, 1947.

Van Gogh and the painters of Auvers-sur-Oise. Musée de l'Orangerie, Paris, 1954.

Vincent van Gogh Exhibition. Musée Jacquemart-André, Paris, 1960.

Collection of the National van Gogh Museum, Amsterdam. Musée de l'Orangerie, Paris, 1971 to 1972.

GONZALÈS *Eva Gonzalès Retrospective.* Salons de la vie moderne, Paris, 1885.

GUIGOU *Guigou Exhibition.* Cantini Museum, Marseilles, 1959.

Guigou Exhibition. Daber Gallery, Paris, 1970.

GUILLAUMIN *Retrospective Exhibition.* Georges Petit Gallery, Paris, 1928.

Exhibition of works by Guillaumin. Durand-Ruel Gallery, Paris, 1953.

JONGKIND *Fiftieth anniversary of the death of Jongkind Exhibition.* Grenoble Museum, 1941.

Jongkind Exhibition. Musée de l'Orangerie, Paris, 1949.

LÉPINE *Lépine Exhibition.* Daber Gallery, Paris, 1949.

MANET *Manet Exhibition.* École des Beaux-Arts, Paris, 1884.

Manet, thirty-five pictures from the Pellerin Collection. Bernheim-Jeune Gallery, Paris, 1910.

Edouard Manet Exhibition. Mathiesen Gallery, Berlin, 1928.

Manet Exhibition. Musée de l'Orangerie, Paris, 1932.

Edouard Manet Exhibition. Wildenstein Galleries, New York, 1937.

Masterpieces by Manet. Paul Rosenberg Gallery, New York, 1947.

Manet Exhibition. Wildenstein Galleries, New York, 1948.

Edouard Manet Exhibition. Philadelphia Museum of Art and Art Institute of Chicago, 1966 to 1967.

MONET *Claude Monet Exhibition.* Durand-Ruel Gallery, Paris, 1928.

Claude Monet. Galerien Thannhauser, Berlin, 1928.

Claude Monet Retrospective. Musée de l'Orangerie, Paris, 1931.

Claude Monet. Rosenberg Gallery, Paris, 1936.

Claude Monet. Wildenstein Galleries, New York, 1945.

Claude Monet. Kunsthaus, Zürich, 1952.

Claude Monet. Marlborough Galleries, London, 1954.

Claude Monet. Edinburgh Festival and Tate Gallery, London, 1957.

Claude Monet. Seasons and Moments. Museum of Modern Art, New York and Los Angeles County Museum, 1960.

Claude Monet, last works. Beyeler Gallery, Basle, 1962.

Monet and his friends. Michel Monet Bequest. Marmottan Museum, Paris, 1972.

MORISOT *Berthe Morisot.* Boussod-Valadon Gallery, Paris, 1892.

Berthe Morisot (Mme Eugène Manet). Durand-Ruel Gallery, Paris, 1896.

Berthe Morisot. Musée de l'Orangerie, Paris, summer, 1941.

Berthe Morisot. Ny Carlsberg Glyptotek, Copenhagen, 1949.

Berthe Morisot. Paintings and Drawings. Arts Council of Great Britain, London, 1950.

Berthe Morisot and Her Circle. Itinerant Exhibition shown in Canada and the United States, 1952-1953.

Berthe Morisot. Dieppe Museum, 1957.

Berthe Morisot. Toulouse-Lautrec Museum, Albi, 1958.

Berthe Morisot, Wildenstein Galleries, New York, 1960.
Berthe Morisot. Jacquemart-André Museum, Paris, 1961.

PISSARRO *Centenary of the Birth of Camille Pissarro.* Musée de l'Orangerie, Paris, 1930.
Camille Pissarro. Wildenstein Galleries, New York, 1945.
Pissarro Exhibition. André Weill Gallery, Paris, 1950.
Camille Pissarro. Matthiesen Gallery, London, 1950.
Camille Pissarro, a Collection of Pastels and Studies. Leicester Galleries, London, 1955.
Camille Pissarro. Durand-Ruel Gallery, Paris, 1956.
Camille Pissarro. Wildenstein Galleries, New York, 1965.

REDON *Odilon Redon Exhibition.* Musée de l'Orangerie, Paris, 1956-1957.

RENOIR *Renoir Exhibition.* Bernheim-Jeune Gallery, Paris, 1913.
Renoir's Classical Period (1875-1886). Knoedler Galleries, New York, 1929.
Renoir Exhibition. Musée de l'Orangerie, Paris, 1933.
Masterpieces by Renoir. Durand-Ruel Galleries, New York, 1935.
Renoir, his Paintings. Metropolitan Museum of Art, New York, 1937.
Renoir as a Portraitist. Bernheim-Jeune Gallery, Paris, 1938.
Renoir Centennial. Duveen Galleries, New York, 1941.
Pierre-Auguste Renoir. California Palace of the Legion of Honor, San Francisco, 1944.
Renoir. Wildenstein Galleries, New York, 1950.
Renoir. Edinburgh Festival, 1953.
The Last Twenty Years of Renoir's Life. Rosenberg Gallery, New York, 1954.

Renoir, Masterpieces in French Private Collections. Galerie des Beaux-Arts, Paris, 1954.
Renoir, Maurice Gangnat Collection. Durand-Ruel Gallery, Paris, 1955.
Pierre-Auguste Renoir, Paintings, Drawings, Prints and Sculptures. Los Angeles County Museum and San Francisco Museum of Art, 1955.
Renoir. Marlborough Gallery, London, 1956.
Auguste Renoir. Städtische Galerie, Munich, 1958.
Renoir. Wildenstein Galleries, New York, 1958.
Hommage à Renoir. Durand-Ruel Gallery, Paris, 1958.

SEURAT *Ninth Salon des Vingt, Seurat Retrospective.* Museum of Modern Art, Brussels, 1892.
Eighth Salon des artistes indépendants, Seurat Retrospective. Grandes Serres de la Ville, Paris, 1905.
Seurat Exhibition. Jacquemart-André Museum, Paris, 1957.

SIGNAC *Paul Signac.* National Museum of Modern Art, Paris, 1951.
Paul Signac. Louvre Museum, Paris, 1963-1964.

SISLEY *Pictures, Studies, Pastels by Alfred Sisley.* Georges Petit Gallery, Paris, May 1899.
Sisley's Studio. Bernheim-Jeune Gallery, Paris, 1907.
Sisley. Durand-Ruel Gallery, Paris, 1957.
Alfred Sisley. Berner Kunstmuseum, Berne, 1958.
Sisley. Paul Rosenberg Gallery, New York, 1961.

TOULOUSE-LAUTREC *Exhibition in honour of the fiftieth anniversary of Toulouse-Lautrec's death,* Musée de l'Orangerie, Paris, 1951.
Toulouse-Lautrec Centenary. Palais de la Berbie, Albi, and Petit-Palais Museum, Paris, 1964.

List of Illustrations

Index

Nittis, Giuseppe de 143, 258
Novalis 42

Offenbach, Jacques 210
Oller, Francisco 115
Ortega y Gasset 7
Ottin, Auguste 258
Ottin, Léon-Auguste 258

Palmer, Samuel 53
Pauwels, Ferdinand 120
Pellerin, Auguste 246
Pelletan, Camille 96
Petit, Georges 135, 143, 222, 251, 259, 260, 261
Petitjean, Hippolyte 24
Picasso, Pablo 79, 212, 222, 246
Piette-Montfoucault, Ludovic 143, 146, 258
Pigear, Amédée 96
Pissarro, Camille 8, 12, 20, 24, 39, 56, 57, 73, 74, 80, 83, 98, 115, 143, 144, 180, 183, 186, 191, 207, 211, 213, 217, 218, 220, 221, 223, 224, 225, 226, 227, 228, 229, 231, 233, 235, 236, 237, 238, 241, 242, 243, 244, 245, 246, 248, 249, 250, 251, 253, 254, 258, 259, 260
Pissarro, Lucien 24, 27, 47, 131, 148, 234, 259
Poe, Edgar 233
Pontillon 142
Poussin, Nicolas 9, 55, 58, 62, 70
Prince of Wales 196, 197
Princeteau, René 199, 215
Prins, Pierre 126
Proust, Antonin 14, 124, 214, 219, 240
Proust, Marcel 18, 21, 57, 214
Puvis de Chavannes, Pierre 26, 28, 60, 243

Quevedo 7
Quisdorf 42

Rachou, Henri 215
Raffaëlli, Jean-François 219, 231, 258
Raimondi, Marc-Aontoine 69, 123
Ranson, Paul 27
Raphael 121, 123, 164, 180
Rappard, van 104
Ravier, Auguste 34, 53, 58, 59
Redon, Odilon 26, 28, 151, 180, 211, 224, 231, 235, 259, 261
Regoyos, Dario de 154
Régnier, Henri de 26
Reid, Alexander 240
Reid, Robert 206, 241
Rembrandt 45, 80, 82, 82, 212
Renard, Jules 239
Renoir, Edmond 220
Renoir, Pierre-Auguste 7, 9, 12, 13, 18, 20, 22, 41, 80, 89, 96, 114, 131, 135, 142, 143, 144, 147, 155, 183, 185, 189 199, 208, 210, 211, 212, 213, 214, 215, 216, 217, 219, 220, 221, 222, 223, 224, 225, 226, 228, 229, 230, 231, 232, 233, 234, 235, 237, 238, 241, 242, 243, 245, 246, 248, 249, 250, 251, 252, 253, 254, 255, 256, 257, 258, 261
Reynolds, Joshua 56
Ribera, Jusepe de 54, 124
Ribot, Théodule 54, 59, 61
Rico, Martin 66
Rimbaud, Arthur 96
Rivière, Georges 241
Rivière, Henri 186
Robert 258
Robinson, Théodore 174
Rodenbach 154
Rodin, Auguste 18, 28, 135, 229, 235
Rondel, Henri 214
Rood, N.O. 16, 177, 179, 181
Rosenberg, Paul 260, 261
Rossetti, Dante Gabriel 38, 61
Rottmann, Carl 55
Rouart, Henri 241, 243, 258, 259
Rouault, Georges 59, 206, 232
Rousseau, Henri 222, 223, 243

Photographs

Bildarchiv Foto Marburg: 81, 120, 121, 193, 194; Blauel: 193; Eva Bollert: 82; Bulloz: 32, 38, 50, 54, 58, 59, 64, 68, 154, 174, 194, 210, 223, 226, 230; Colorphoto Hans Hintz: 175; Durand-Ruel: 89, 224; Giraudon: 9, 14, 19, 21, 32, 33, 35, 38, 39, 40, 41, 44, 45, 51, 55, 56, 62, 66, 67, 69, 70, 81, 82, 98, 114, 115, 117, 118, 122, 133, 134, 138, 139, 142, 143, 148, 149, 174, 176, 177, 180, 181, 185, 187, 188, 190, 191, 197, 199, 202, 203, 214, 215, 216, 217, 218, 221, 224, 227, 229, 230, 231, 232, 233, 234, 235, 237; Hauck: 207; Keystone: 253, 255; Kleinhempel: 82, 119, 195; Mas: 129, 154; National Gallery of Art, Washington: 92, 102, 136, 138, 150, 200, 201; Réunion des musées nationaux: 232; Roger-Viollet: 112, 151, 175, 206, 208, 226, 229, 232; The Tate Gallery, London: 185.